BLOOD AND CHAMPAGNE

ALSO BY ALEX KERSHAW

The Bedford Boys

Jack London

BLOOD AND CHAMPAGNE

THE LIFE AND TIMES OF
ROBERT CAPA

ALEX KERSHAW

DA CAPO PRESS
A Member of the Perseus Books Group

Cataloging-in-Publication data for this book is available from the Library of Congress.

ISBN 0–306–81356–4

First Da Capo Press edition 2004
Originally published in Great Britain in 2002 by Macmillan.
Originally published in the United States in 2003 by St. Martin's Press, New York; reprinted by arrangement.

Published by Da Capo Press
A Member of the Perseus Books Group
http://www.dacapopress.com

1 2 3 4 5 6 7 8 9—08 07 06 05 04

for Warren Trabant

For me, Capa wore the dazzling matador's costume, but he never went in for the kill; a great player, he fought for himself and others in a whirlwind. Destiny was determined that he should be struck down at the height of his glory.

HENRI CARTIER-BRESSON

Contents

List of Illustrations, xi

Acknowledgements, xiv

Three Thousand Miles From Omaha, 1

1 Conversation in Budapest, 5

2 Barbarians at the Gate, 15

3 The Man Who Invented Himself, 22

4 The Passionate War, 33

5 'The Falling Soldier', 38

6 'La Paquena Rubena', 48

7 'The 400 Million', 66

8 The Final Defeat, 73

9 Splendid Isolation, 82

10 Muddling Through, 90

11 The Desert, 98

12 It's a Tough War, 107

13 The Longest Day, 116

14 The Bocage, 132

15 Victory, 144

16 'Here's Looking At You, Kid', 158

17 The End of the Affair, 167

18 Back in the USSR, 177

19 The New Look, 192

20 A Road of Death, 201

21 The Realm of the Senses, 214

22 How Can I Be Old?, 225

23 Forward Lies the Delta, 241

Epilogue: The Legend, 252

Notes, 256

Bibliography, 277

Index, 290

List of Illustrations

1. 'He had a gambler's sense of priorities.' Capa with multiple betting slips, Longchamps, Paris, 1952. (Copyright © Henri Cartier-Bresson/ Magnum Photos.)
2. 'The little red fox', Gerda Taro. (Photo by Fred Stein.)
3. 'She was the great love of his life.' Gerda Taro's funeral procession in Paris, 1937. (*Ce Soir*, 2 August 1937. Collection Bibliothèque Historique de la ville de Paris.)
4. 'He had gone in search of death.' Fernhout, Ivens and Capa, second from left, in China 1938 with three Chinese officials. (Copyright © European Foundation Joris Ivens.)
5. 'Among the 400 million.' Ivens and an unidentified man are on top of the tank, Capa, Fernhout and a Chinese man are in front, China 1938. (Copyright © European Foundation Joris Ivens.)
6. Capa and 'Papa' Hemingway, Sun Valley, Idaho, November 1940. (Copyright © Lloyd Arnold/John F. Kennedy Library.)
7. 'He [Capa] could speak seven languages but none of them well.' Ernest Hemingway listens to 'Capanese', Sun Valley, Idaho, November 1940. (Copyright © Lloyd Arnold/John F. Kennedy Library.)
8. Capa dances the night away at Sun Valley, November 1940. His 'soul sister', Martha Gellhorn, is second from left. (Copyright © Lloyd Arnold/John F. Kennedy Library.)
9. 'He was the worst driver in the world.' Capa, late 1944. (Hutton-Getty.)
10. 'Listen, old goat, it's the end of the game that counts and how many chips you've got in your pocket – if you're still playing.'

Capa and 'old goat' George Rodger, Naples, 1943. (Copyright © Magnum Photos.)

11. 'I was under fire with him.' Capa's friend and editor at *Life*, John Morris, London, 1944. (John G. Morris Collection/University of Chicago Library.)
12. The waterfront after bombing, Anzio, 1943. (Hulton-Deutsch/Corbis.)
13. Ernie Pyle, the great America war correspondent, lights up after a direct hit on the correspondents' beachfront hotel, Anzio, 1944. (Courtesy The Lilly Library, Indiana University, Bloomington, Indiana.)
14. 'He was phenomenally brave.' Capa, second from left, about to jump with the 17th Airborne over Wesel on the Dutch border, March 1945. (Hulton-Getty.)
15. Capa with close friend and fellow Magnum founder David 'Chim' Seymour, Paris, early 1950s. (Copyright © Henri Cartier-Bresson/Magnum Photos.)
16. Magnum founders toasting the liberation of Paris at a party at the home of *Vogue* editor Michel de Brunhoff. Capa far left, Chim Seymour centre without tie, Cartier-Bresson far right. (John G. Morris Collection/University of Chicago Library.)
17. 'You are my sort of creature.' Capa with the writer Gael Elton Mayo. (Copyright © The Estate of Gael Elton Mayo.)
18. Ingrid Bergman with her father, a Bohemian photographer. (Swedish Film Institute Stills Archive.)
19. 'She was like a great painting.' Ingrid Bergman in *Notorious*, 1946. (RKO Radio Pictures/Ronald Grant Archive.)
20. Capa playing poker with John Huston (far right) while Burl Ives plays guitar, London 1953. (Copyright © Ernst Haas/Getty Images.)
21. Capa with John Steinbeck and his wife Gwyn in a Paris hotel in 1947, just a few days before crossing the Iron Curtain. (Center for Steinbeck Studies, San Jose State University.)
22. Back in action. A newsreel cameraman captures Capa photographing the wounded from Dien Bien Phu, Indo-China, May 1954. (Collection Patrick Jeudy.)

23. 'He asked me to take his camera'. The last photo of Capa alive, taken by friend and colleague Michel Descamps. (Photo by Michel Descamps/SCOOP/*Paris Match*.)
24. 'She could talk of nothing else.' 'Julita' Friedmann at the grave of her favourite son in upstate New York. (Copyright © Lisl Steiner.)
25. 'The man who invented himself.' André Friedmann, alias Robert Capa, 1954. (Hulton-Getty.)

Acknowledgements

Over a four-year period of research for this book, many people provided enormous help and encouragement. While this book was not authorized, almost every contemporary of Capa agreed to be interviewed. Those who were too ill, or felt they had nothing new to bring to the table, still provided generous help. I am particularly grateful to Henri Cartier-Bresson for permission to quote in full his poem about Capa.

Many people in several countries provided hospitality. In Paris, Suzy Marquis and her husband Jean-Gabriel were particularly generous with their time. Bettina Graziani, Warren Trabant and Pierre Gassmann also welcomed me into their homes. The Paris-based British photographer and Magnum veteran Jimmy Fox also provided invaluable assistance, subtle clues and many contact numbers for people who had long disappeared from the public eye. John Morris, a surviving colleague and friend of Capa's, was eventually just as helpful and painstaking in efforts to provide a balanced portrait of Capa's life. The distinguished film-maker Patrick Jeudy kindly showed me wonderful newsreels and film of Capa in action.

Lara Holman at the Hulton-Getty Picture Collection in London tracked down crucial pictures, and Macmillan's Josie Meijer laboured long and hard to secure those that appear in this book. Hers was no easy task in these days of corporate profiteering from historic images and I am most appreciative. Staff at Colindale Newspaper Library in London, including Jackie Pitcher and Michael Nash, provided copies of all Capa's stories from *Illustrated* and *Picture Post*, which showcased Capa's work better than any other publication. Although *Time-Life* restricts access to non-employees to its archives, I was nevertheless able to find key information thanks to several staff, particularly Bill Hooper, who specifically located a radio interview with Capa that threw important light on many controversial issues.

The writer Jozefa Stuart, who knew Capa and researched an unpublished biography of him in the early 1960s, spoke to me at length and even lobbied on my behalf to access crucial information she had gathered and which is now held by ICP in New York. Nor can the executor of the Robert Capa estate, Richard Whelan, go unacknowledged in any work about Capa, for his ground-breaking 1985 biography, in part based on Stuart's pioneering work, is an impressively detailed account of Capa's life.

Others helped explain key events and issues in Capa's life. In Lynchburg, Virginia, while listening to Glenn Miller, Professor Bill McIntosh of the National D-Day Foundation provided a military overview of the most important day in Capa's career, and helped me understand some of the strategic complexities of the battle for Normandy and Overlord.

My father trudged along beaches in the rain and spent several days in Normandy and Paris, tracing Capa's footsteps. My mother showed me southern Spain. Jay Deutsch of the Leica Gallery in New York provided contacts and a technical understanding of the Leica. Professor Wolodymyr Stojko of the *Ukrainian Journal* contacted sources in Kiev, and provided a sharp perspective on Capa's visit to the Soviet Union. The art and photography dealer Howard Greenberg spoke candidly about the commercial value of Capa's work. Susan Shillinglaw, director of the Steinbeck Center, helped point me to several important sources. Patty Cottingham, executive director of the Scripps Howard Foundation, provided several contact numbers for journalists and photographers. Rick Bray of the Ernie Pyle Historical Site unearthed a great deal of information about Capa's exploits with Ernie Pyle. The legendary George Silk helped me understand another photographer's perspective on covering the Second World War. Bernard Crystal at Columbia University pointed me in the direction of correspondence concerning Capa's business dealings with John Steinbeck. Michael Edwards at the Eisenhower Center tracked down several important transcripts of D-Day veterans. Steven Plotkin at the JFK Library in Boston helped locate wonderful pictures of Capa with Hemingway and Martha Gellhorn.

In Budapest, Éva Keleti and Katya Steiner went out of their way to make my stay as enjoyable and illuminating as possible. Without them, I would never have gained a sense of Capa's Hungarian background. In Spain, Maria Paz spent several months chasing rogue leads, poring over documents and arranging interviews. Chris Littleford translated key newspaper articles and chased reluctant sources. I am also indebted to his wife Amor for her hospitality. Miguel Angel Jaramillo Guerreira, director of the Archivo General de la Guerra Civil Española in Salamanca, endured a barrage of questions. Manuel Melgar of the Military Archives in Madrid was also very helpful.

In Germany, Professor Hans Puttnies helped provide a context for my research into Weimar Germany. The biographer Irme Schaber generously helped me track down several of Capa's contemporaries, including Ruth Cerf Berg and Irene Spiegel. Irme Schaber also spoke to me about her own pioneering work on Gerda Taro. I am deeply grateful to her for her time and help – if only all biographers were so open-minded and positive. In Switzerland, Ruth Cerf Berg's daughter, Kathrin Berg Müller, was particularly helpful in securing answers to many questions I posed to her mother, a truly remarkable woman. In Amsterdam, Eva Besnyö provided a crucial insight into Capa's childhood. In Washington, Ben Bradlee provided a pithy account of his time in Paris and at Klosters. John Fox of the FBI's information unit explained several details in Capa's FBI file. John Kelso, Section Chief of Freedom of Information Privacy Acts Section Office of Public and Congressional Affairs, provided me with all those documents he is authorized to release. David Wallis in New York provided many important articles from several databases.

Leslie Calmes of the Center for Creative Photography in Tucson provided a trove of wonderful material, particularly many sections of memoirs and several letters written by Hansel Mieth, and which I have quoted at length. I am extremely grateful to Mieth's long-standing friend, Georgia Brown, for permission to do so. Dr Norman Allan in

Toronto also generously provided the manuscript for an unpublished biography of his father, and gave permission to quote from it. I am similarly indebted to Jinx Rodger in Britain who allowed me to quote from her late husband's lyrical diaries. Georgia de Chamberet in London sent me her mother's insightful memoir and pictures of Gael Elton Mayo with Capa. In Vermont, Patti Stratton, Lucy Steele and Amanda Hoag worked tirelessly to transcribe well over a hundred hours of interviews. I am particularly grateful to Amanda for the many hours she spent collating ancient copies of *Life* and *Picture Post*.

Jonathan Drubner, Tom Garagis, Paul and Amanda Armstrong, David Boyle, Tessa Souter, David McBeth, Serge Glansberg, Paul Spike, George Waud, Michael Watts, Michael and Cynthia Perry, Kevin and Maria Smith, and the inimitable Bettina Viviano also provided friendship and relief during the last five years. In particular, Dave Bernath and his family in Venice, California, tolerated my presence on their couch several times. In Dave's case, I also enjoyed countless hours of discussion and at one point he even provided German translation.

I am as always grateful to Lindsay Stirling for her superbly professional help and advice with the manuscript. I would also like to thank Irish Dreamtime's Pierce Brosnan, Beau St. Clair, and Angelique Higgins, and CAA's Robert Bookman and John Levin, as well as Nigel Sinclair of Intermedia, for their keen interest in this project.

Staff and editors at the *Guardian*, the *Observer* and *Sunday Times Magazine* have long supported my freelance travels, and provided income when I needed it most.

In America and abroad, I was also given assistance by the staff of many institutions and libraries, ranging from the Lanesboro Public Library in Minnesota to the New York Public Library. The staff at the Sawyer Library at Williams College tolerated my presence until the early hours for one particularly long winter. I also benefited from the resources of the Park-McCullogh Free Library in Bennington, Bennington College, The British Library, London's Imperial War Museum, Magnum's New York office archives, Salamanca's Spanish Civil War Archives, the National Archives in Washington DC, the US

Military History Institute, The Eisenhower Center in New Orleans, The National D-Day Foundation in Virginia, the British Film Institute Library, the Foreign Press Association in Washington, Columbia University, the *New York Times*' archives, the Academy of Motion Pictures Arts and Sciences, the Getty Museum in Los Angeles, Eastman Kodak House in New York, the Russian and Hungarian Embassies in Washington, Colindale Newspaper Library, Westminster Public Library, the Library of Congress and the Paris-Match Archives in Paris.

The following kindly agreed to answer questions and provide information – many endured several hours of interviewing: Dr Alexander Matthews, Alfred Gellhorn, John Hammond Jr., Hart Preston, Jim Nachtwey, Ray Nance, Betty Hooper, Earl Wilson, Elizabeth Teas, Lucille Hoback Boggess, Roy and Helen Stevens, Eva Besnyö, Karoly Kincses, Nina Beskow, Robert Brau, Alan Goodrich, Jim Lager, Steven Burstin, Andrew Mauldin, John Morris, Inge Morath, Dirck Halstead, Elliot Erwitt, Jean-Gabriel and Suzy Marquis, Flury Clavadetscher, Ruth Guler, the late Larry Adler, Ruth Hartmann, Larry Collins, Bettina Graziani, John Loengard, Peter Viertel, Russell Miller, Donald Spoto, Harry Benson, Anjelica Huston, Eve Arnold, Myron Davis, Jimmy Fox, Thomas Gunther, Marc Riboud, Pierre Gassmann, Ruth Cerf Berg, Russell Burrows, Anthony Saua, Irme Schaber, Hans Puttnies, Patrick Jeudy, Michel Descamps, Marie-Claude Cogny, David Douglas Duncan, Judy Freiburg, Yvonne Halsmann, Patricia Wheatley, Ben Bradlee, Jean-Jacques Naudet, Georgia Brown, Marie-Monique Robin, Jinx Rodger, Rosemarie Scherman, Frank Zachary, Slim Aarons, Dr Norman Allan, George Silk, Inge Bondi, Liesl Steiner, Irene Spiegel, Carl and Shelley Mydans, Milton Wolff, Audrey Jarreau, Henri Cartier-Bresson, Burt Glinn, Lois Mercier and Maria Borrel Garcia.

This book originated in conversations with my wife and several exceptional photojournalists with whom I have worked very closely in the last decade. Simon Norfolk, Charles Ommanney, John Snowdon and Greg Williams have all shared many insights and done more than their fair share of the driving on many difficult assignments. Through them, I discovered first-hand what enormous resilience is required today in order to be a photojournalist and still pay the rent.

ACKNOWLEDGEMENTS

The most positive result of writing this book was a new friendship with another lifelong journalist. I will for ever be indebted to ex-*Heute* editor Warren Trabant, a man of great humour, insight and gentility, who wined and dined with Capa and spent many wonderful evenings doing the same with me.

I have been fortunate to have such an incisive and supportive editor at Macmillan – Georgina Morley, who stuck by through thick and thin and waited beyond reasonable expectation for the book to be completed. Nicholas Blake did a superb job of copy-editing the manuscript. My agent, Derek Johns, was as always a model of diplomacy and patience, and many others at AP Watt, specifically Linda Shaughnessy, provided invaluable help.

Finally, this book would never have been completed had it not been for the infinite tolerance and patience of my wife Robin. She and my son Felix allowed me the time and space to pursue what became a five-year-long obsession. I would also like to thank her family, and especially my own, for their long-standing support.

Sadly, and despite being led to believe that the incorporation of Capa's photographs might be possible, I was not granted permission to use a single image because of this book's unauthorized nature.

Three Thousand Miles From Omaha

'It does seem to me that Capa has proved beyond all doubt that the camera need not be a cold mechanical device. Like the pen, it is as good as the man who uses it. It can be the extension of mind and heart.'

JOHN STEINBECK, *Popular Photography*[1]

One late autumn afternoon, I drove north through Virginia, watching the Blue Ridge Mountains loom larger as I neared Bedford, home of America's first D-Day memorial. As the sun set, I visited the memorial with eighty-five-year-old Sergeant Roy Stevens, a veteran of Company A of the 116th Infantry Regiment of the 29th Division. Several times, elderly men approached and shared memories with Mr Stevens, sometimes with tears in their eyes – veterans of 'the Bulge', the beach at Anzio, and the Battle of Normandy.

Later, Stevens told me in detail his own story. In the early hours of 6 June 1944 he prepared to board a landing craft destined for Omaha Beach. Just as he was about to clamber in, he spotted his identical twin brother, Ray. 'He stuck out his hand for me to shake,' Roy told me. 'I didn't shake it. Instead, I said: "Look, I'll shake your hand in Vierville-sur-Mer up at the crossroads, later this morning sometime."'

Ray bowed his head and said he wasn't going to make it. He wouldn't survive. He was certain of it. Roy Stevens didn't make it to Vierville-sur-Mer that morning either. His landing craft sank a few hundred yards from the beach, minutes before the first wave of American troops arrived. Stevens was saved from drowning by a fellow member of Company A and finally arrived four days later on Omaha

Beach, where he found a makeshift grave for his brother and several other friends.

His brother and eighteen other young men from Bedford had been killed within minutes of reaching 'Bloody Omaha', scene of the greatest slaughter on D-Day. Of the thirty-five Bedford soldiers who belonged to Company A, twenty-one were dead by nightfall. War historians believe Bedford suffered the highest per-capita loss of any town or city in America.

In Mr Stevens' modest ranch-style home we talked late into the night about his brother, Bedford and war. Finally, I handed him a tattered book I'd found in a rare-book store in New York: *Images of War*.

'Who wrote this?' Stevens asked as he turned to the chapter on page 105, labelled 'The Invasion'.

'Robert Capa,' I replied. 'He was the only photographer to land with the first wave on Omaha, with the 116th on Easy Red.'

'Easy Red?' Stevens asked. 'The first wave? Was he a soldier or in the coast guard?'

'Neither. He was a journalist. A Hungarian Jew. He volunteered.'

'Some of the best men – they volunteered. But they didn't last long.'

Stevens read a quote from Capa: 'I would say that the war correspondent gets more drinks, more girls, better pay, and greater freedom to choose his spot and being allowed to be a coward and not be executed for it is his torture. The war correspondent has his stake – his life – in his own hands and he can put it on this horse or that horse, or he can put it back in his pocket at the very last minute. I am a gambler. I decided to go in with . . . the first wave.'[2]

Stevens turned to a picture of several GIs struggling to get ashore under heavy fire.

'What was his name again?'

'Robert Capa.'

'He must have wanted those photographs very badly.'

Stevens sat in silence and flicked through another eighty pages, finally reaching one of Capa's last pictures, taken only days before he died, aged forty, in Indo-China in 1954. He closed the book and leaned back in his recliner. He suddenly looked tired.

'Have you been back to Omaha?' I asked.

'Yes,' he said proudly. 'Oh yes.'

He pointed to a wall lined with framed photographs. Among the snapshots were two mounted Purple Hearts, his and his brother's. There was also a small picture of him walking along Omaha Beach in 1994, his face contorted with emotion.

'Have you been?' he asked.

'Yes, this spring.'

'Did you visit the graveyard?'

I nodded. That Easter Sunday, I had parked my car beside the rows of tour buses emptying eighty-year-old Americans and their families into the cemetery where thousands of their peers are interred beneath marble headstones on a cliff top overlooking a four-mile-long beach.

At first, I marvelled at the simple dignity of the monuments and the way that the graves all faced one direction, west, towards home. But then I watched a middle-aged woman standing alone, sobbing, before a grave. The father she had never known had died two hundred yards away, along with several hundred other Americans who hit the beach that dreary June day.

On the beach itself, a two-hundred-yard section has been left pretty much undisturbed for almost sixty years. The mines and unexploded shells and all the other lethal defences have been removed, but not the ghosts. It was raining hard as I walked along Easy Green and then the half-mile of Easy Red where Robert Capa photographed possibly the most important moments of the twentieth century, certainly the biggest story of his short but relentlessly dramatic career.

There was a haunting silence on Easy Red, even amidst the howling wind and crash of surf. For many of those who actually landed that day and still return, the silence is deafening. Only in the capsule of a car speeding towards Bayeux or in a tour bus headed back to Paris does the cacophony of dying become a nagging whisper.

Over several months, I interviewed Stevens and other Second World War veterans, photographers as well as soldiers. Every time I met a veteran, I would show him *Images of War*. Many had never seen Capa's pictures of Omaha Beach, let alone his coverage of other momentous days in five different wars. One eighty-year-old bit his lip and closed the book of images: like nothing else, a still photograph conjures up vivid memories. An officer, one of 500,000 Americans who by 1945 had suffered combat fatigue (mental and nervous breakdown), sat and stared for several minutes at images from D-Day, shaking his head every few seconds. Another veteran laughed at an image of a Frenchman handing a carafe of wine to weary GIs, and recalled a similar moment on his long journey from Omaha Beach to Berlin.

Lieutenant Ray Nance, Roy Stevens' commanding officer, struggled to contain his emotions as he saw Capa's pictures of Omaha Beach. He lost every single man in his landing craft in the first wave – boys he'd known since he could remember, cut down before they even touched the sand. Nance spoke slowly at first, as if not wanting to remember, but after several hours he told me Omaha had been his redemption: there must be a God, for why else had he survived? Only God could have spared him from the German machine-gunner who played 'cat and mouse'[3] with him as he crawled alone, badly wounded, across two hundred yards of mined sand.

Others commented that they could not see a single image of violence among Capa's work, only pictures of beauty and sadness. They all wanted to know more about this man who had captured in black and white the most unforgettable moments of their lives. Who was this gambler who left a visual legacy showing the purity of the human spirit?

1 Conversation in Budapest

'It's not enough to have talent. You also have to be Hungarian.'

ROBERT CAPA, quoted, *Life*, 19 April 1997

Autumn 1948: a red star had been painted over the old Hungarian colours on the tail of the lend-lease American Dakota. Robert Capa looked down on the patchwork of farms little changed since feudal times. Then he glimpsed the river of his youth, the Danube. A few minutes later, his plane was bumping along a runway towards a bullet-holed building where grim-faced communist officials stood waiting.

Capa was returning to his birthplace after an absence of seventeen years. He had mixed feelings: nostalgia and intense curiosity as well as anxiety at what he would find in this new communist state. There would be reminders everywhere of his former self: the Jewish kid who'd hustled, fought and bluffed his way to fame.

For many years, Capa's past had largely remained a mystery, even to those who thought they knew him well. But then in 1947 an old friend, John Hersey, the brilliant author of Hiroshima *(1946), had ripped away his debonair mask, revealing the haunted face of a refugee from pain and horror. 'Capa, the photographer who is credited by his colleagues and competitors with having taken the greatest pictures of the Second World War, does not exist,' Hersey had written in an obscure literary magazine,* 47. *'Capa is an invention. There is a thing in the shape of a man – short, swarthy, and carrying itself as if braced for something, with spaniel's eyes, a carefully cynical upper lip, and good luck in the whole face; and this thing walks along and calls itself Capa and is famous. Yet it has no actuality. It is an invention all the time and in all respects.'*[1]

The 'Man Who Invented Himself', as Hersey had dubbed Capa, now moved through the airport lobby. The Communist Party officials waiting for him knew he was in Hungary to report for Holiday *magazine, the glossy American bible of the new jet set. Soon, he was in the outskirts of Buda, the aristocratic town across the Danube from the upstart Pest. A once magnificent city now lay in ruins because of a bitter two-month siege by the Russians during the winter of 1944–45. 'Looking down on the burned-out row of hotels and the ruined bridges,' Capa later wrote, 'Budapest appeared like a beautiful woman with her teeth knocked out.'*

Once Paris's rival in architecture and sophistication, Budapest had been first scarred by Nazism and finally robbed by Stalinism of her once phenomenal powers of seduction. The city was being rebuilt but at an agonizingly slow pace and mostly by hand: on top of the old Ritz Hotel, tiny figures attacked walls with picks. Then Capa arrived at the Danube. Here again, something was missing from the familiar vista. Capa suddenly realized that the Elizabeth Bridge, in his youth the longest suspension bridge in Europe, had disappeared, as had three others. In 1945, the retreating Nazis had blown them up. Many of the riverside cafes had also vanished. The Café Moderne, where his father had played pinochle into the small hours, was one of the few that had escaped German and Soviet bombing.

Capa's driver began to negotiate the narrow streets of Pest, passing the extravagant pre-war buildings of a once ebullient Jewish bourgeoisie. Domes, spires, turrets and cupolas jostled for attention. Balconies boasted bizarre mythological figures. Some buildings still had a gaudy confidence with their imitation marble, fake bronze, art deco stained glass, and peeling stucco walls in every pastel shade imaginable.

The streets were now lined with rubble. Whole blocks had disappeared altogether. The Jewish neighbourhood where Capa had grown up was eerily quiet, many of its former residents having met their end in the gas chambers of Auschwitz. Here and there, from wrought-iron lampposts, hung banners supporting Hungary's new communist regime.

Strange memories began to haunt Capa, creeping like ghosts from familiar alleys. There was the baby elephant that did tricks on the dance floor of the Arizona nightclub. Then there was that unforgettable night when his blood had trickled across the stone floors of the dictator Admiral Horthy's police headquarters. Capa had returned to Budapest, he wrote, 'to listen to a new music'.[2] *But now he remembered an old, terrifying tune: Horthy's Chief of Police, Peter Heim, had whistled Beethoven's Fifth while beating up long-haired revolutionaries like Capa.*

Capa checked into the Hotel Bristol, the lone survivor of a famous pre-war row of elegant hotels. The head desk clerk examined his passport and asked him if he had ever been to Hollywood. Was he well connected there? The man's questions reminded him of his arrival in America for the first time, at Ellis Island, and an equally inquisitive clerk who'd asked him if he had ever been to Moscow.

Capa was given a discount on his room and the address of a bar where he would find the last vestiges of bourgeois decadence in Budapest. He arrived there later that evening, and chatted to its owner, Anna, a beautiful twenty-five-year-old, who complained that the communists were unspeakably dull and bad for business. Capa photographed her smoking a cigarette, wearing fake jewels and a sexy black top. She had full lips and lustrous dark hair but a haunted look in her eyes. She came from an aristocratic family and had been a very accomplished rider before the Nazis had stolen her horses. Then the communists had taken her lands. She had tried to escape Hungary, she told Capa, but had been caught by the police, and was now waiting for a passport.

By 2 a.m., Capa was feeling sentimental. He decided to ask Anna to take a stroll with him along the banks of the Danube. There, under the flickering lamplight, he had charmed his first conquests, and soon he did the same with Anna. Months later, he boasted to friends in Paris that he had bedded a genuine Hungarian blue-blood. Before the war, his class had doffed their caps and addressed Anna as Countess Fehervary.

The next morning, Capa left the Hotel Bristol, Leicas dangling around his neck. Demolition experts were clearing the ruins of nearby hotels. After every explosion, a hail of bricks flew overhead. He made for Vaczi Street, once the most elegant shopping area in Budapest, if not Europe. In his youth, he had known a Jewish boy, Sandor, who worked in a furrier's shop there. Because only one out of twenty of Hungary's Jews survived the Holocaust, he was surprised to find him alive, and shocked by how old he looked: his hair had fallen out; horror had etched his face with deep wrinkles. He had been an inmate in the death camps and then a prisoner of the Russians. Now he repaired the torn furs of once-rich ladies.

After several days in Budapest, Capa met with another old friend, a writer called György Markos. Capa played his usual part of droll raconteur, the laconic charmer with one tall story after another. He told Markos he had once become entangled in a tree because his parachute had snagged several branches. Not knowing if he was behind enemy lines or not, he had hung there calmly sipping from a bottle of Scotch until he was cut down. Then there was the time President Roosevelt, no less, had asked him if he could help him in some way. 'Yes, get me a passport,' he had replied.[3]

As the night drew to a close, Capa confessed to Markos that he'd been a displaced person since 1931. He was still travelling on a refugee's passport. In fact he had been drifting from one hotel to another, from one war zone to another, since the age of seventeen.

'And what will you do now?' Markos asked.

'What can a jobless war reporter do?' shrugged Capa. 'I'll travel around wherever I can.'

'So you are still looking for adventure? Do you admit deep down inside that you are an adventurer and need the excitement of war?'

'You're crazy!' snapped Capa. 'I hate violence and the thing I hate most is war.'[4]

On 22 October 1913, André Friedmann was born with a shock of thick black hair and a surplus little finger on one hand. The deformity confirmed his mother Julia's belief that he was a special child, one of Jehovah's chosen.[5] World war and constant conflict between his parents were André's earliest experiences. He was less than a year old when Hungary entered the Great War of 1914–18 on the side of the Germans. Until he left Hungary as a political refugee in 1931, barely a week passed when his parents did not fight bitterly with each other, usually over his father's compulsive gambling and subsequent lies.[6]

André's parents had little in common other than that they were non-practising Jews who had come from desperately poor backgrounds. Born in June 1880, his father Dezsö Friedmann had grown up in a remote village in Transylvania: a hinterland of ancient superstition, medieval culture and Romantic sensibilities. In his youth, Dezsö escaped the backwoods and roamed Europe for several months, making his way from Budapest to London and then to Paris. For the rest of his life, he romanticized this period of wanderlust: the young André sat and listened for hours as his fast-talking, diminutive father told stories about living on his wits and charm as he drifted, looking for money and excitement, from one unfriendly city to another.

Dezsö married Julianna Henrietta Berkovits, André's mother, in 1910 and together they set up a small salon in the Belvaros area of Pest, to this day the heart of the city's commercial district. They made their first home in a new U-shaped apartment building on Városház Utca, a few yards from the Pilvax Café where leaders of an 1848 revolution had once met.

Dezsö called himself a master tailor but quickly showed himself to be an aspiring bon viveur, far more interested in wearing smart suits than making them. Luck explained failure or success. Life's rules were as simple as pinochle, his game of choice. All the best players acted like winners, and looking the part was what got you into the right game at the right table. That was the hard part. Then fortune would show her hand. It was a philosophy his young son would never forget.

André's mother believed the opposite. The daughter of a careworn peasant, she had grown up in a feudal corner of the Austro-Hungarian Empire, one of ten children, and had toiled all her life. Apprenticed to a dressmaker at twelve, Julia was fiercely determined to save her sons from the same fate, and was often seated at her sewing table from morning until the early hours, fantasizing that her special child would do more than peddle uniforms of hope to the Jewish bourgeoisie.

When she wasn't working, Julia often spoiled André and dressed him in beautifully made sailor's outfits and lacy ensembles. A 1917 image shows a pensive André, dressed in one of his mother's elaborate costumes, sitting with his smiling family. The Friedmanns never looked quite so happy again. In October 1918, a few weeks before the war ended, revolution rocked Budapest, and the family watched massive crowds throng the streets, waving chrysanthemums, the symbol of the communist uprising of Leninist Béla Kun. Hungary's experiment in Soviet dictatorship ended, however, on 1 August 1919, after just 133 days, with a coup d'état supported by the Romanian army.

By the late autumn Admiral Horthy, a prototype fascist, was firmly in control of Hungary. Within a couple of months, Horthy ordered the execution of 5,000 Leftists. More than 70,000 went to jail or internment camps. In what soon became known as the White Terror, organized pogroms swept Hungary, fuelled partly by Horthy's characterization of Béla Kun and others as Jewish traitors. The Friedmanns kept their sons safe at home while in a nearby alley Rightists beat up several Jewish students, emboldened by anti-Semitic laws that set quotas for Jewish entry into universities and law schools.*

But the greatest psychological blow to André's homeland was not defeat in the Great War nor Horthy's dictatorship but rather a piece of paper – the Trianon Peace Treaty, part of the much broader peace settlements at Versailles. On 4 June 1920, Hungary was forced to cede 70 per cent of its territory and 60 per cent of its total population. The new borders reduced Hungary by two-thirds. Of all the defeated powers, Hungary lost most. Patriotic Hungarians' bitter protest, '*Nem, nem, solia!*' (No, no, never!), echoed throughout André's youth.[7]

In 1923, André entered the Imre Madách Gymnasium on the Barcsay Utca. A below-average pupil with a short attention span, he often failed to complete his homework and appeared to his classmates to be a rather shabby daydreamer. '[His] trousers were always torn,' according to his mother 'Julita'. 'He was always walking into a lamp-post because he was talking too hard. He was a good-natured child, with no rudeness in him. Always the face smiled. Sometimes he was a little clumsy, and his clumsiness made him shy. And he loved the girls already – even when he was a baby.'[8]

By the time André reached adolescence, Julia was far too busy trying to keep the family business going to pay much attention to the son she

* The proportion of Jewish students in Hungary fell from 34 per cent in 1917–18 to only 8 per cent in 1935–36.

had once spoiled. After school, he roamed Pest's Jewish quarter with a gang of other children who lived on their wits.* 'André seemed to do whatever he liked,' remembers childhood friend Eva Besnyö, then a dark-haired, rather sombre girl with eyes so dark that a man riding a tram once told her to go home and wash them.

When he wasn't roaming Pest's back streets, André played with Eva and her two teenage sisters, Panna and Magda. 'André later told me, great romantic that he was, that he was in love with my sisters and me. André couldn't choose which one of us he loved most,' says Eva, whose upper-middle-class mother fiercely disapproved of the uncouth André. 'He hoped some day that someone would steal us away, so he could be the hero and rescue us. Then my parents would finally approve of him. He was very, very romantic at heart.'

Eva, now ninety-one years old and a Jewish survivor of a century of horrors, lives alone in Amsterdam – her home since fleeing Hitler in 1933. Though physically feeble, she is still sharp, and her memories are bitter, romantic and vivid. A celebrated photographer in Holland, she has thought in images all her life. 'I used to call Capa "Bandi" back then,' she says (Bandi is short for André). 'That was his nickname. We also used to call him "Capa", which meant shark. His [brother] Cornell's nickname was crocodile.'*

As Besnyö remembers him, Bandi often complained of being bored and would seek out conflict and danger. It was with her that he discovered a passion for skiing – in spite of Julia's angry protests.† Aged

*While researching his childhood for an unpublished biography, the writer Jozefa Stuart formed an image of the young André Friedmann as a 'little rascal, with great charm, who was forever running. He never stopped running, all his life. He never had a real home, a place where there were regular meals, where the family sat down together for dinner . . . it was a chaotic childhood.'

† She had slipped the day before I spoke to her, and had gashed her head, which she had wrapped in a silk-flowered scarf. She poured green tea with shaking hands, stubbornly refusing help. Outside, Amsterdam's canals were silent, as still as reflecting pools. Inside, she sat surrounded by photographs, books and Bauhaus furniture – relics of the last heady days of Weimar Germany. She remembered all the Friedmann boys vividly. The eldest, László, born in 1911, began working in the family business at fifteen but died young in 1936 of rheumatic fever. The youngest was Cornell, born in 1918, the year Hungary plunged into chaos following defeat in the First World War.

fifteen, he borrowed some skis and headed with Besnyö to Svabhegy Hill overlooking Budapest. Neither had even tried on a pair of skis but that didn't stop them climbing on a ski lift and heading to the summit.

'I'm going to do it,' said André with determination as Budapest faded into the distance, the icy Danube forming a giant curve below.

'But you don't know what to do,' replied Besnyö.

André shrugged: 'I'm going to do it anyway.'

'He was never afraid to try new things, especially any adventure that involved a little danger,' Besnyö now says. 'I hoped he wouldn't break a leg, and he didn't. He went down and then climbed back up. He always wanted to discover everything for himself.'

A swarthy youth with heavy brows, full lips and delicate hands, André was increasingly popular with his classmates and the neighbourhood's girls. Often, he could be found kissing in the shadows beneath the Elizabeth Bridge, a popular venue for Pest's youngest lovers. But it seems he did not lose his virginity to a doe-eyed Slavic girl from Pest. He later claimed that he first had sex with a wealthy middle-aged client of his mother's who seduced him when he delivered a new dress.[9]

Not long after, he became involved with Leftist revolutionaries. The climate demanded bold action: in Hungary, bloody social unrest erupted throughout the late twenties between Left and Right. On the streets of the capital, pitched battles between rival factions became a weekly fixture, and by the time he was sixteen, André had become a veteran street fighter, often joining thousands of other young radicals as they marched through the working-class districts of Pest. 'André became politically active for several reasons,' explains Besnyö. 'He was discriminated against as a Jew. But he was also interested in the danger.'

During the McCarthy witch-hunt in the 1950s, André was afraid that his past would catch up with him and repeatedly denied joining the Communist Party in Hungary, or indeed any other country. He

*Besnyö's favourite pastime was photography. The proud owner of a Kodak Brownie camera, she spent much of her free time taking photographs around Budapest. On some occasions, André joined her, but she insists, 'He was not interested in photography when we were together in Budapest. We never talked about photography.'

explained his political stance during this period in a 1953 affidavit: 'During my last two years in high school, I became interested in literature and politics and decided to make my career as a journalist. I was, at that time, highly critical of the anti-Semitic dictatorship of Admiral Horthy. I studied socialism, but found myself in immediate disagreement with the aims and methods of the Communist Party.'[10]

André did not tell the FBI in this affidavit that late one night he met a Communist Party recruiter in Budapest. According to his brother Cornell, the recruiter told André that 'the party was not interested in young bourgeois intellectuals.* Conversely, [André] decided he was not interested in the party.'[11] This late-night flirtation with communism cost André dearly, if his brother is to be believed: 'The damage had been done,' he wrote later. 'The walk was observed by the secret police.'[12] When André got home, two agents arrested him. Julia begged them to not take her son: so many other subversives had never returned from Horthy's police cells. But her pleas were ignored, and André was bustled into the back of a police van and taken for interrogation. In a small cell, where other political prisoners had scrawled their names on the walls, thugs hired by Peter Heim punched and beat him.

'It was usual for young firebrands like André to get roughed up as a deterrent,' says Besnyö. 'But they couldn't scare André. He laughed in their face when they hit him, for they could only insinuate that he was a Leftist. They could not prove that he was a communist.' André apparently laughed at his interrogators until they knocked him unconscious.

How and on what condition he was later released remains a mystery. The wife of Imre Hetényi, a deputy chief of the state police, was, according to Cornell, 'a good customer' of his parents' salon. 'Through that connection our father was able to secure [my brother's] release on the condition he leave Hungary at once.'[13]

Could a minor Jewish tailor really have influenced the strong man of a police state? Perhaps Hiem had lost to Deszö at pinochle? Eva Besnyö suggests there was a far less dramatic reason for André finally leaving Hungary: he simply followed her example.* As a young Jew she

* It is highly unlikely that the Communist Party would have rejected André when it needed every young, streetwise militant it could find. Besides, he was no bourgeois intellectual.

yearned to escape the rising anti-Semitism in Hungary. In 1930, her father agreed to send her to study photography in Berlin, the epicentre of experimentation in photography. When Besnyö told André she was leaving for Berlin, he replied nonchalantly: 'Perhaps I'll also come.'

'How are you going to manage to get there?' she asked. She knew the Friedmanns barely had enough money to put him through college in Budapest, let alone pay for expenses to Berlin. 'Never you mind about that,' replied André. 'I'll get there.'

*Her father had arranged to send her to an expensive art college in Budapest after she left school. In due course, she became aware of several documentary trends in Hungarian photography and of the ideas of the left-wing writer and artist Lajos Kassák, who believed photography was an art form with unexplored social utility. Photographs could be a socially conscious artist's means of showing truth to the world, thereby helping to change it. While André was throwing rocks at fascists, Besnyö was using a Rolleiflex camera to document dockers and peasant women in local villages.

2 Barbarians at the Gate

'I am a camera.'

CHRISTOPHER ISHERWOOD, *Goodbye To Berlin*

In July 1931, André left Budapest by train. After a roundabout journey, he arrived in Berlin in early September. Alone and suddenly feeling vulnerable, not yet eighteen years old, he sought out Eva Besnyö and eventually found her living in a small studio.*

'How did you manage to get here?' Besnyö asked him.

André had not hitchhiked nor found his way by some other romantic means. Instead, he had cannily traded on his Jewish identity to make good his vow to follow her to Berlin. 'André was always very street smart,' Besnyö recalls. 'He had discovered that the Jewish community in Budapest sent gifted students abroad to study. So he had applied to them for a grant, and they had accepted his application.' But the grant had not allowed him to travel directly from Budapest to Berlin: he had had to hop from one Jewish host family to another, finally arriving via Prague, Vienna and Dresden.

When Besnyö asked what he was going to do in Berlin, he told

*Since leaving Hungary, she felt as if she had come alive: 'In Berlin, the doors opened and light flooded in. Light in the darkness. I became a new person.' Already, she had taken wonderfully detailed pictures of the city's architecture and wide streets. Through her viewfinder, Berlin was a futuristic metropolis of 'powerful diagonal lines, bird's and worm's eye views, tilted images and extreme close-ups.' (Eva Besnyö, *Eva Besnyö* (Amsterdam: Focus Publishing, 2000).

her he was going to study political science at the famous Deutsche Hochschule Für Politik, and on 27 October he duly registered for the winter term. But he was too restless and inquisitive about Berlin – too hungry for experience – to sit through the endlessly theoretical lectures and before long he started to skip classes.

These first months in Berlin were not uncomfortable. Relatives sent him small amounts of money and his parents sent a monthly allowance. But then, as the world economy sank into depression following the 1929 Wall Street crash, the Friedmann salon lost customers and Julia stopped sending the few marks he needed each month. As autumn turned to bitter winter, he started to learn about desperation. According to his cousin Suzy Marquis, he soon became so hungry that he stole veal cutlets from the dog-dish of his landlady, Frau Bohen.[1] Having gone several weeks without paying rent, André bolted as soon as Frau Bohen began to suspect where her beloved dachshund's dinner had gone.

By early 1932, André needed to make money if he was to continue his studies without starving. Having briefly considered journalism as a career in Budapest, he now started to consider photography seriously. 'While pursuing my studies,' he stated in 1953, 'my parents' means gave out, and I decided to become a photographer, which was the nearest thing to journalism for anyone who found himself without a language.'[2] (His German was still limited at this stage.)

He asked Eva Besnyö if she could help find him a job with an agency or in a studio. 'This photography business,' he wondered, 'is it a good way to make a living?'

'You can't talk like that!' Besnyö replied. 'It's not a profession. It's a calling.'

'Never mind about that. Is it good fun?'

'Yes. It's very enjoyable.'

Eva Besnyö knew several people who might be able to help André find work. Perhaps his best bet would be to contact a photographer called Otto Umbehrs, an ex-miner who had studied design at the Bauhaus school of art and design, and was now director of portraiture and advertising work at a prestigious agency called

Dephot.* Besnyö called Umbo (the name most people used for him) and asked if he could use a 'very clever boy'. Umbo told Besnyö to send André to see him. When she next heard from André, he was working in Dephot's darkroom as an assistant, refilling bottles of fixer and developer, hanging prints up to dry, and learning the rudiments of exposure and printing.

André was enthralled by the agency's exciting, fast-paced environment. Deadlines loomed, tempers frayed, and the chase for pictures and stories was relentless. Although he had been hired for a pittance to slave in the darkroom, it wasn't long before he was also helping to arrange assignments and doing general administrative work in the agency's main office. His days were frenetic and long – Dephot fed many of Germany's 2,500 newspapers and periodicals, and at least a dozen of Berlin's papers that issued an illustrated supplement each week.

Calling the shots at Dephot was Simon Guttmann, a small bespectacled man with boundless energy and a genius for originating story ideas. In 1928, he had set up Dephot to profit from the rapid growth in illustrated magazines in Germany. By the time André joined the agency, his photographers included several esteemed photojournalists such as Felix Man, who since 1929 had worked for the *Müncher Illustrierte Presse*, for a guaranteed 1,000 marks a month. André may have been working at Dephot when Man shot his most celebrated photo series, 'A Day in the Life of Mussolini'. Today, it is regarded as a classic of early reportage, a photo-story that brilliantly and subtly caught Il Duce's vanity and absurdity.[3]

By the summer of 1932, André had given up college (his excuse for getting to Berlin) and was assisting Man and others on assignments to

*A wildly Bohemian enthusiast of the Dada movement, Umbo bridged the divide between Besnyö's world of experimental photographers, influenced by the ideas of Moholy-Nagy and György Kepes, and the first golden age of photojournalism. A superb 'flash-bulber', as André called experts in flash-photography, Umbo was peerless in capturing the startled look of Berlin's doomed decadents: graceful women caught unawares in a moment of illumination in a cellar nightclub, lesbians giggling at a sweaty cabaret, and fur-clad libertines high on Berlin's 'Süssen Liebe' – sweet life.

record daily life in the city. Often he would be handed a small camera to reload – one of the first models of the now famous Leica.* The Leica made the impossible feasible, with its high-speed lens and focal plane shutters that brought exposure times down to 1/1000 of a second. It allowed Dephot's photojournalists to take action pictures and work in low-light conditions without relying on complicated and expensive lighting equipment.[4]

André borrowed a Leica from the Dephot office and quickly learned how to maximize its technical advantages. There was no better place or time to practise reportage: Berlin was a fascinating brew of political and cultural extremes. The German photographer Gisèle Freund was a student in Berlin during this period; she later befriended André after fleeing Germany and smuggling out harrowing photographs she'd taken of Hitler's political victims. 'The capital of the young Republic,' she recalled, was 'the centre of German and artistic and intellectual movements. Its theatre became celebrated for the plays of Bertolt Brecht, Ernst Toller and Karl Zuckmayer and for the work of the directors Max Reinhardt and Edwin Piscator. The silent films of U.F.A., directed by Fritz Lang, Ernst Lubitsch, and others were internationally known.'†

By 1932, Berlin was also a battleground where Left and Right fought in the streets for Germany's future. On 4 June 1932 the Reichstag was dissolved and national elections were scheduled for 31 July. On 15 June, a ban on the SA (the *Sturmabteilung* – Storm Battalion), a Nazi paramilitary organization, was lifted and Germany plunged into political violence. In Berlin, hundreds died in street battles in working-class districts. By mid-July, civil war threatened to engulf the country. Every political party, except the warring Nazis and communists, demanded the restoration of law and order. Martial law was declared in Berlin.

On 31 July, the National Socialist Party won more seats than any

*Later models dangle from the neck of almost every respected photojournalist to this day.

†But the Nazis had already made their cultural intentions clear. At a 1931 premiere of Erich Maria Remarque's pacifist *All Quiet on The Western Front*, they organized riots to protest against the film, even invading a Berlin cinema where they threw stink bombs and let loose mice before finally succeeding in getting the film banned.

other party, gaining 13,745,000 votes. Germany's middle and upper classes had turned out in force for Hitler, partly because of widespread fear of a communist uprising. Although the communists seemed to be quickly gaining working-class support – they won twelve seats to become the third largest party in the Reichstag, with eighty-nine members – they could form no opposition to the Nazis' 320 seats.

It was that autumn, with Germany in political disarray, that André got his first big break at Dephot. One day, he saw incredibly exotic images take form in the agency's red-lit darkroom. They were of a bewitching India, as seen by Harald Lechenperg, one of Dephot's most intrepid reporters. Enthralled, André rushed into Guttmann's office and told him how superlative the pictures were. Recognizing his passion, Guttmann decided to nurture André and several weeks later sent him on his first major assignment.[5]

On 27 November, André slipped into the Copenhagen Stadium – the Sportpalast – and waited for his first subject to appear before a large crowd. Guttmann had asked him to photograph Leon Trotsky as he lectured on 'the meaning of the Russian Revolution'. As Trotsky spoke, André snapped away, capturing grainy images of Stalin's arch-enemy in his last moments before a large audience. When Trotsky fell silent, the Sportpalast erupted in loud applause. André watched Trotsky standing alone, suddenly looking exhausted. The rousing ovations were not for the speech. The students were saluting a man already being hunted by Stalin's assassins who had been rejected by one country after another in a desperate quest for a refuge. As Trotsky left the stage, it seemed as if death hovered over him.

André was not the only photographer in the Sportpalast that Sunday with a Leica but his pictures were by far the most dramatic. Crucially, he had got within a few feet of his subject. Although technically they were far from perfect, his images had what would become a trademark intimacy and intensity. When André arrived back in Berlin, he discovered that the magazine *Der Welt Spiegel* had given his pictures a full-page layout. In small print, at the bottom of the page, were the intoxicating words: '*Aufnahmen: Friedmann – Dephot*'.[6]

But André's first byline did little to improve his precarious financial situation. Often penniless, he started to visit the Romanisches Café, a gathering place for the émigré community, where he could usually scrounge something to eat or a cup of coffee from his fellow Hungarians. But there were fewer of them in Berlin by the day. His friend Besnyö had already left Berlin that summer. 'The streets had been taken over by Brown Shirts [the SA],' she explained. 'Everywhere in the city you could see Nazis with clubs hanging from their belts. I began to feel terribly insecure.'[7]

André stayed on, unwilling to return to Hungary where Admiral Horthy's fascist regime had stepped up its persecution of Jews and democrats. And so, as intellectuals and artists fled Berlin, a homeless André roamed the city, often sleeping in parks and doorways, witnessing from the gutter Hitler's rise to power.

On 30 January 1933, President Hindenburg's advisers persuaded him to appoint Hitler as chancellor. As dusk descended on a chaotic Berlin, the sound of jack-boots grew louder and louder. André watched as Nazi storm troopers marched through the streets in perfect formation, holding blazing torches high in the air to celebrate the Austrian corporal's ascent to power. By the thousand, Germany's new elite emerged from the woods of Tiergarten, stamped through the Brandenburg Gate and down Wilhelmstrasse. The words of their favourite marching song, '*Horst Wessel*', echoed throughout Germany. At the Chancellery, Hitler basked in his moment of astonishing glory.

The Nazi revolution mesmerized the German people. Hitler promised national revival, jobs, restored German pride, and the destruction of the decadent forces that had given rise to the abominations of the Weimar Republic: homosexuals, communists and Jews. After Hitler's night of triumph, it was clear to André that his days in Berlin were numbered. Sooner or later he would be arrested and perhaps sent to an internment camp. If he slept in the wrong doorway, or bumped into a group of drunken Hitler Youth, he could be knifed or even beaten to death.

On 27 February, the Reichstag disappeared into raging flames and along with it all hope of a democratic future for Germany. The next day, Hitler banned the Communist Party, which he claimed had set the fire, and declared a state of emergency. The Third Reich had begun. As the Reichstag's embers still smouldered, over 4,000 Communist officials and a great many Social Democrat and liberal leaders were arrested. Ernst Röhm's SA thugs broke into homes and shot suspected subversives on the spot. The fortunate were tortured and beaten. Others were sent to the first concentration camps.

André finally decided to leave Berlin and contacted the Jewish organization that had helped him get to the city in the first place. [8] As soon as he received the money for a ticket, he took a train to Vienna. Among the tens of thousands also fleeing Nazi Germany were many of the century's artistic and scientific luminaries: Albert Einstein, Thomas Mann, Bertolt Brecht and Wassily Kandinsky.

In Vienna, André stayed with Dephot photographer Harald Lechenperg for several weeks. But history continued to snap at his heels. A week after the Reichstag fire, the Austrian Chancellor, Engelbert Dollfuss, instituted a totalitarian regime. By June 1933, André had returned to Budapest, where he found Julia, Dezsö and his older brother László still making dresses, but barely making ends meet.

For several weeks, André found work with the Veres travel agency, taking pictures of local landmarks. By late summer, however, he was again desperate to leave Hungary. The Hungarian Left had been ruthlessly crushed during his absence and his prospects of becoming a professional photographer in his native land seemed dim. The obvious place to go next was Paris, where thousands of other Jewish Hungarians had already found refuge from fascism.[9]

3 The Man Who Invented Himself

'There are some people who are born to be Parisian and Capa was one of them. Worldly, handsome, languid, and dandyish when it suited him . . . [Capa] might have been born near the Bastille or in one of the great houses of the sixteenth arrondissement.'

IRWIN SHAW, *Vogue*, April 1982

Paris proved to be just as cruel as Berlin. At first, André struggled even to eat. For several months, he drifted from one ramshackle hotel to another, leaving before the managers could force him to pay his bills. Hustling odd jobs, drinking heavily when he could find a few francs, he was by the winter of 1934 a frequent visitor to a pawnshop in the Latin quarter. Simply to survive, he would trade in his most prized possession – a Leica. 'Mostly [André] carried this instrument – a Leica, with one lens and one button to push – to and from [the] pawnshop,' according to John Hersey. 'The camera spent three weeks in pledge at the shop to each week it spent in Friedmann's hands.'[1]

When André had nothing left to pawn and couldn't afford to buy food, he tried fishing for his supper in the Seine but without much luck. Occasionally, he would visit his mother's cousin, Szeren Fischer, who lived in a modest apartment near the Madeleine with her husband, Béla, and six-year-old daughter, Suzy. A bowl of soup was always on hand and he was even able to make use of an old enlarger which Suzy's father, a keen amateur photographer, kept in a windowless closet.[2] Suzy remembers André's visits to this day, for he would always bring her some small item as a gift and play with her. Eventually, she became one of André's few confidantes. 'Bandi always had an aura – charisma,' she says. 'From the first time I remember him, when I was three on a visit to Budapest, Bandi was the kind you couldn't ignore. You could hate him, you could love him, you could worship him but you were not indifferent to him.'

Living in rooms not much bigger than a bed, André and his fellow refugees made their true homes in Left Bank cafes. One of André's favourites was the Café du Dôme in Montparnasse, where Anaïs Nin had whispered her love to Henry Miller. It was at the Dôme in early 1934 that André befriended a Polish Jew, David 'Chim' Seymour. Quiet, with thick glasses and an owlish face, Chim was a witty intellectual who worked for the communist weekly *Regards* and would become perhaps André's closest friend. Born on 20 November 1911 in Warsaw, the son of a respected Yiddish publisher, Chim had dreamed of being a concert pianist before discovering the graphic arts at college in Leipzig and then trying his hand at photography while studying physics at the Sorbonne.

One day at the Dôme, Chim introduced André to another working photographer: Henri Cartier-Bresson, an *haut-bourgeois* Norman whose family owned one of the most successful textile businesses in France.* Cartier-Bresson had grown up in Chanteloup, near Paris, the son of an artistic businessman and a mother who was descended from Charlotte Corday, who had been executed for assassinating the famous revolutionary Jean-Paul Marat. After an exclusive private school and a year at Cambridge, he had travelled widely in Europe, Mexico and Africa. He had already held exhibitions of his work in Spain and Mexico.

In Cartier-Bresson's eyes, André would always be an anarchist who treated everyone the same and a wonderfully romantic 'player',[3] but not a photographer of outstanding intellect. 'Before I met [André] and

* 'With one stroke,' the French photographer Jean Lacouture has written, 'the little Polish refugee forged an alliance between the decade's two most antithetical pursuers of the image – movement and structure, nature and culture – a partnership as improbable as that of the torrent and the rock.' (Jean Lacoutre, *Introduction to Robert Capa* (Paris: Pantheon Photo Library, 1988).)

Chim,' Cartier-Bresson recalled, 'I was living with writers and painters more than photographers . . . [André] was not primarily a vision man, he was an adventurer with a tremendous sense of life. But the photography was not the main thing, it was what he had to say, his whole personality. Chim was a philosopher, a chess player, a man who though not religious at all carried the burden of being Jewish within him as a kind of sadness.'[4]

Of the three, André and Chim were the true *copains* – intimates, bonded by their Eastern European sensibilities and experiences of anti-Semitism. The fate of European Jewry was already plastered on the walls of Paris, just as it had been in Berlin and Budapest: anti-Semitic election posters, pasted up by fascists, disfigured metro stations and other public places. As photographers, all three soon documented brilliantly the social and industrial strife in France as the country lurched from one political crisis to another during the mid-1930s. In Eugen Weber's masterly 1994 book, *The Hollow Years: France in the 1930s*, the three men's photographs combine to provide a dazzling portrait of the doomed Third Republic.

Another refugee who soon joined this group of ambitious, politicized photographers was Pierre Gassmann, a German photographer and printer.* 'From the moment I met [André] until he died, he was always great fun, always very much one to live in the moment, absolutely passionate about life – especially food, wine and women. He was very instinctive, a very natural photographer. He wanted to show people things they had never seen. He wanted to shock and surprise.'[5] He was soon fixing prints for Chim, André and Cartier-Bresson in a bidet in his apartment.

Not long after André had made these new friends, Simon Guttmann visited Paris, tracked him down through contacts in the Hungarian community and then offered him a job: taking publicity

*Although he has worked with many of the century's great photographers, there is just one photograph mounted in Gassmann's living room. It shows André smiling winsomely in 1952, aged thirty-eight, just two years before he died. Today, Gassmann is the owner of the famous Parisian printing lab, Picto.

shots for a Swiss life insurance company's brochure.[6] For one picture, he would need to find a beautiful young blonde and then pose her in a local park.

André knew where to find likely candidates: the Left Bank cafes where he'd spent the last several months hustling centimes for a glass of wine and plotting how to make enough money to take his Leica out of pawn. One afternoon, he met Ruth Cerf, a stunning Swiss refugee. She remembers that they got talking and André asked her to pose in a park in Montparnasse. '[He] looked like a tramp. He said he was looking for a model. I agreed to the picture but I was worried about being alone with him so I decided to take a friend.'

She arrived at the park with her flatmate, Gerda Pohorylles: a spirited five-foot redhead with a tomboy haircut and sparkling green eyes who would soon change the entire course of André's life.[7] Like Cerf, she found André rather uncouth but also very charismatic and handsome. Born into a bookish family on 1 August 1911 in Stuttgart, Gerda was also a refugee from fascism. During the last years of the Weimar Republic she attended a commercial school, learned secretarial skills, wore high heels to classes and got engaged, much to the fury of her rich aunt, to a suave thirty-five-year-old cotton trader, Hans Bote. The engagement lasted a matter of weeks before Gerda fell in love with a Russian medical student, Georg Kavitkes, who introduced her to Bolshevism.

By the time Hitler came to power in 1933, Gerda was already an active member of communist organizations, and had distributed anti-Nazi flyers and pasted left-wing manifestos on walls at night. In a letter to one friend she had even speculated about being beaten to death by the Nazis. On 19 March 1933 the Nazis arrested her on suspicion of involvement in a Bolshevik conspiracy against Hitler. While searching her bedroom, they found a letter to her boyfriend, Georg, that made reference to communism. She managed to convince her interrogators that she was simply a silly young woman with no political convictions and in August she crossed into France with a Polish passport and made her way to Paris, where she was helped by several communist organizations that provided food and shelter to political refugees. Ruth

Cerf worked for one such organization and the pair shared an apartment that was so badly heated that they spent winter afternoons huddled up to stay warm.[8]

Shortly after meeting Gerda, André picked up a piece of stationery from the Café Dôme and scribbled his mother a brief letter. He explained that Simon Guttmann had again come to the rescue and found him his first foreign assignments – he was going to Spain.[9] Filled with excitement, he had no idea that Guttmann had arranged to sell the stories to the *Berliner Illustrierte Zeitung*, a magazine with a nasty habit of running pretty pictures of Nazis on its cover.[10]

Spain captivated André from the moment he arrived in San Sebastián, just across the French border. The country had much in common with Hungary, from the influence of Islam to the food, the prevalence of gypsy folklore and the expressive culture. Indeed, Spain was a home from home, a country whose soul André instantly understood, and whose vibrancy thrilled him to the core.

His first assignment was a story about the boxer Paolino Uzcudun, who was scheduled to fight the German heavyweight champion Max Schmeling in Berlin on 7 July 1935: his photographs showed a much more dignified, yet tougher, sport than the corrupted pugilism we see on television today.[11] His next stop was Madrid, where he photographed the daredevil Lieutenant Colonel Emilio Herrera beside a specially designed hot-air balloon. According to *Vu* magazine, Herrera planned to break the world record for a balloon ascent.[12] On 14 April, André witnessed a parade to mark the fourth anniversary of the Spanish Republic – a fragile experiment in democracy. He then travelled to Seville for Holy Week, the most boisterous and exotic festival in the Spanish religious calendar.

The gypsy in André thrilled to the images that soon flashed past his viewfinder. Sixty-four immense bronze statues were borne in a procession several miles long through the city.[13] Among the revellers were señoritas with azure eyes, silk-clad flamenco dancers, pomaded toreros and others in costumes reminiscent of the Inquisition and the Ku Klux Klan. Firecrackers fizzed until first light as the spectacular religious processions wound through the ancient city's narrow streets. In a letter to Gerda back in Paris, André described these scenes in vivid detail, and how he and the townspeople drank the night away. He ended the letter by saying in ungrammatical German that she was often in his thoughts.[14]

With the income from the two stories, André was able to take a much-needed holiday. That summer, he joined Gerda, Willi Chardack, a medical student, and another friend, Raymond Gorin, on the island of Sainte Marguerite, off the Côte d'Azur. André and Gerda were soon inseparable. 'They fell in love in the South of France,' recalls Ruth Cerf.

Gerda began to dream. André was blessed with enormous potential but he was too undisciplined, too bohemian, often arrogant and feckless. She also recognized André as something of a 'rogue and a womanizer' according to Ruth Cerf. But perhaps his charm and daring, once allied to a professional attitude to his work, would save them both from poverty. She found to her delight that André did not protest when she nagged him about drinking and told him to smarten himself up. Here was a woman who didn't suffocate with affection, and who was as unashamed of her sexuality as she was self-conscious of her outsider status in Paris as a German Jew.* He started to call her 'the boss',[15] taught her in a matter of days how to handle a Leica, and even developed some of her first pictures. Soon they were living together in a studio apartment near the Eiffel Tower.

'Without Gerda, André maybe wouldn't have made it,' says Eva Besnyö. 'She picked him up, gave him direction . . . He had never wanted an ordinary life, and so when things didn't go well, he drank and gambled. He was in a bad way when they met, and maybe without her it would have been the end for him.'

In a letter to his mother that autumn,[16] André said he'd found Gerda a job selling pictures for a new agency called Alliance, run by a formidably efficient and beautiful woman called Maria Eisner. He

* She once washed before André's friends in the nude and, according to Ruth Cerf, failed throughout her short life to be monogamous. 'For Gerda, men were somewhat disposable,' says Cerf. 'She was no feminist. Rich men were always her favourites.'

himself was also working as a part-time picture editor for a Japanese monthly owned by the Mainichi Press.*

Around this time, Julia informed André that she was going to visit her sisters who had moved to New York. What she may not have told him was that her marriage to his father was over. According to one of André's surviving relatives, Dezsö's gambling had finally forced the family business to go under and the Friedmann marriage along with it. Within a year, according to this relative and Ruth Cerf, Dezsö would play his final hand and 'take his own life', in Cerf's words.

Before Dezsö allegedly committed suicide, his youngest son, Cornell, joined André in Paris, hoping to become a doctor. When not studying French, he began to develop André's pictures, and before long, he was also doing the same for Chim and Cartier-Bresson. Eventually, he converted the bathroom across the hall from his hotel room into a darkroom. 'It was in rue Vavin in a small hotel facing the Café Dôme. I had a room on the top floor, and if I stuck my head out from my roof window, I looked right down on the Dôme, where all the photographers, artists, foreigners, philosophers and Parisians met and drank coffee.'[17]

In April 1936, again on stationery from the Café Dôme, André told his mother that his transition from waster to respectable bourgeois had taken a new and surprising turn. Thanks to Gerda, he had become reborn. But it was not a religious conversion or a rededication to Judaism – far from it. He had taken on a new name befitting his new persona.[18]

In 1947, John Hersey explained how André Friedmann was 'reborn' as Robert Capa.[19] 'André and Gerda decided to form an association of

* In other letters to his mother dated from this time, he said that film-making interested him more than photography. Many other photographers in his circle, including Cartier-Bresson, were occasionally working in film and since leaving Budapest he had become a passionate admirer of French cinema. He was not alone. France was just as enthralled by the new medium. Cinema's share of Paris entertainment revenue rose from 40 per cent in 1929 to an astonishing 72 per cent by 1939. In May 1940, as German Panzers rolled through the cornfields of northern France, Paris cinemas counted more than three million admissions. (Eugen Weber, *The Hollow Years, France in the 1930s* (New York: Norton, 1994).)

three people. Gerda, who worked in a picture agency, was to serve as secretary and sales representative; André was to be a darkroom hired hand; and these two were to be employed by a rich, famous, and talented (and imaginary) American photographer named Robert Capa, then allegedly visiting France.'*

Robert Capa explained to a radio interviewer in 1947 how he came to change his name: 'I had a name which was a little bit different from Bob Capa. That real name of mine was not too good. I was just as foolish as I am now but younger. I couldn't get any assignment. I needed a new name badly.'

'Well, what was your name?' asked Capa's interviewer.

'Oh, it's very embarrassing for me to say. It began with André and it was Friedmann and the two of them hang together and let's discard it for me.'

'All right.'

'So I was figuring on a new one . . . Robert would sound very American because that was how somebody had to sound. Capa sounded American and it's easy to pronounce. So Bob Capa sounds like a good name. And then I invented that Bob Capa was a famous American photographer who came over to Europe and did not want to bore the French editors because they didn't pay enough . . . So I just moved in with my little Leica, took some pictures and wrote Bob Capa on it which sold for double prices.'[20]

Some have speculated that Capa named himself after Frank Capra, already a popular director of movies such as *Platinum Blonde* (1931) and *American Madness* (1932). But why the first name Robert? The veteran Hungarian photojournalist Éva Keleti, who organized the first exhibition of Capa's photographs in his homeland in 1976, thinks she may have the answer. In one of her favourite restaurants in Budapest, she scribbles on a notepad: 'André – Bandi – Bob'. 'They called him Bandi when he was a boy in Budapest,' she tells me. 'It's not much of a stretch to go from Bandi to Bob to Robert.'

*Around the same time, Gerda, too, reinvented herself, changing her surname from the unpronounceable Pohorylles to the snappier Taro. Inspired by a popular Japanese artist in Paris called Taro Okamoto, 'Taro' was short and punchy, like Capa.

According to Hersey, Capa had mastered his new disguise by early summer 1936. On Gerda's recommendation, he had a new haircut (short back and sides) and had even taken to wearing a smart coat and a hat. Yet, ironically, it was not such bourgeois attire but the blue overalls and pinafores of *les ouvriers* (manual workers) that were suddenly all the rage among young radicals that summer. On Sunday 3 May 1936, a Leftist coalition movement, dubbed the Front Populaire (Popular Front), won office.*

Through a fellow Hungarian refugee, André Kertész, Capa learned about opportunities with *Vu* magazine, an influential pro-Front Populaire publication. *Vu* did not pay well, but it needed contributors badly.† Impressed by André's pictures of Trotsky, the editor, Lucien Vogel, assigned him to cover political events in Paris. Many of André's subsequent pictures were often badly composed and out of focus, but they caught the mood of a heady period.[21]

In an attempt to pacify workers, Premier Léon Blum announced a 'new deal' of 12 per cent pay rises, a forty-hour working week, two weeks' paid holiday each year and collective bargaining. Working-class France was overjoyed. Women danced in each other's arms on factory floors, red flags fluttered over ministries in Paris, and the international forces of fascism appeared finally to have met their match: a united front of progressives who would surely stop Hitler and Mussolini in their tracks.

Capa photographed the Front Populaire with increasing flair. As Hersey wittily put it, the strikes and civil disturbances associated with the growing new party 'afforded the unreal American and his dark-room man [Gerda] opportunities to make amazing pictures'.[22] For several weeks, Hersey also claimed, there was 'a kind of Capa craze'. André and Gerda started to make a living. It seemed like the perfect

* While this victory delighted Capa, it did not pacify France's distraught workers: in June 1936, with an anti-fascist government running the country, there were 12,142 strikes, involving nearly two million people.

† *Vu* was one of the most influential magazines of its time. The April 1932 issue, *The German Enigma*, had carried no fewer than 438 photographs over 125 pages, many of them courtesy of Guttmann's Dephot.

arrangement, for 'Capa loved Gerda, Gerda loved André, André loved Capa, and Capa loved Capa'.[23] When André failed to get a picture that others brought back from the latest protest or strike, Gerda would cover for him. 'That bastard has run off to the Côte d'Azur again,' she would say, 'with an actress.' 'Friedmann took the pictures,' Hersey elaborated. 'Gerda sold them, and credit was given to the nonexistent Capa. Since this Capa was supposed to be so rich, Gerda refused to let his pictures go to any French newspaper for less than 150 francs apiece – three times the prevailing rate.'

In late June 1936, Capa covered a meeting of the League of Nations in Geneva where the former Abyssinian Emperor, Haile Selassie, made an impassioned speech against Mussolini. As Selassie spoke, several Italian correspondents loyal to Mussolini heckled loudly and scuffles broke out between left-wing journalists, one of them a Spaniard, and Il Duce's fascist scribes. When Swiss policemen removed the Italians and tossed the Spaniard on to the street, André was waiting outside and managed to photograph several policemen as they gagged the Spaniard's screams of protest.[24]

According to John Hersey, when André's pictures – labelled 'Robert Capa' – landed on Lucien Vogel's desk, he called the famous American photographer's agent. Gerda picked up the phone. 'Mr Capa says the Geneva picture will cost 300 francs,' she told Vogel. 'This is all very interesting about Robert Capa,' Vogel replied, 'but please advise the ridiculous boy Friedmann who goes around shooting pictures in a dirty leather jacket to report to my office at nine tomorrow morning.'[25] He had apparently spotted Capa outside the Geneva meeting.

Thomas Gunther, the leading authority on the Alliance agency, says André was caught red-handed on another occasion. Gerda had told Maria Eisner that she had come across some remarkable pictures by a man called Capa – a superb photographer but very expensive. As it happened, André was visiting the agency when Eisner looked at samples of this expensive American photographer's work. She had such a 'good eye for pictures', according to Gunther, that she instantly recognized them as André Friedmann's. She immediately called him into her office and, before an embarrassed Gerda, pointed out that the pictures were his. Eisner was, however, sufficiently impressed by his work, whatever the byline on the captions, to sign him to her agency for 1,100 francs a month in return for three stories each week: he was making less than Gerda, but at long last he could afford to eat regular meals.[26]

In early July 1936, Eisner sent Capa to Verdun to photograph the twentieth anniversary of one of the bloodiest battles of the First World War. The surrounding landscape was a haunting reminder of a war that killed 1.4 million Frenchmen and mangled another 1.1 million, the so-called *mutilés*. Even twenty years later, vast areas remained a no-man's-land of blackened trees and craters filled with stagnant water.

Capa's pictures show the military cemetery in Verdun, lit by hundreds of floodlights. Veterans are solemnly lined up behind the tombstones of dead comrades. As with many French veterans, they still regarded their officers as '*idiots*' and the war of attrition as an insane exercise in bleeding France white. Columns of survivors refused to march in step as a way of showing their continued disgust at what their generation had suffered. Many were now ardent pacifists. None wanted another war.

Yet war looked increasingly likely. On 3 October 1935 Mussolini had spat in the face of the League of Nations, set up after the First World War to preserve the peace, by invading Abyssinia. In March 1936, goose-stepping German troops had marched into the Rhineland, defying the Versailles peace treaty and sending a cold chill throughout France.

Capa returned from Verdun to cover Paris's Bastille Day festivities on 14 July. A week later, he picked up one of the newspapers he worked for and read about an uprising against a Front Populaire government abroad. A small fat man called Generalissimo Franco, who would soon enjoy both Hitler's and Mussolini's support, had arrived in Cadiz on 19 July at the head of Spanish foreign legionaries known as 'Moors'. He and his fellow Moroccan Insurgents planned to overthrow democracy in Spain. 'The energy we will employ,' Franco had warned the elected government of Spain, 'will be in proportion to the resistance you may put up. We urge you especially to avoid useless shedding of blood.'

4 The Passionate War

> 'The Spanish Civil War was the happiest period of our lives. We were truly happy then for when people died it seemed as though their death was justified and important. For they died for something that they believed in and that was going to happen.[1]
>
> ERNEST HEMINGWAY, 1940

The Spanish Civil War was Capa's first chance to fight totalitarianism in the trenches with a potent weapon – the Leica. In the journalist Martha Gellhorn's words, 'Spain was the place for all free men to fight Hitler, the Nazis, and the corrupt ideas which the Hitler imitators also practiced. [Capa] did not expect to fight, since he had never held a rifle; he expected to take pictures which would force everyone to see what there was to fight.'[2]

As soon as Capa and Gerda heard about Franco's uprising, they decided they would go to Spain together. Capa's coverage of the Front Populaire had made his name among publications sympathetic with the Republicans such as *Ce Soir*, *Vu* and *Regards*. It shouldn't be difficult, he reckoned, to get an assignment in Spain, and he quickly contacted his editors.

Lucien Vogel of *Vu* agreed to send both Capa and Gerda to Spain. He would hire a small plane to take them to Barcelona, and would accompany them himself: he intended to organize the coverage for a special issue of his magazine on the Civil War. Ignoring his mother's protests, in early August Capa, with Gerda, Vogel and several other journalists, flew to Spain. It was an inauspicious start. As they crossed the Pyrenees, their plane suddenly lost altitude, crash-landed in a field outside Barcelona and broke apart.[3] Astonishingly, there were no fatalities; Capa and Gerda emerged from the wreckage badly shaken but unharmed. At the same time, sixty miles to the south in the port of Cadiz, the first Nazi shipment of planes and soldiers landed on Spanish soil.

Capa and Gerda reached the outskirts of Barcelona late on 5 August. The crash was soon forgotten amid the crazed atmosphere of Catalonia's capital, then in the throes of an anarchist revolution. In one street, Capa and Gerda found several anarchist couples, wearing blue boiler suits and enjoying the afternoon sun, elated by the sudden transfer of Barcelona's majestic buildings and institutions to the masses. Most of the city's factory owners had either fled or shared the same fate as the thousands of nuns, monks and priests the Republicans butchered in the first months of the war.

In 1959 the German writer, Gustav Regler, vividly recalled these first heady days of the anarchist uprising against Franco: 'There was a spirit of intoxication in the people, an infectious eagerness for sacrifice, a hot-blooded belief in freedom . . . To judge by their outward aspect, the militiamen might have been pushed out into the streets by the French Revolution, and no doubt many of the acts of violence in the first days of the war had been prompted by unconscious imitation of the sans-culottes.'[4]

Perhaps Capa's first contact in Barcelona was Jaume Miravitlles, the twenty-eight-year-old General Secretary of the left-wing Esquerra Party. Miravitlles recalled helping Capa and Gerda obtain permits to photograph in Barcelona and official French press passes. He also clearly remembered how Capa was intoxicated by the anarchist cause. Its anti-authoritarian, decadent disavowal of all tradition, bourgeois rules, laws and moral codes left a permanent impression on the young photographer.*

*Capa was just one of many young idealists, including George Orwell and André Malraux, for whom the Spanish Civil War would be the most affecting experience of their lives. For thousands of other young men and women around the world who volunteered to fight Franco, the war also represented the front line in an ideological battle against totalitarianism. If Franco was allowed to defeat democracy in Spain, there seemed little hope of fascism being successfully stopped elsewhere.

Capa and Gerda then toured banks and grand hotels seized by a baffling array of anti-Franco activists. The anarchist union, CNT FAI, had set up a disorganized camp in the sprawling Calle Layetana, which would soon be renamed Via Durriti. The Trotskyite Partido Obrero de Unificación Marxista (POUM) had made the Hotel Falcon, close to the Plaza Catalunya, its base. In one square, Capa and Gerda came across an all-female unit. Gerda saw role models; Capa saw their first saleable story. French and British magazines, he correctly sensed, would snap up pictures of these fighting women with their ivory faces, long curling locks and smart new jodhpurs. They photographed one particularly beautiful soldier sitting on a cafe terrace, absorbed in a women's magazine – a gun propped between her knees.

At Barcelona's central train station, Capa and Gerda watched thousands of jubilant troops leaving to fight the Insurgents on the Aragon front. None of their pictures showed the usual wrenching goodbyes of separating lovers, but rather the boundless optimism of Barcelona's working class as it departed to crush Franco's infamous Moors. On the side of one car, someone had daubed in white paint: 'JURAD SOBRE ESTAS LETRAS HERMANOS ANTES MORIR QUE CONSENTIR TIRANO' – Swear upon these fraternal letters that you will sooner die than consent to tyranny. Most of the young men leaning out of windows and enthusiastically waving their fists would never see Barcelona again.

In late August, Capa and Gerda drove 150 miles to the nearest front lines around Huesca, a town lying in the shelter of the Pyrenees, midway between the Mediterranean and the Atlantic coasts. But there was no action and so, eager to record images of a first Republican victory, they continued south after learning of hundreds of German communists serving in POUM militias a few miles away. In Leciñena, north-east of Saragossa, Capa and Gerda briefly joined the same unit with which George Orwell would spend the winter before being wounded and leaving Spain disillusioned and embittered in spring 1937.[5]

They were again disappointed: the unit's motley soldiers, most of them wearing mismatched caps and carrying antiquated guns, simply lounged around. But then they learned that the Republican government in Madrid had ordered the first major attack on Franco's forces, in Córdoba.* In early September they set out, now determined to record actual combat and hopefully even a first defeat for fascism.

En route, they stopped in Toledo. For several weeks, the Republicans had laid siege to the famous Alcázar in the middle of the city. Insurgent Colonel Moscardo and several hundred of his followers had managed to withstand repeated assaults. When Capa and Gerda arrived, they learned that the Republicans were plotting to breach the fortress with dynamite, but it would take at least another fortnight before sufficient explosive could be placed under the walls, and so the couple quickly headed further south towards Córdoba. Finally, in the vicinity of a small village called Cerro Muriano, the two photographers found the action they were looking for.[6]

On the morning of 5 September, the fascists had bombed Cerro Muriano. That afternoon, Capa and Gerda took several pictures of terrified villagers fleeing the town. On radios, Insurgent General Queipo de Llano could be heard vowing that his men would soon arrive and then rape the village's 'female reds'.[7] Also in the area that day was the German writer Franz Borkenau, who later recalled in his book, *The Spanish Cockpit* (1937), that when he arrived 'the whole village was in flight; men, women, and children; on foot, by donkeys, by cars, and motor-lorries.' Borkenau was dismayed to see many members of the anarchist militia, CNT, also running away 'like cowards'. 'Rifles are no good against bombs and shells,' some of them shouted.

When Borkenau entered Cerro Muriano itself, he found all the houses deserted, doors locked, abandoned livestock wandering the streets. At the front lines, he discovered that 'three or four' men had died. Later that afternoon, he watched many more men desert, except for a 'small group of militia from Alcoy, an old revolutionary centre in the province of Murcia . . . they stood the bombardment . . . with the proudest gallantry and indifference . . . Discipline, however, was lacking to an almost incredible extent.'[8]

* Franco's followers were now waging a war of fratricidal terror. Almost every time a town fell to Insurgent troops, scores of public executions followed.

That afternoon, it is thought, Capa joined the militia from Alcoy in a trench at the front and then miraculously took the most famous photograph of the entire Spanish Civil War, 'The Falling Soldier'. It depicted a militiaman from Alcoy a split second after he'd apparently been shot to death.

5 'The Falling Soldier'

> 'No tricks are necessary to take pictures in Spain. You don't have to pose your camera. The pictures are there, and you just take them. The truth is the best picture, the best propaganda.'
>
> ROBERT CAPA, interview with *New York World-Telegram*, 2 September 1937

'The Falling Soldier' is the most debated picture in the history of photojournalism. To question its authenticity is to earn the undying ire of eighty-three-year-old Cornell Capa, who controls his brother's estate and has spent many years fiercely defending his brother's legend. Richard Whelan, Cornell's chosen biographer of his brother, has called 'The Falling Soldier' 'perhaps the greatest war photograph ever made'.[1] Esperanza Aguirre Gil de Biedma, while Spain's Minister of Education and Culture in Spain in the mid-nineties, described it as a 'universal icon . . . of such visual potency that it is on a par with Picasso's *Guernica*'.[2]

Yet Capa's most famous picture may be no more than what it is titled – a picture of a soldier falling over.* The distinguished French documentary maker Patrick Jeudy believes this could be the case. In his Paris office, he showed me unseen footage of Capa, as well as a sequence taken during the Spanish Civil War of a man losing his footing as he runs down a hillside. If the film is stopped, a single frame looks similar to Capa's famous picture. As Jeudy argues, there is no way of knowing from Capa's still image itself whether the man has

* 'The Falling Soldier' came to haunt Capa just as Eddie Adams came to be haunted by his famous 1968 shot of a man being executed in Vietnam.

accidentally slipped, is being killed, or has been asked to simulate the moment of death.

Jeudy is but one of many film-makers, historians and photographers, all of them ardent admirers of Capa's work, who have doubts about the picture. According to the photographer and ex-Magnum archivist Jimmy Fox, these doubts should not distract people from Capa's overall work, which remains unquestionably the most evocative photographic record of the most turbulent years of the twentieth century. But he himself has questioned what he says are rather odd aspects of the only contemporary report of how Capa took the picture:

> I remember bringing up with Cornell the saga of the dying soldier during the Spanish Civil War, as Cornell had asked me several years ago to go to Spain to see the newly discovered family of [the man allegedly depicted in Capa's photograph]. What sounded strange to me is [that] Capa came back to [New York] by boat about 6 months after the photo was published in *Life* and had an interview with a journalist in which he explained he spent several days with the man, including the fact that the man was shot next to him and that he remained by his body until dark and retreated from enemy fire.[3]

The journalist in question was from the *New York World-Telegram*, and he interviewed Capa on 1 September 1937 in New York. Capa told him how he had come to take his sensational photograph. The newspaper reported:

> [Capa and his subject, the soldier] were on the Cordoba front, stranded there, the two of them, Capa with his precious camera and the soldier with his rifle. The soldier was impatient. He wanted to get back to the Loyalist lines. Time and again he climbed up and peered over the sandbags. Each time he would drop back at the warning rattle of machine-gun fire. Finally, the soldier muttered something to the effect that he was going to take the long chance. He clambered out of the trench with Capa behind him. The machine-guns rattled, and Capa automatically snapped his camera, falling back beside the body of his companion. Two hours later, when it was dark and the guns were still, the photographer crept

> across the broken ground to safety. Later he discovered that he had taken one of the finest shots of the Spanish war.[4]

Capa was notorious throughout his career for not including key information such as names on his captions. Even so, Fox remains curious as to how Capa could have spent several days with the soldier and his unit and yet not know his name. Why did he not find the identity of the man when he was killed? Wouldn't some member of the man's unit have been able to identify the man for him?*

In 1982, one of Capa's friends, Hansel Mieth, wrote about 'The Falling Soldier'. She described in a letter how in the late forties she returned to her New York apartment from an assignment to find her husband Otto and Capa arguing bitterly about the picture.

'Otto was angry and Bob was very dejected and yet defensive. Otto talked harsh and critical and Bob bit back like a beaten puppy. I was tired from days of work and did not jump into the fray. But I thought Otto unnecessarily didactic.'

When Capa left the apartment, Otto fumed in silence.

'What are you accusing Bob of?' Mieth asked. 'Do you believe he faked the picture?'

'I wish to God he had.'

'So what's all the controversy about?'

'I don't want to talk about it. I hope what I'm forced to think is wrong.'

Otto Mieth had argued bitterly with Capa about the circumstances in which the picture had been taken.

'I knew him [the Falling Soldier] when he was alive,' Capa told him. 'They were fooling around. We were all fooling around. We felt good. There was no shooting. They came running down the slope. I ran too.'

*Capa was not the only photographer who apparently captured a moment of death in the Spanish Civil War. The left-wing *London Daily Herald* on 15 October 1936 showed men drowning at sea, and *The Illustrated London News* carried a picture of seven men running across a clearing, captioned: 'Two men brought down in a rebel charge, one of them actually falling.' (Quoted, Caroline Brothers, *War and Photography, A Cultural History* (London: Routledge, 1997).) But Capa's picture was extraordinary for its proximity to the victim – no more than twenty yards – and its dramatic symbolism.

'Did you tell the men to stage an attack?' asked Otto.

'Hell no. We all were happy. A little crazy, maybe.'

'And then?' asked Otto.

'Then, suddenly it was the real thing. I didn't hear the firing – not at first.'

'Where were you?'

'A little ahead and to the side of them.'[5]

If this account is to be believed, Capa felt guilty because he had asked the men to run down an exposed hillside and this request had cost a man his life. According to Professor Hans Puttnies, a biographer of Gisèle Freund, Capa told Freund a similar story, admitting that he had 'killed' the man in the picture.

As demonstrated by the above accounts, neither given by Capa himself, Capa's version of events changed significantly in the telling. However, an account given by Capa himself does exist, in a 1947 radio interview to promote his memoir *Slightly Out of Focus*.

At 8.30 a.m. on 20 October, Capa told New Yorkers listening to WNBC New York what had happened on that fateful day in 1936. He brought up 'The Falling Soldier' without prompting, stressing that 'the prize picture is born in the imagination of editors and public who sees them'.

He had once taken such a picture 'which was appreciated much more than other ones'. When he took it, he 'certainly did not know' that it was a special picture. 'It happened in Spain,' he explained. 'It was very much at the beginning of my career as a photographer and very much at the beginning of the Spanish Civil War. And war was kind of romantic, if you can say anything like that . . .'

Capa told listeners he had taken the picture in Andalusía while accompanying a group of raw Republican recruits. 'They were not soldiers,' he added, 'and they were dying every minute with great gestures and they figured that it was really for liberty and the right kind of fight. They were enthused.'

Capa said he'd been in a trench with around twenty men armed with old rifles – a flat contradiction of his statement to the *New York World-Telegram*. On a facing hill, he added, there was an Insurgent machine gun. The men fired towards the machine gun for five minutes. Then they stood up and said '*Vamos!*' ('Let's go!'), and crawled out of the trench and advanced towards the machine gun. 'Sure enough,' Capa continued, 'the machine gun opened up and, dim dom! So what was left of them came back and again take pot shots in the direction of the machine gun [that] certainly was clever enough not to answer. And after five minutes again they say "*Vamos*" and they got mowed down again. This thing repeated itself for about three or four times so the fourth time I just kind of put my camera above my head and even didn't look and clicked a picture when they moved over the trench.'

Capa explained that he did not develop his film from that day himself. He sent it back to Paris with many other rolls and then stayed on in Spain for three months. When he returned to France he discovered that he 'was a very famous photographer because that camera which I hold above my head just caught a man at the moment when he was shot.'

'The Falling Soldier' first appeared in *Vu* magazine on 23 September 1936, and was given further exposure in *Paris-Soir* and *Regards* the next year. According to Professor Puttnies, the Swiss backers of *Vu* magazine dismissed Lucien Vogel after Capa's photograph appeared. 'The appearance of [Vogel's] special issue on the Spanish Civil War in the fall of 1936,' Gisèle Freund has confirmed, 'supporting the Republican point of view, utterly outraged *Vu*'s backers and Vogel was forced to resign.'[6]

The picture appeared on page 19 of *Life* magazine on 12 July 1937, and was captioned: 'A Spanish soldier the instant he is dropped by a bullet through the head.' As in Europe, it created a sensation. Several readers wrote angrily to the editor complaining about such graphic depiction of violence. No such image had ever appeared in the homes of Middle America.

It was not until 1974 that the veracity of 'The Falling Soldier' was first publicly questioned, in Phillip Knightley's *The First Casualty*.[7] Knightley had interviewed O. D. Gallagher, a correspondent with the *Daily Express* during the Civil War, who told him 'The Falling Soldier' was one of a series of action shots staged during a lull in the fighting.

According to him, Capa and other photographers complained to a Republican officer that they had nothing to photograph. The officer said he would round up some troops and stage manoeuvres. When the picture was later published, Gallagher commented on how genuine it looked, given its slight blurring. He told Knightley that Capa 'had a good laugh and said, "If you want to get good action shots, they mustn't be in true focus. If your hand trembles a little, then you get a fine action shot."' This testimony was partly undermined, however, when he said in an interview with the historian Jorge Lewinski in 1978 that Capa had taken the picture in Insurgent-controlled Spain. There is no evidence that Capa ever visited Nationalist Spain. Indeed, such a visit would have been highly unlikely, given his passionate support of the Republican cause.

Another important source in Knightley's book was Ted Allan, a Canadian veteran of the Civil War who fell in love with Gerda aged nineteen and became a good friend to Capa in the late 1930s. He wrote to Knightley, telling him that he once discussed the picture with David 'Chim' Seymour, who also covered the Civil War, as did Cartier-Bresson. 'Chim told me that Capa had not taken that photograph. Whether he then told me that he, Chim, had taken it or that Gerda had taken it, I cannot now remember.'[8] Gerda Taro's biographer, Irme Schaber, says she chose not to discuss 'The Falling Soldier' at length in her book because she did not see it as crucial to understanding her subject. She thinks it very unlikely that Gerda took the photograph. But it is possible. The Spanish cultural historian Carlos Serrano, who has examined photographs by Capa and Gerda from this period, has written that it is often impossible to tell who took what picture. Until 1937, almost all of Gerda's photographs appeared either without a by-line or with Capa's.

By closely examining Capa's negatives, one could see whether or not his shot really was a fluke, or whether it formed part of a staged sequence of different men, or just one man, pretending to be shot. Apparently, many of the negatives for the sequence to which the picture belongs do not exist. Nor is there an original print or negative of the actual photograph.

If Capa did stage the picture, he would probably have taken several pictures of militiamen falling over, pretending to be shot, and would probably have used a tripod to prevent blurring. Ironically, evidence of this nature is arguably to be found in *Vu* magazine itself. Under a double-page headline 'The Civil War in Spain', *Vu* printed the famous photograph above a second picture of another dying militiaman. Both pictures were sub-headed: 'How they fell'. The magazine's caption clearly refers to two different men: 'Legs tense, chest to the wind, rifle in hand, they tear down the stubble-covered slope . . . Suddenly their flight is broken, a bullet whistles – a fratricidal bullet – and their blood is drunk by their native soil.'[9]

The soldier in the first, more famous image is wearing a white shirt and dark trousers. The second is dressed in dark overalls. The man in the first picture has dark shoes. The second wears white espadrilles. The first has three ammunition pouches on a leather shoulder strap. The second has two pouches on his belt. The motion of their fall is quite different in each photograph. It is clearly very unlikely that both pictures could be of the same man. Yet could Capa really have taken first one picture of a man dying, a fluke as he himself said, and then a second fluke picture of a man being shot on the very same hillside? Or are we seeing the same moment staged with two different actors?

For every doubter, there is a far more impassioned defender of 'The Falling Soldier'. Gerda's and Capa's surviving friend, Ruth Cerf, has not been quoted on the record about the photograph, yet knew both photographers far more intimately during this period than anyone alive today. She now insists that the picture 'is authentic': 'I saw the [photographs] that followed it, when the soldier was dead on the ground.' But she is not specific about how she came to see the subsequent shots and what happened to them.

Following Knightley's revelations, the Spanish Civil War veteran Georges Soria insisted vehemently that the picture was authentic. 'Capa's professional honesty was such that it is impossible to believe for a single moment that he could have invented a hoax as mediocre as it is contemptible.'[10] He wrote that he had gone north of Madrid in August 1936 with Capa to the Sierra de Guadarrama. After a

Republican counter-attack, Soria recalled that Capa did not dive for cover when shots rang out but stood 'taking photographs as if nothing was happening'[11] while men were mown down.

Soria did not actually see Capa take the picture of the 'Falling Soldier', and he admitted that he dived to the ground from 'the first splutter of the enemy machine gun'. He nevertheless maintained that the picture was taken in August in a mountain range a day's drive from Madrid. Yet in 1936 Cerro Muriano was at least three days' drive from Madrid, and in any case the picture was taken in September and not August.

In recent years other defenders have become ever more emphatic that the picture is in fact true. The most recent assertions have been based on the findings of an unknown Spanish amateur historian called Mario Brotons, also a veteran of the war.[12] He claimed the man in Capa's photograph is Federico Borrell, who died aged twenty-four on 5 September 1936, the day the picture was supposedly taken. Borrell was a mill worker from a small town called Alcoy, also Brotons' home town. While researching a book on the Spanish Civil War in the early nineties, Brotons apparently scoured military archives in Madrid and Salamanca. To his amazement, he later stated, he found in both archives evidence that only one man died on 5 September on the Cerro Muriano front: Federico Borrell. When he showed Capa's picture to Borrell's surviving relatives in 1996, they apparently recognized Federico without being prompted.

Federico had a younger brother named Everisto, who also fought near Cerro Muriano. In 1996 Rita Grosvenor, an English journalist, interviewed Everisto's widow, Maria, for the *Observer*. 'Everisto told us Federico had been killed. He hadn't seen what happened because he had been in a different position. But his friends had told him they saw Federico fling up his arms and immediately crumple to the ground after being shot in the head. He died instantly, they said.'[13]

Capa's picture is one of the most famous photographs in Spanish history. Why had none of Borrell's relatives recognized him in the preceding sixty years when it appeared countless times in magazines, newspapers and on television? Sadly, Maria died only weeks before a planned interview with the author of this book. Mario Brotons died in 1997.

Brotons' book does not include notes on sources. So what document did he find to prove his assertion that just one soldier died that day, a claim that contradicts Franz Borkenau's eyewitness report and every one of Capa's accounts? He wrote that he found his evidence in the Spanish Civil War archives in Salamanca and military archives in Ávila, near Madrid. Yet a thorough search of these archives has produced nothing to support Brotons' thesis. The head of the Salamanca archives, Miguel Angel Jaramillo, says there is no mention of Federico Borrell in his archives, and Manuel Melgar, a curator of the Ávila records, says there is no trace of Federico Borrell in his archive either.

Angel Jaramillo has worked in the Salamanca archives for ten years, and was never even contacted by Brotons:

> According to our records, Mr Brotons did not come here. Our archives have many documents listing dead and missing. It is crucial information for people claiming pensions . . . And I can tell you we have found nothing with Borrell's name on any list of men who went missing or died in the war . . . If Brotons found evidence here, why did he not reproduce it in his book? For such an important claim, a professional historian would be very careful to provide exact attribution, and show it. It is strange that he did not.

Even if one accepts that the man in the picture is actually Federico, can one then say that he died at the moment the picture was taken? He could have died hours later. And what of the second man in the *Vu* magazine spread? Why has he not been identified? Why did Capa never mention his existence? Crucially, why was Federico's body never found?

Caroline Brothers, a British academic, recently examined the 'Falling Soldier' controversy in exhaustive detail, and concluded: 'The fame of this photograph is indicative of a collective imagination which wanted and still wants to believe certain things about the nature of death in war. What this image argued was that death in war was heroic, and tragic, and that the individual counted and that his death mattered.'[14]

One may well ask whether there is any truth to Capa's 'Falling Soldier' beyond its representation of a symbolic death. Capa was not an impartial reporter. He ignored atrocities committed by the Republicans, and would soon stage at least one documented attack as well as serve as an ideological cheerleader to the communist cause in Spain.

'The Falling Soldier', authentic or fake, is ultimately a record of Capa's political bias and idealism. Both would be severely tested in the remaining battles of 'the Passionate War'. Indeed, he would soon come to experience the brutalizing insanity and death of illusions that all witnesses who get close enough to the 'romance' of war inevitably confront.

What has never been in doubt is that the publication of 'The Falling Soldier' marked a point of no return. The photograph ensured that André Friedmann would for ever be remembered as Robert Capa, the American photographer so daring, so determined to get as close as possible to the intensity of war, that he was even able to record the very instant of a man's death.

6 'La Paquena Rubena'

> 'When you think of all the fine people we both know who have been killed . . . you get an absurd feeling that somehow it's unfair to be alive.'
>
> GERDA TARO, 9 July 1937[1]

Dawn, 18 September 1936: Capa and Gerda waited among a crowd of photographers and reporters gathered outside the Alcázar in Toledo. At 6.31 precisely, a massive explosion breached the fortress and shook the city but failed to dislodge the besieged Insurgents. Hans Namuth, a German photographer, was beside Capa and Gerda when Republican troops then attacked the Alcázar only to be quickly repulsed. 'We [see] how they climb up the steep hill,' Namuth recalled. 'We [see] how some are being shot dead, the injured are carried back next to us so close that the blood is dripping on our shoes and we [look] into the white eyes of the dead, our ears almost deaf from the noise of grenades and from dynamite explosions.'[2]

Capa and Gerda left Toledo shaken and dejected by the slaughter. On 30 September, the two-month siege was raised when Franco routed the Republicans and took the city. The fall of Toledo was of enormous propaganda value to the Insurgents, and opened the way to Madrid, forty miles north. Franco, who had been made commander-in-chief of the Insurgent armies, issued a statement the day the Alcázar was relieved: 'Madrid's plans of resistance make me smile. We shall get there as fast as we can march, crushing whatever ridiculous resistance is attempted.'

Gerda and Capa were already in the capital, waiting with the rest of the city's frightened inhabitants for Franco's forces to attack. Around this time, just north of Madrid, Capa met the intense young German writer Gustav Regler, who was by now the political commissioner of the 12th International Brigade, commanded by the flamboyant and handsome Mate Zalka, a Hungarian writer also known as General Lukacz.*

Regler thought Capa looked like a gypsy and took him to be even younger than his real age, a few weeks short of twenty-three. According to him, Capa joined the 12th Brigade as it marched towards the Manzanares River, where other Republican forces were said to be preparing to defend Madrid from Franco's first major assault. In pitch darkness, they scrambled through a no-man's-land of stark scrub scalded by frost, but when they reached the river, they found deserted trenches. Regler was shocked: 'Madrid lay as open to attack as a doe overtaken by hounds.'[3]

As they returned to Lukacz's headquarters, Capa got his first taste of the heart-pounding terror of war. 'The young man [Capa]', Regler recalled, 'disliked the noise of the shells which soon whistled over us, though they exploded far in the country. Later, he asked leave to change his trousers saying with humour that it was his first battle and that his bowels had been weaker than his feet.'

Capa probably discovered several things during this first experience of combat. At five feet eight inches, he was short but still several feet too high to survive heavy shelling – the best way to keep his head was to lie with it pressed into the earth or better still in the base of a deep foxhole. Silence was golden near the front lines – a sniper's bullet sometimes greeted even a whispered '*hola*'. In war, only the now – the moment – filled a man's head. Instinct and visceral concerns crowded out all subjective emotions and thoughts. And as many war photographers have subsequently attested, the adrenaline rush of combat can be a highly addictive experience.

In late September, with bombs raining down on Madrid day and night, Capa and Gerda returned to Paris via Barcelona, having com-

* Even Franco grudgingly respected Lukacz's military skills and tenacity.

pleted their project for Vogel. Exhausted, uncertain whether they would see Madrid again, they had so far failed to show how the Spanish people could defeat fascism. Life in Paris was unbearably lethargic compared to the intensity of every waking moment in Spain. After pushing their pictures on communist propaganda magazines, they made plans to return to Spain as soon as possible, needing to fix again on the rush of fighting fascism with their cameras.

Capa was the first to get another commission and he made the journey back to Madrid in November, alone. In his absence, fear of torture and rape at the hands of Franco's troops had galvanized many Madrileños into a fierce defence of the city. The epicentre of the new resistance was the Casa de Campo, a park at the west of the city, where the Republicans had dug in and created elaborate barricades with doors, suitcases, or whatever they could find to hand. Beneath skeletal oak trees, in the hilly streets, three men often shared one rifle, waiting for the perfect moment to fire on the enemy. Teenage girls, having tossed away their gold crosses and chains, padded their shoulders to prevent bruising from Spanish Mauser rifles that had a kick like a mule.

For several weeks, as bitter winter gripped Madrid, Capa photographed close-quarter fighting in the Casa de Campo and around the several slaughterhouses to the north-west of the city, joining several Republican units as they fought from one bombed-out house to the next. His photographs that winter also showed bearded gunmen huddled for warmth in shell-holed university dormitories. Weeping mothers sat with their children on the platforms of metro stations – as trains passed, sleepers appeared to instinctively move their feet away from the edge of platforms. In the central Telefônica building, fellow correspondents wired censored reports, ducking as shells passed overhead. A hundred yards from the front lines, cafes on the Gran Via still served creamy coffee in tall glasses and *pasteles*, sickly sweet pastries.

The magazine *World Illustrated* praised this coverage in its pages, which also showed men tossing grenades over walls at their brothers, noting that 'good pictures from Madrid are scarce. Neither side welcomes photographers. There is danger in reaching the spots where good pictures can be taken.'[4] Capa was, however, able to move from one killing zone to another with remarkable ease. All he needed to do was hop on a tram. For the price of an espresso in Montparnasse, he could ride into battle as many times as he wanted. 'You can take a streetcar to the front line,' Madrileños told him, 'but don't take the metro, you might come up on the wrong side.'[5]

Capa also recorded the saddest faces of war, focusing on petrified mothers and their children. In so doing, he became the first photographer to bring the full horror of the war into the homes of readers around Europe and beyond. In his images, the battle for Spain was pitiless, sparing none. Modern war's aerial bombardment slaughtered more innocents than actual combatants. Capa's most moving pictures were of shell-shocked women from the working-class suburb of Vallecas, one of the areas that suffered the heaviest bombing. He placed his Leica only inches from some women's faces only minutes after they had returned to find their homes destroyed and neighbours beneath bloody rubble. When Capa returned to Paris in December, he discovered that these photographs had been sold through Alliance to magazines in several countries. On 28 December, they earned him his first spread in *Life*, a new American magazine that had begun publication on 23 November and quickly sold out its initial printing of 466,000 copies.

In early 1937, Capa returned to Spain and teamed with Gerda again to cover the refugee situation on the Andalusían coast, where thousands were fleeing the Insurgent advance on the port of Málaga. From Málaga, it was several days' walk along the coast road to the nearest Republican refuge – Almería. Parents begged drivers to cram their children into already overloaded trucks and wagons, knowing they stood little chance of seeing them again. Hundreds collapsed and died of exhaustion and hunger by the roadside. One afternoon, Insurgent planes attacked. Caught unawares, entire families were mown down. A Canadian doctor, Norman Bethune, watched German and Italian planes return to strafe the refugee columns time and time again, their 'machine guns weaving intricate patterns among the fleeing'.[6]

Capa and Gerda returned to Paris with their pictures of this tragedy in early March. Perhaps aware of his own mortality, Capa proposed marriage to Gerda. To his surprise, she refused the offer. She had become as involved as he with the fate of the Republic and 'marriage was out of the question', says Ruth Cerf, so long as fascists were still to be beaten in Spain. Besides, if she were ever to stop being a 'polygamist' it would only be for financial reasons – a potential husband would have to be wealthy, not a struggling freelance photographer.

Gerda had other reasons for not tying the knot with her creation. She had taken many extraordinary photographs during her visit to Spain, but not one had so far appeared under her own byline, and when she did get a credit her name followed Capa's: 'Photos: Capa et Taro'. Tired of seeing most of her pictures also attributed to 'Capa' alone or not at all, she was determined to make her own name. It was high time she stepped out of her teacher's shadow. 'She felt insulted that her name was not mentioned,' says Ruth Cerf. 'She no longer saw a future with Capa.'

Nevertheless, they returned together to Madrid later that month, checking into the Hotel Florida. Among their fellow guests they discovered the thirty-seven-year-old American writer Ernest Hemingway, already famous for his first novel, *The Sun Also Rises* (1926), and his epic of the First World War, *A Farewell to Arms* (1930). Capa's and Hemingway's paths would cross many times in the coming years. From their first meeting, Hemingway admired Capa's guts and self-deprecating humour. The intense young Hungarian had a talent for helping others smile in the worst of times. For his part, Capa respected 'Papa' for his passionate support of the Republicans and willingness to actually report from a trench or foxhole in the front lines rather than a well-stocked hotel bar or cosy bomb shelter. Here was a man to imitate, if not in speech and prose, then at least in presenting one's life as a huge canvas of romance and heroism. 'Our friendship dated from the good days,' Capa recalled in *Slightly Out of Focus*. 'We first met in 1937 in Loyalist Spain, where I was a young freelance photographer, and he was a very famous writer. His nickname was "Papa" . . . and I soon adopted him as a father.'[7]

On 21 April, Franco's forces shelled Madrid in the heaviest bombardment of the war so far. On the 27th – market day in Guernica –

Hitler's Condor Legion pilots massacred the inhabitants of the Basque country's cultural and spiritual home. A few days later, Capa headed north to the Basque port of Bilbao, where the Insurgents had started to make crucial advances. By the time he arrived, Hitler's bombers were raiding Bilbao several times a day. Capa photographed mothers and their young daughters as they ran for shelter, and others trying to douse the fires that raged for days on end in the city's fuel dump.

The American journalist Vincent Sheean recalled one particular bombing: 'Capa was going along taking his pictures when a Stuka or a JU-88 came bang over. He jumped for a ditch and two other people jumped into the same ditch at the same time. He thought it only right and proper that he should introduce himself somehow, so he said: "I am a photographer." The next man said: "I am a Basque Catholic." The third man said: "Those are two professions that are of no use at this moment."'[8]

Around this time, another American correspondent, the laconic Jay Allen, met Capa at Bilbao's airport, where Capa had just dispatched film to *Regards* in Paris, and shared a ride back into the city with him in an old Packard truck. Capa looked at him with disgust. 'I had obviously brought no food,' Allen recalled. ' "Another one to feed and a big one," [Capa] told the chauffeur in bad Spanish.'

A few days later, Allen and Capa took a break from reporting the war, and watched a cabaret in the city centre. Suddenly, the air-raid sirens sounded yet again, shrieking four heart-stopping blasts. Outside the theatre, Capa returned to work. 'I saw him calmly get the faces until the street was empty of all save a *guardia* with a rifle,' Allen recalled in the preface to *Death in the Making*, a collection of Gerda and Capa's photographs published in America in 1938. '[The *guardia*] drove us to a refuge. I saw [Capa] at the front, grave eyes, expressionless to agony. But not [his camera's] eye.'

On 7 May 1937, Franco's troops attacked Mt Sollube, an important buttress surrounding Bilbao. A week later, Republicans began to flee the city. Capa returned to Paris where he had an important meeting with the imperious but charming Richard de Rochemont, head of the *Time-Life* office there. Having seen his impressive coverage of the war in *Life*, de Rochemont asked Capa to work for him on a documentary series, 'The March of Time'. Capa agreed.

He would now be working indirectly for Henry Luce, de Rochemont's boss, and the founder of *Life*. Ironically, Luce was convinced that Franco was a 'great white knight who was going to save Spain from those dirty communists'.[9] However, the film de Rochemont intended to make, *Rehearsal for War*, was blatantly anti-fascist; Luce, to his credit, was often at variance with the editorial content of his films and magazines.* As a cameraman, however, Capa did not endear himself to de Rochemont and other producers. 'I was very fond of Capa but he was completely undisciplined,' de Rochemont recalled. 'I sent him to the Spanish War with an Eyemo camera on a sort of stringer basis . . . [but] he gave the camera to his girl friend to operate.'[10] Tom Orchard, an associate producer on *Rehearsal for War*, was equally unimpressed. 'Bob, being a still photographer, didn't know how to use a movie camera. So as a result we had perfectly marvellous shots, but they were perfectly marvellous still shots. He'd do ZZzzzt! And you'd have five feet.'[11]

In late May, Capa reunited with Gerda at the Navacerrada Pass, near Segovia, to cover a Republican attack. This time, he hoped, he and Gerda would finally record a Republican victory – with both a movie camera and in stills.† They worked furiously, recording vivid scenes of tanks and men advancing, but the Republican attack failed. Again, they returned to Madrid without the images they craved.

In mid-June, Capa and Gerda headed south from Madrid, ever more desperate for scenes of victory, arriving early on the 24th at the headquarters of the communist Chapaiev Battalion near Peñarroya. Later that day, the battalion's political commissar, Alfred Kantorowicz, a brave and witty German intellectual, met Capa and Gerda as they climbed into the mountains of the Sierra Mulva. In his diary, Kantorowicz noted that Capa was struggling with a large film camera,

* A former *Life* picture editor, John Morris, says Capa's stills helped balance pro-Franco coverage in the pages of *Life*.

† Hemingway later recreated key events from the attack in *For Whom the Bell Tolls*, published to enormous acclaim and financial success in 1940.

and that Gerda was extremely attractive, wearing 'trousers, a beret pulled down over beautiful red-blond hair, and dainty revolver at her waist'.[12]

The diary entry also described in detail how Gerda and Capa used Kanto's men later that afternoon to stage several attacks. 'Capa arranged a whole attack scene: an imaginary fascist position was stormed as men, with terrifying roars and passionate battle-lust, leapt and bounded doubletime into victory . . . [Capa] was very pleased with the result.'[13]

Unable to record the real thing, they had finally resorted to fakery. Capa was impressed by his men's 'passionate fighting spirit', and told Kanto that staged attacks would look 'more real' than if they'd actually taken place.* Two days later, Capa and Gerda headed with Kanto to the front lines of the Battle of La Granjuela. Kanto wrote in his diary: 'Nothing could hold her [Gerda] back as she tossed her camera on to her shoulder and, with profligate foolishness, in broad daylight, ran across 180 meters to the position without cover. A few daring ones followed her. It was the time of the siesta; the fascists seemed to be sleeping. All went well. Gerda Taro filmed at length the position and the comrades of the second company. It was almost with force that the men held her and Capa until dusk.'[14]

Having successfully recorded apparently victorious Republican attacks, Capa left for Paris to hand over his and Gerda's footage to Richard de Rochemont. Meanwhile, Gerda stayed in Madrid for the 2nd International Writers' Conference. Now widely known as *la Paquena Rubena* (the little red fox), Gerda covered the self-important gathering of left-leaning writers for *Ce Soir*, a communist daily. Her photographs would bear the stamp 'Photo Taro'. She was now a photojournalist in her own right.

Before leaving for Paris, Capa asked Ted Allan, a young Canadian volunteer, to keep an eye on Gerda. 'I leave Gerda in your charge,

*Staging scenes was not uncommon among the 'March of Time' film-makers. Luce had notoriously told directors to employ 'fakery in allegiance to the truth'. Often, actors would even be employed to play figures such as Haile Selassie when interviews couldn't be obtained.

Teddie,' Capa told him. 'Take good care of her.'[15] Allan, an aspiring writer, worked as a political commissar for the Canadian Dr Norman Bethune's blood transfusion unit. He had spent several evenings with Gerda and Capa drinking in the bar of the Hotel Gran Via in Madrid, and sometimes with Hemingway and John Dos Passos: on first meeting Gerda in Capa's company, Allan looked at her and thought 'yum, yum'.[16]

While waiting for her editors at *Ce Soir* to assign her another story, Gerda moved into a suite at the hotel Casa de Alianze, popular among the most glamorous anti-fascists in Spain for its all-night bed-hopping and its artist-residents such as the Chilean poet Pablo Neruda. Gerda quickly became the Alianze's star attraction, hosting several parties at which die-hard socialist correspondents such as Claud Cockburn and the Russian Ilja Ehrenburg listened to handsome young poets recite florid lines.

Several foreign correspondents in Madrid, including the 'cadaverous' Cockburn, who was writing overly optimistic pieces for the *London Worker*, were quickly besotted with Gerda.[17] Two pictures taken by Capa before he left for Paris capture something of her allure during this period: in the first, Gerda, in green fatigues, squats down beside a boulder behind a soldier, a look of ecstasy on her face, high on the adrenaline rush of war. The other shows her with arms draped dramatically against a headstone with PC (Communist Party) engraved on it.*

For much of July 1937, Allan and Gerda chased stories late into the night. It was emotionally draining – seeing hysterical orphans, starving women and children and countless corpses. Gerda remained buoyant, however, and drove from one story to another singing Republican marching songs. Her favourite was 'Los Quatros Generales', which poked fun at the 'four Insurgent generals' and lauded the spirit of Madrid's resistance.[18]

In his hotel room one afternoon, Allan showed Gerda some short

* The photograph was evidence of both Capa and Gerda's sympathy with communism. 'Both [Capa and Gerda] were communists,' says Ruth Cerf, who along with Capa and Gerda attended many political meetings of communist émigrés in the early thirties.

stories he'd written – he later drew on them for a novel, *This Time A New Earth* – and was thrilled when she said she liked them. She went to the bathroom and returned brushing her teeth, dressed in only her underwear. She lay down on the bed.

'Do you feel like taking a nap before we go to dinner?' she asked.

Allan lay down beside her, making sure their bodies didn't touch. He knew how much Capa adored her, how serious he had been when entrusting her life to him. Gerda decided to test his resolve, touching his eyelid with a delicate fingertip.

'I'm not going to fall in love again!' she said. 'It's too painful.'

Allan asked whether she still loved Capa.

'Capa is my friend,' she stressed, 'my *copain*.'

According to Allan, Gerda then asked if he liked to be touched near his groin. He nodded. Gerda took his hand, placed it on her groin and said she liked to be touched there also. Allan caressed her gently then stopped. He felt guilty.

'Are you going to marry Capa?' he asked.

'I told you, he's my *copain*, not my lover. He still wants us to marry, but I don't want to.'

'He acts like you are lovers,' said Allan. 'He put you in my charge. He asked me to take care of you.'

'Yes. He was clever. He saw how I looked at you.'[19]

While Gerda flirted with other men, to the west of Madrid more than 100,000 Spaniards were butchering each other in the battle for Brunete. Gerda finally arrived in the city on 12 July as Insurgent snipers were picking off Republican soldiers at will. For several hours, she shot a successful Republican assault on the last Insurgent strongholds. One of her images was of a Republican painting a hammer and sickle on to a whitewashed wall beside a fascist slogan, 'Arriba España', which had been crossed out.

Several days later, Gerda accompanied the grey-faced, cynical London *Daily Worker* correspondent Claud Cockburn back to the front lines. He later recalled how in the middle of a field they came under heavy fire from German planes. 'We arrived at the conclusion that we had, this time, very little chance of getting out alive,' Cockburn wrote. '[Gerda] then stood up and began to make [sic] photos of the planes.'

'In case we do somehow get out of this,' she told him, 'we'll have something to show the Non-Intervention Committee.'[20]

Gerda no longer saw any difference between herself and the Republican combatants. She had lost all notions of objectivity. She now wore her dainty revolver on her hip, day and night. She told a fellow German photographer, Walter Reuter, that she also wore stockings and high heels to the front lines because it boosted men's morale.[21] To others, such as Alfred Kantorowicz and the Soviet writer Michail Koltsov, she had become an anti-fascist fighter: blind to the political infighting that was splitting the Republicans but ever more sensitive to the suffering of Spanish civilians. Ideology was irrelevant. Victory over fascism was all that counted. 'When you think of all the fine people we both know who have been killed even in this offensive,' she told Cockburn, 'you get an absurd feeling that somehow it's unfair still to be alive.'[22]

Gerda was due to return to Paris on Monday 26 July. By Friday the 24th, the Republicans had regained some ground, and she decided to return to Brunete one last time. Just after dawn on Sunday morning, she telephoned Ted Allan and asked him to accompany her – she'd already managed to find a car to take them. 'I must get some good pictures to take to Paris,' she told him. 'If they are still fighting near Brunete it will be my chance to get some action pictures.'[23]

When they arrived on the outskirts of Brunete the French driver refused to go a yard further, and Gerda and Allan took off on foot across a cornfield. In the town itself they met General Walters, commander of Republican forces in the area. Heavy losses had unnerved him and other officers, and he ordered them to leave immediately. Gerda pleaded with Walters, who again ordered her to leave, this time shouting at her. But she wouldn't listen. Anticipating a fierce Insurgent attack, she and Allan took cover in a shallow foxhole. Frightened Republican troops were dug in nearby.

Then came the ominous sound of Franco's planes. Twelve Heinkel bombers filled the sky. Seconds later, bombs exploded all around them.

Gerda snapped into action, taking picture after picture as earth showered down on the foxhole. One German Condor Legion pilot, Werner Beumelburg, looked down from his plane and saw so much destruction that he felt as if he were present at the 'last day on earth'.[24]

At about 4 p.m., Gerda and Allan spotted biplanes fitted with powerful machine guns. One swooped directly towards them. Allan realized the pilots must have seen the flash of metal from Gerda's camera in the sun. She stayed calm as one plane flew in low and opened up on their foxhole. As more planes dived towards their position, she lay on her back and simply reloaded her Leica camera. Capa's Eyemo camera lay a few feet from the foxhole, and Allan grabbed it and tried to use it as a shield from bullets, shrapnel and flying rocks. Around 5.30 p.m., Allan and Gerda suddenly spotted men running in retreat towards them. Several were blown to pieces only yards from where they lay. Chaos ensued as more men turned and ran. But then several Republican soldiers nearby pointed their rifles at their retreating comrades. This was enough to halt the rout, and soon the Republican lines re-formed. Allan pleaded with Gerda to leave. Finally, she agreed.

They accompanied a Scottish doctor towards new lines that had formed between Brunete and the nearby village of Villanueva. Dead and dying men lined the road. Gerda did not photograph them. She had run out of film. In Villanueva, two men begged the doctor to help a wounded friend. They lifted a blanket covering their comrade: his legs had been mangled beyond recognition. A Republican tank passed by. They placed the wounded man on it and hitched a ride. Again, enemy planes opened up. The tank stopped outside a whitewashed farmhouse, crammed with the dead and dying.

A black touring car, carrying three wounded men, approached. Gerda and Allan stopped it and asked for a lift. Gerda jumped on the running board. 'Tonight we'll have a farewell party in Madrid,' she said. 'I've bought some champagne.'[25]

Suddenly, another Republican tank approached, veered towards them as its driver lost control, and then smashed into the side of the car, crushing Gerda and throwing Allan into a nearby ditch. The next thing Allan knew he was lying on the road. His trousers were torn and bloodied but he felt no pain. He cried out for Gerda as two soldiers ran to him and dragged him into a ditch. Then he saw Gerda's face. She was screaming, her eyes imploring him to help her, but he could not move his legs.

Insurgent planes dived again. Soldiers ran for cover. The planes passed. Allan called out for Gerda. He was told she had been taken away in an ambulance. He asked where her camera was. No one knew. Then someone handed him Gerda's belt – its wooden buckle had been smashed into pieces. Minutes later, he passed out. He came to in a hospital in the town of El Escorial.

The hospital was a former Jesuit children's school, with large dormitories and separate rooms for the badly injured. Allan was told that Gerda had been admitted. She had just undergone a serious operation. An English nurse said that she was in shock but would pull through. Apparently, she had been conscious when she had arrived on a stretcher, and had asked a doctor to send cables to her editor at *Ce Soir* and to Capa.

Late that night, Irene Spiegel, an American nurse, tried to keep her 'comfortable'.

> The tank had slashed her belly open. She had very bad abdominal injuries – all her intestines had spilled out. I remember Ted Allan being there, and asking to see her. But I couldn't let him because I'd been told to keep her comfortable, out of pain. If I had known she was going to die, I would have let him see her. But she didn't ask for him. The only thing she said was: 'Are my cameras OK? They're new. Are they OK?' When she died, she just closed her eyes. I had given her morphine – we had no penicillin or antibiotics, and she was not in pain at the end. I remember very clearly that she was very beautiful, she could have been a movie star, and she was not afraid.[26]

Just after 6 a.m. on Monday 26 July, Allan was told that Gerda had died. His son, Dr Norman Allan, says that when his father died in Montreal in 1995, he was still haunted by Gerda's death.[27]

*

On 27 July, Capa picked up a copy of *L'Humanité* in Paris. It contained a brief report from Spain: 'A French journalist, Mlle Taro, is reported to have been killed during a combat near Brunete.' Capa was stunned. Could it be true? Later that day, he received a phone call from Louis Aragon, editor-in-chief of *Ce Soir*. Gerda was indeed dead.

While Capa waited in Paris for his lover's body to return from Spain, Europe's left-wing press canonized Gerda, elevating her from reckless reporter to anti-fascist saint. *Ce Soir* printed hundreds of tributes and devoted page after page to commemorating her life. *Life* described her as 'probably the first woman photographer ever to be killed in action'.[28] Finally, on Friday 30 July 1937, Gerda's coffin reached Paris, where hundreds of fellow communists and friends, including Capa and Gerda's family, gathered at the Gare d'Austerlitz to greet it. Ruth Cerf was among them, and vividly recalls the crowd of tens of thousands of mostly Communist Party members who also witnessed the funeral procession the next day – Gerda's twenty-sixth birthday – from the Maison de la Culture to Père-Lachaise cemetery.

According to several eyewitnesses, Capa was inconsolable as he followed behind the coffin and, as Gerda's father started to recite from the Torah, he collapsed in tears. Seeking solace in solitude and the bottle, he locked himself in his studio and mourned alone for a fortnight, barely eating, crippled by survivor's guilt. It was Capa who had taught Gerda how to use a Leica. He had introduced her to combat photography. He had seen her extraordinary pictures appear under his byline. He had become a world-famous photographer according to plan but his inventor had died. Why her? Why not him?

In Henri Cartier-Bresson's eyes, it was as if a veil had been thrown over Capa. The man who eventually emerged from behind it was, as others saw him, altogether different: cynical, ever more opportunistic, at times deeply nihilistic, afraid of attachment, permanently broken-hearted.

Capa's old friend Pierre Gassmann tried to console him: it had been an accident, he was not to blame. Gassmann says he remembers Capa telling him that he felt responsible for her death. 'It was the only time he was truly serious with me. Capa told me: "I left her in danger – she would never have died if I'd been there. As long as she was with me, she was safe. As long as I was there, she'd do what I did. I would never have let her stand on the running board. That was a reckless thing to do. I would never have allowed it." '

Gerda's family may have blamed Capa for the loss of their daughter. Her brothers were so furious with him, according to Hansel Mieth, that they set upon him after their sister's funeral: 'They had a terrible fight . . . Bob got beaten up.'[29] Ruth Cerf adds: 'Everyone in one way held Capa at fault – responsible for Gerda's death – because he had taken her to Spain with him.'

A Hungarian friend, György Markos, also tried to console him. He recalled that Capa, who continued to drink heavily for the rest of his life, 'raged and drank' for several days after the funeral. 'Capa, you cannot go on like this,' György pleaded. 'You will go mad and destroy yourself; you have no right to do it. You are needed, you have great things to accomplish.'

'Yes, yes,' Capa muttered, 'you are right. I must do something.'[30]

But what? According to a fellow Hungarian photographer, Willy Ronis, Gerda's death prompted Capa to consider giving up photojournalism to work in the film industry. He also considered taking a job as a photographer on a round the world cruise.[31] Unable to wander the *quartiers* he'd explored with Gerda, or sit at cafes where they'd schemed and dreamed, Capa escaped to the damp streets of Amsterdam instead. 'Perhaps it is a romantic notion,' says Eva Besnyö, who was then living in the city. 'But in a way I think part of Capa died with Gerda. You see, she was his true soul mate.'

In later years, Capa often referred to Gerda as his wife, and colleagues and friends repeated the fiction that he had in fact married her. As if his word were not enough, for several months after her death he carried pictures of Gerda in his wallet, and handed them around in bars or in the flickering light of campfires, describing their glory days in Spain. 'After Gerda died, he would always talk about her with me, over and over again,' says Ruth Cerf. 'She was the great love of his life.'

*

By November 1937, Capa had recovered sufficiently from Gerda's loss to be able to function again, and he returned to Spain once more. The Civil War had reached a critical point. Increasingly, the Republic's forces and the International Brigades were proving no match against Franco's armies and Hitler's and Mussolini's tens of thousands of professional, well-armed soldiers, battleships and, above all, hundreds of modern aircraft. Franco was winning key battles throughout Spain, and on 21 October, Gijón, the last stronghold of Republican forces in northern Spain, fell to the Insurgents.

In early December Capa teamed up with the *New York Times*' Herbert Matthews, one of the most objective correspondents covering the war. Like George Orwell and others who cut their teeth in Spain, Matthews did not see the war as a simplistic, 'good versus evil' crusade. In his eyes, both sides committed atrocities, and the war was no longer a fratricidal affair – the Republicans and Insurgents were by now supplied by foreign powers that increasingly viewed Spain as a dress rehearsal for a broader war in Europe and beyond. He was particularly sceptical about Soviet actions in Spain. Stalin's emissaries appeared intent on turning the Republic into a communist state, rigidly disciplined by a murderous secret service.*

On 15 December 1937, the Insurgents attacked Teruel, a bleak 3,500 foot high mountain-ringed natural fortress that blocked their advance towards Valencia, on the Mediterranean coast. Capa and the ascetic, scrupulous Matthews arrived there on 21 December. The town had almost been encircled. If it fell, Franco would finally have a chance to sever communications between Barcelona and Madrid, thereby fatally dividing the Republican forces.

For several days, Capa and Matthews joined Ernest Hemingway and the ruddy-faced, middle-aged Sefton Delmer of the *Daily Mail* in covering the battle for Teruel, retiring each evening to a comfortable hotel sixty miles away in Valencia. On Christmas Eve, Hemingway

* One can only speculate as to how Capa himself felt about the violent divisions opening up among Spain's Popular Front resistance to Franco. There is no evidence that he felt the bitterness that Orwell did over the slow betrayal of the Republic by self-interested extremists blinded by dogma to the broader fight against fascism.

bade them farewell and returned to America to complete a documentary film, *Spanish Earth*, and raise money for the Republican cause. On New Year's Day 1938, news arrived that Teruel had apparently fallen.

Matthews and Capa set out the following morning. It was bitterly cold and heavy going on the snow-bound roads. That afternoon, they came across a group of frozen Republicans breaking ice off their vehicles with picks and others manning tractors with cranes, used to lift vehicles over the steepest stretch of the last open road into the mountain town. Tired and hungry, they finally crossed over Puerto Ragudo, the last mountain before Teruel, around 7.30 p.m.

When they arrived in the village of Baracas, on the other side of the mountain, they soon forgot the day's ordeal, spending the night with several *Carabinero* officers before a cheerful fire, and feasting on salt cod, bread, wine, and coffee. They even managed a few hours' sleep rolled up in a dusty rug. The next morning, they set out once more. The detritus of war began to litter the pot-holed road: rotting carcasses and smashed furniture and burnt-out vehicles. In one tree's wiry branches sat a Republican soldier's stiff corpse. The man's face screamed death – he had been wrapping a telephone line around the branches when a sniper's bullet had found him.

Just outside Teruel, they learned that the Republican lines had held, but only just. The fiercest fighting was concentrated around the Civil Governor's building in the centre of the town. Matthews and Capa followed a group of Republican soldiers into the building, scrambling over broken plaster and rubble, and up a flight of stairs.

They had crawled into a killing zone designed to grind down a man's nerves and send him insane with terror and shock: the building echoed with rifle fire, interrupted by suicidal pistol shots, screams for mercy from Republican hostages, and grenade explosions. Undeterred, Capa and Matthews, backs against shell-holed walls, crept further inside. After several minutes, the pair arrived on the third floor.

'*Viva Franco!*' screamed several Insurgents. '*Viva España!*'

Franco's men were on the floor below, and suddenly fired through the floor at Capa and Matthews. Several Republicans returned fire, blasting holes through the floor, and then tossed grenades into rooms below.

Hearts pounding, Capa and Matthews inched their way up several steps and then down a corridor, glancing into one room after another where Spaniard was busy slaughtering Spaniard. In one room, they spotted a lone Republican, poised to kill.

'Here's one for you and one for Franco!' the soldier cried, firing twice with a revolver. There was a scream. Then sounds of weeping and moans of agony. Looking for their source, Matthews glanced through a hole in the floor and saw a young Insurgent holding a grenade, about to pull the pin. The Republican fired again, pumping three more bullets into his compatriot.

'Rather terrible, isn't it?' said Matthews.

Once the Insurgent resistance in the building had been dealt with, Capa joined the search for civilians who were known to have hidden in the basement. Eventually, more than fifty people, mostly women and children, had to be helped out of the rubble. In a moving report for *Ce Soir*, Capa described how they had survived for over two weeks on leftover scraps from the defenders' meals and a few rotten sardines. They looked like corpses, he noted, and didn't even have the energy to crawl from their hiding-places. Deeply affected by their suffering, Capa wrote that words failed him in trying to describe 'this pitiful scene'.[32]

In mid-February 1938, Franco seized the town and then advanced towards the Mediterranean. Republican Spain, it appeared, was now doomed.[33] Elsewhere in Europe, totalitarianism was also on the march, ever more triumphant. On 14 March, exultant crowds greeted Hitler as he drove into the capital of his homeland, Austria. On 19 April, Franco captured Vinaròs and other towns along the coast between Valencia and Barcelona, finally cutting Republican Spain in two.

Capa did not cover any of these depressing stories. On 21 January, he had left Europe, bound for a different war against totalitarianism, even more savage than the one in Spain, on the other side of the world.

7 'The 400 Million'

'It was the same kind of fight: the people's war in Spain against an aggressor, and the people's war in China against Japan.'

JORIS IVENS, *The Camera and I*

In January 1938, Capa agreed to work on a documentary film, *The 400 Million*, to be shot in China. His job would be to take stills and act as assistant cameraman. He would be working in extreme heat and under brutal conditions at the height of the Sino-Japanese War, which had already claimed over a million lives. The film crew would also include Joris Ivens as the director and John Fernhout as the cameraman, both of whom Capa had befriended in Spain. Ivens had a personal reason for taking Capa to China to work on his film: believing he had married Gerda, he felt it was his 'responsibility to get [Capa] into work to distract him' from his continued grief.[1]

The 400 Million was an even more ambitious project than the propagandist *The Spanish Earth*: Ivens wanted to show how the United Front, an alliance between communists and Chiang Kai-shek's nationalists, was successfully combating brutal Japanese imperialism. It would also be far more dangerous. As a precaution, Ivens told a co-producer how she should interpret coded messages calling for help. The words 'John very ill', for example, should be read as: 'Get us out of this country as soon as possible.'

Capa and Fernhout were to meet Ivens in Hong Kong before travelling deep into China, and the two set out together from Marseilles on 21 January 1938. Also aboard their steamer, the *Aramis*, were two young British writers heading to the Eastern Front in the international fight against fascism: W. H. Auden and Christopher Isherwood.

Isherwood later recalled how Capa and Fernhout were 'the life and soul' of the second-class section of the ship, constantly pinching bottoms, horsing around and swearing at each other in French, and cracking jokes about chickens. 'Capa is Hungarian, but more French than the French; stocky and swarthy, with drooping black comedian's eyes . . . Fernhout is a tall, blond young Dutchman – as wild as Capa but slightly less noisy.'[2]

The *Aramis* docked in Hong Kong on 16 February. Ivens and his cameramen then flew to the city of Hankow, where Chiang Kai-shek's government had its temporary base. Through fellow correspondents in Hankow, Capa learned that invading Japanese forces had racked up remarkable victories in recent months, but were badly overstretched. Though many in the West had predicted China would be a second Abyssinia, the Japanese had been held at bay, thanks largely to Mao Tse-tung's communists.

Within days of arriving in Hankow, Ivens realized he'd bitten off more than they could chew. Chiang Kai-shek's wife, the formidable American-educated 'Madame Chiang', a beautiful and ruthlessly charming favourite of press magnate Henry Luce, had decided to make *The 400 Million* her pet project. Only with her permission could Ivens and his crew film the war against Japan. For six weeks after their arrival, she confined the film-makers to Hankow and had them followed by her spies.

In his memoir, *The Camera and I*, Ivens recalled that he wanted to cover the communist Mao Tse-tung's forces, but 'Madame' would not allow it. The Nationalists were the true, heroic defenders of China, not Mao and his army of peasant revolutionaries, who had kidnapped her husband before agreeing to release him in order to combat the 1936 Japanese invasion more effectively.

To help pay his way in China, Capa had agreed to provide *Life* with stories on an ad hoc basis. For Sinophile Luce's magazine, which made no bones about its support for the 'heroic' Chiang Kai-shek, he was soon supplying picture after flattering picture of China's golden couple. A story for Stefan Lorant's British magazine *Picture Post* on 5 November 1938 was, if anything, even more blatantly propagandist. 'Fantastic had been the career of China's 50-year-old Commander-in-Chief,' trumpeted the magazine, 'the most-bombed man in the world, and his charming wife – the backbone of China's resistance to Japan.' Capa apparently met Madame Chiang several times. On one occasion, he later told a friend, he had to pour several of her cocktails into potted plants to stay sober. Madame Chiang Kai-shek, 'the strict puritanical Methodist', allegedly mixed a lethal martini.

At 4 p.m. on 16 March, Capa picked up his cameras and went to work on a story for *Life*, titled 'Chinese Children Barnstorm for Recruits'. On a stage in a public square, children imitating a Chinese soldier and peasants pretended to lie asleep. Suddenly, another child, playing a cruel boss, lashed into a peasant. The performance ended with Chinese soldiers carting off both Japanese invaders and rich landowners – the twin enemies of the Chinese masses. The propaganda piece – no more subtle than *Life*'s picture spreads – was put on especially for an audience of young soldiers crouched down in the dirt in uniforms so thin that they shivered at night.

By that spring, *The 400 Million* had become a miserable experience for all involved. 'Things didn't go well at all,' recalls Eva Besnyö, then married to Fernhout. 'John [Fernhout] told me there were bitter disagreements. Capa didn't really work out for them.' Capa, who within the year was tagged by *Picture Post* as 'the greatest war photographer in the world',[3] resented being a mere assistant. And when he focused on his own stills work, he discovered he was in direct competition with the highly talented Walter Bosshard, a former Dephot photographer who was also on assignment for *Life* magazine and was beating him to the best stories.

In early April, the team finally left Hankow by train, along with a party of military advisers and yet more spies, for the Suchow front in the north-east. It was a nerve-racking journey: the Japanese had decided the only way to take and then hold vast swaths of Chinese territory was to control the railways, and that meant constant surveillance and dive-bombing of any trains.[4]

Capa and his colleagues arrived in Suchow station at 6 a.m. on the 3rd. They found four dying civilians on the platform. 'One still moves a little,' Ivens noted. 'We have arrived just in time. The Chinese army is surrounding the Japanese near Taierchwang . . . As Capa photographs our group, I consider this unique situation in this war for independence. For the first time in China's history all her armies are united . . .'[5]

On 4 April, Capa examined Japanese lines four miles away through a Chinese gunner's artillery glasses. Suddenly, the Japanese started to shell the observation post. Capa took cover in an old barn. That night, in the company of Ivens and Fernhout, he sang in a 'hoarse melancholy voice' of the Hungarian plains. The next day, he got his first lesson as a second cameraman. 'The censorman, General Tu, makes himself very important by forbidding a close-up of the gun,' Ivens noted, 'which is nonsense, because it is a German gun, made in '33, and well-known.' Quickly, Capa learned his first Chinese words: *Bu yao kan* – 'Don't look at the camera.'

At 6 a.m. on 7 April, Capa woke to learn that the Chinese had taken Taierchwang. He was furious. General Tu had prevented him from getting close enough to take pictures, forcing him to miss the first Japanese defeat in living memory, and the first Chinese victory of the war. Around midday, he joined the equally angry Ivens and Fernhout in a truck headed into the town. As they reached the outskirts, a Japanese plane appeared on the horizon, and then swooped towards them. They took cover behind a 'small sand heap of a grave'. 'We lie close to the ground,' Ivens recorded, 'with our faces down so that the Japanese pilot cannot see the skin of the face which is so easy to spot.'

A nearby armoured train opened fire, the plane circled and then left. That afternoon, Capa entered the city and found utter desolation. In one street, when Capa and Fernhout began to film, an old woman began to scream, thinking the camera was a gun. Another old woman sat alone 'among fragments of clay and board'. 'This is my house,' she said.

Capa's report for *Life*, published on 23 May, reflected Luce's intense joy that the Chinese had for once beaten the Japanese. 'A Victory

Makes Taierhchwang China's Most Famous Village', it declared, above pictures of soldiers after the town had fallen. 'To the names of small towns famous as turning points in history – Waterloo, Gettysburg, Verdun – add still another . . . Next day all China celebrated a great victory. Next day, too, great War Photographer Robert Capa, who eyewitnessed the battle, developed his film, sent it flying by China Clipper to *Life*.' Although *Life* stated that Capa had covered the fighting on the night of 6 April, in fact he had been fast asleep.

On 11 April, the crew rode out of the city to film a wounded Chinese farmer and his family. They returned at a gallop as darkness fell, camera cases bouncing against their backs. 'These are the rugged tiny horses on which the army of Genghis Khan conquered all of Asia and some of Europe. Sometimes in the dark we lose each other. Galloping at full speed Capa suddenly imagines he is really Genghis Khan and yells war cries to us. From the rear he looks more like Sancho Panza. His squat silhouette bounces up and down in the saddle – he is riding for the second time in his life.'

The following evening, a frustrated Capa and exasperated Ivens sat up trying to work out where the front lines had shifted. 'Far away in the night we hear heavy shots in the low foothills,' Ivens wrote. 'It is like the regular beating of heavy blankets, something you might hear in a fever. There is a gong sound, mixed with machine guns . . . There is a long silence. Through the young green cornfields near us an unbroken line of panting soldiers trot quickly on their way to get the heavy gun. But we are not allowed to go with them.'

Capa and his colleagues arrived back in Hankow for Easter, by now bitterly resentful of Madame Chiang Kai-shek and her phalanx of censors and spies. On 29 April, Ivens and Fernhout left for north-west China, Capa promising to follow two days later. Hours after their train pulled out, the Japanese launched a massive bombardment to mark Emperor Hirohito's birthday. The raid claimed over a thousand civilian casualties, and among blazing streets and destroyed buildings, Capa saw images as painful as in Madrid. Again, he focused on the horror and terror of the civilian population: a father grasping his small child, running towards an air-raid shelter; a woman hiding her tearful face from his camera; a man vainly fighting a huge blaze with a wok.

The bombing also destroyed any residue of enthusiasm he had for the whole China adventure. He was soon a regular at the 'Dump Bar', where a tight-knit group of Western correspondents, including the American writers Agnes Smedley and Edgar Snow, swilled back gin and cheap Scotch. 'Our old values seemed to vanish and we lost regard for material things,' Smedley recalled, 'for no one knew whether there would be a tomorrow. We were like passengers on a ship foundering in a stormy sea who at last had found their humanity . . . In the tense atmosphere of war even poetry, song, and wit blossomed among us and a magical glow shone over our friendship.'[6]

In early July, Capa pulled himself away from the marathon craps games in the Dump Bar to cover the flooding of the Yellow River, done deliberately to prevent the Japanese advance. The spectacular bursting of dams stopped the Japanese for a few weeks, but left two million homeless. Capa's pictures showed bedraggled peasants trying desperately to reach dry land, their homes engulfed by the river's muddy torrents. Capa returned to Hankow on the 4th and a few hours after arriving rejoined Ivens and Fernhout at a meeting of Chiang Kai-shek's Supreme War Council. Such meetings had never been open to the press and Capa's pictures of the 'Generalissimo' syndicated widely.

On 19 July, the Japanese deliberately targeted the civilian areas of Hankow for the first time. As Capa roamed the devastation beneath a fierce midday sun, flames engulfed the city. In some areas, the heat was so intense that people's faces appeared bloated. The air swirled with ash. Homes were reduced to sooty skeletons.

In early August, Ivens and Fernhout left for New York. Not long after, with the mercury still above 100 degrees at noon, Capa met a remarkable character in Sino-American relations, 'Vinegar Joe' Stilwell, the American military attaché in China. Stilwell's nickname was well deserved: he was famously caustic regarding naive Western assumptions about the Chinese. Capa came across him in an army camp outside Nanchang, 150 miles from Hankow, where the American and other advisers were trying to assess the relative strengths of the warring armies. The situation looked ugly to both Stilwell and Capa:

the Japanese were within a few days' march of Hankow itself.

On the morning of 7 September, Capa joined Stilwell as he and a group of British and French military attachés made for the front lines. Stilwell noted in his diary that Capa was 'quite a guy'. Another entry reads: 'Moved by night, hard going and guard went astray. Pack transport, coolies, exhausted men curled up to die . . . Jap plane at 200 feet machine gunning the road . . . Bread and cheese for breakfast, by Capa. Mouldy but O.K. . . . Hot as hell.'[7]

Back in Paris, György Markos and Suzy Marquis saw the pictures Capa was sending. Marquis knew he was still alive only when another picture appeared. Markos guessed that he had decided to show the world the kind of horrors that had robbed him of Gerda. The pictures were the most unsettling he had seen: 'Children with protruding bellies, pregnant mothers in blood and filth; Chinese digging their own graves under the supervision of Japanese soldiers; Japanese soldiers practicing bayonet assaults on living Chinese.' Capa had gone in search of death, he concluded, but had not found it: 'Not yet, anyway.'[8]

As Capa sweated it out with the other correspondents waiting for Hankow to fall, dubbed the 'Last-ditchers', he asked himself whether being a freelance photographer was how he wanted to spend the rest of his life, and in a letter to a communist friend, Peter Koester, whom he had met while working for Dephot, he broached the idea of forming an agency of young photographers who could control their own work.[9]

In late September, with Hankow not yet captured, he left for Paris. A few days before he left China for good, he shot the first photographs of war ever to appear in colour, using Kodachrome 35mm film. *Life*'s 17 October issue devoted two pages to images showing the aftermath of yet another bombing raid. 'The slums of Hankow, capital of China's retreating government,' read a caption, 'are red with flame and black with smoke after a Japanese bombing . . . a blue-shirted coolie woman sits in bleak watch over her household goods as Hankow burns in the noonday heat.'

Hankow finally fell to the Japanese on 25 October 1938. By then, Capa was back in Spain, covering the most heart-rending story of his career: the Republic's final defeat.

8 The Final Defeat

'Countries do not live by victories only, but by the examples which their people have known how to give, in tragic times.'

JUAN NEGRÍN, 1939[1]

Only days after Capa left China, Britain and France signed the Munich agreement: a shameful capitulation to an increasingly bellicose Hitler. On 30 September, Neville Chamberlain famously waved the agreement and declared: 'I believe it is peace in our time.' Stalin soon joined Chamberlain in kowtowing to Hitler, ordering the withdrawal of 6,000 Soviets from the International Brigades. Several European powers had also agreed to withdraw volunteers, most belonging to the International Brigades. The Republic was abandoned to fight alone against Franco and his allies, Hitler and Mussolini.

Capa arrived in Barcelona in early October knowing that 'the Passionate War' was all but lost. Among a new group of 'last ditchers' in the bar at the Hotel Majestic, he ran into Ernest Hemingway. On Papa's arm was a stunning blonde correspondent for *Collier's* with a Bryn Mawr accent and a razor-sharp mind: Martha Gellhorn. Elegant, funny and deeply compassionate, Gellhorn was no lightweight. She had already published a novel and a collection of short stories and had spent enough time in Germany to share Capa's hatred of the Nazis.

Gellhorn later regarded Capa as a kind of brother, one of the few men who truly understood her contradictions and passions. That autumn, they bickered over politics – he mercilessly pointed out her naivety about the *causa* – and made fun of each other, but always with affection. One day, he arrived at the hotel in a new camel's hair overcoat with huge lapels and pearl buttons. She thought the coat 'wildly out of place in Barcelona'. 'If I am killed,' he told her sincerely, 'I wish to die in my polo coat.'[2] Gellhorn's novella *Till Death Do Us Part* portrayed him far more insightfully than any of the many male writers he encountered. She cast him as Bara – 'so dashing in his special gypsy way, loved by women, welcomed by men, a life-giver, the sort of person people claimed to know when they didn't, made up stories about, quoted, were proud to be seen with, happy to be used by' – and disguised herself as Marushka, who, Bara said, 'should have been Russian since she had a pre-Soviet Russian soul, so fierce, so illogical, so elevated, so absurd.'

On 25 October, Capa arrived in Montblanc where the Spanish premier, Juan Negrín, was scheduled to speak to the departing International Brigades. Capa's pictures show hundreds of men reduced to tears but defiantly waving their fists in the air after hearing his speech. They'd survived on foul-tasting diets of dried mule and goat meat through two bitterly cold winters. Now their fight was almost over.

Four days later, Capa woke early. All that morning he fretted, worried that his Leicas were somehow faulty. Finally, word arrived that a farewell parade of the International Brigades would start at four thirty – the exact time of the final march-by had been kept secret in case of a massive air raid. When Capa reached the famous 'Diagonal' at the centre of Barcelona, he found tens of thousands of emotional Catalans waiting to say goodbye, their arms full of bouquets.

Tears began to flow as the first group of volunteers arrived: an honour guard of Republican soldiers and sailors, singing at the tops of their voices. Then the first of the Internationals appeared – Germans of the XIth Brigade, marching eight abreast. Women ran towards them and showered them with flowers. Petals soon formed a carpet beneath their battered boots. Then the sky filled with strips of paper, raining down from windows above. Small boys joined the ranks and were lifted high on to the weary men's shoulders.

Finally, 200 men from the American Abraham Lincoln Brigade

arrived. The flowers, in places ankle-deep, slowed their proud stride. At the head of the column was their tall, handsome commander, Milton Wolff, hoping his fellow 'premature anti-fascists' shaped up in comparison to the other foreigners.

Capa had first met Wolff when he'd taken a picture of him and Hemingway before the pair went into action on the Abril front in early 1938, and Wolff still admires him for his ability to smile on misfortune, to lift the spirits of others around him. 'Capa always put on a good face,' he says. 'No gloomy Gus, that madman Hungarian! We all admired his photographs, his guts. You can see from his pictures in Spain how close he was most of the time to the front. He'd butter up officers to get into their good books, so he'd get close to the action.'

Once all the international volunteers had gathered in the Diagonal, La Pasionaria, the figurehead of resistance to Franco, took her place at a podium to address them. A sombre, middle-aged woman with fiercely intelligent eyes, she had famously declared that it was 'better to die on your feet than live on your knees'. She spoke to the women in the vast crowd first. 'When the years pass by and the wounds of war are stanched,' she instructed, 'speak to your children. Tell them of the International Brigades. Tell them how these men gave up everything, their loves, their country, home and fortune, and came and told us, "We are here because Spain's cause is ours." . . . Thousands of them are staying here with the Spanish earth.'

She spoke to the men next. 'You can go proudly. You are history. You are legend. You are the heroic example of democracy's solidarity and universality. We shall not forget you, and when the olive tree of peace puts forth its leaves again, mingled with the laurels of the Spanish Republic's victory, come back!'[3]

Gerda should have been there beside Capa, working as his ideal partner, if not his wife. So many should have been there. But they were not. Thousands of volunteers, along with the innocence of an entire generation, had been lost.

*

While the withdrawal of the International Brigades was a tragic blow to the Republic, it did not kill all hope of withstanding – at least in Catalonia – the Insurgent advance. Since July 1938, the Republican army had been fighting a bitter battle against Franco on the banks of the Ebro River. With bitter determination, Republican units of the Fifth Army had held a small bridgehead through the autumn. In late October, with Mussolini and Hitler increasingly impatient for Franco to finish off the 'reds' in Spain, the Insurgents launched a massive attack on the bridgehead.

In early November, Capa accompanied Hemingway and the *New York Herald Tribune* correspondent Vincent Sheean to the Ebro front. On the morning of the 5th, Capa and Sheean came under heavy fire while trying to make a rendezvous with Hemingway, who had promised to arrange transport to the bridgehead, and took cover in a stable. Whenever they heard another shell whistle overhead, they dived to the ground. 'This is a bad day for photographers,' Sheean told Capa. 'This is the only kind of day that is any good for photographers,' he replied, removing straw from the polo coat Gellhorn had ridiculed.[4]

When the shelling subsided, they joined Hemingway, and Herbert Matthews from the *New York Times*, on the banks of the Ebro. Hemingway was standing proudly beside a flat-bottomed boat, manned by four peasants whom he paid with cigarettes. Beyond raged the Ebro, exposed to Insurgent artillery and sniper fire. All bridges in the area had long been destroyed and the dams opened to make the river impassable to Republican reinforcements. The only way to reach the bridgehead was to brave the Ebro's currents and rapids.

The group made it through the strong eddies and then walked to General Enrique Lister's last redoubt – a whitewashed cottage on a hill in the destroyed village of Mora de Ebro. Although General Lister knew Hemingway well, and was normally hospitable to journalists, he was not pleased to see the group. He was about to order his men to retreat, and told the reporters to return to the river immediately. As they returned to the Ebro, they passed some Republican tanks. Matthews pulled out his camera and took pictures but Capa didn't bother to even lift his Leica. Matthews was perplexed. 'This kind of

OVERLEAF:
'He had a gambler's sense of priorities.' Capa with multiple betting slips, Longchamps, Paris, 1952.

'The little red fox.' Gerda Taro.

Gerda Taro, suivie d'une foule émue, **a été portée ce matin au Père-Lachaise**

Le corps de notre amie repose non loin des victimes de Clichy sous un immense monceau de fleurs

Le cortège funèbre s'est arrêté devant notre journal pour y être salué par les collaborateurs qui assuraient le service (Lire dans la troisième page)

'She was the great love of his life.' Gerda Taro's funeral procession in Paris, 1937.

'He had gone in search of death.' Fernhout, Ivens and Capa, second from left, with three Chinese officials, China, 1938.

'Among the 400 million.' Ivens and an unidentified man are on top of the tank, Capa, Fernhout and a Chinese man in front, China, 1938.

Capa and 'Papa' Hemingway, Sun Valley, Idaho, November 1940.

'He [Capa] could speak seven languages but none of them well.' Ernest Hemingway listens to 'Capanese', Sun Valley, Idaho, November 1940.

Capa dances the night away at Sun Valley, November 1940. His 'soul sister', Martha Gellhorn, is second from left.

'He was the worst driver in the world.' Capa, late 1944.

'I was under fire with him.' Capa's friend and editor at *Life*, John Morris, London, 1944.

OPPOSITE: 'Listen, old goat, it's the end of the game that counts and how many chips you've got in your pocket – if you're still playing.' Capa and 'old goat' George Rodger, Naples, 1943.

The waterfront after bombing, Anzio, 1944.

Ernie Pyle, the great American war correspondent, lights up after a direct hit on the correspondents' beachfront hotel, Anzio, 1944.

'He was phenomenally brave.' Capa, second from left, about to jump with the 17th Airborne over Wesel on the Dutch border, 24 March 1945.

Capa with close friend and fellow Magnum founder David 'Chim' Seymour, Paris, early 1950s.

Magnum founders toasting the liberation of Paris at a party at the home of *Vogue* editor Michel de Brunhoff, shortly after the event. Capa far left, Chim Seymour centre without tie, Cartier-Bresson far right.

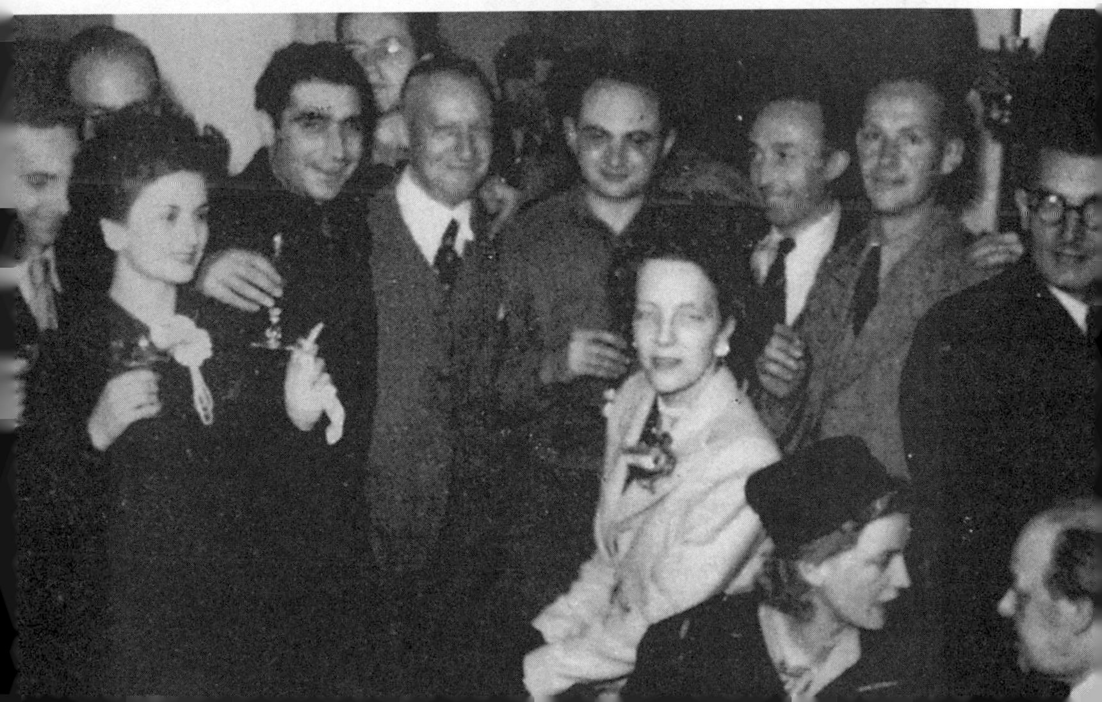

'You are my sort of creature.' Capa with the writer Gael Elton Mayo.

OPPOSITE:
Ingrid Bergman with her father, a Bohemian photographer.

'She was like a great painting'. Ingrid Bergman in *Notorious*, 1946.

Capa playing poker with John Huston (far right) while Burl Ives plays guitar, London, 1953.

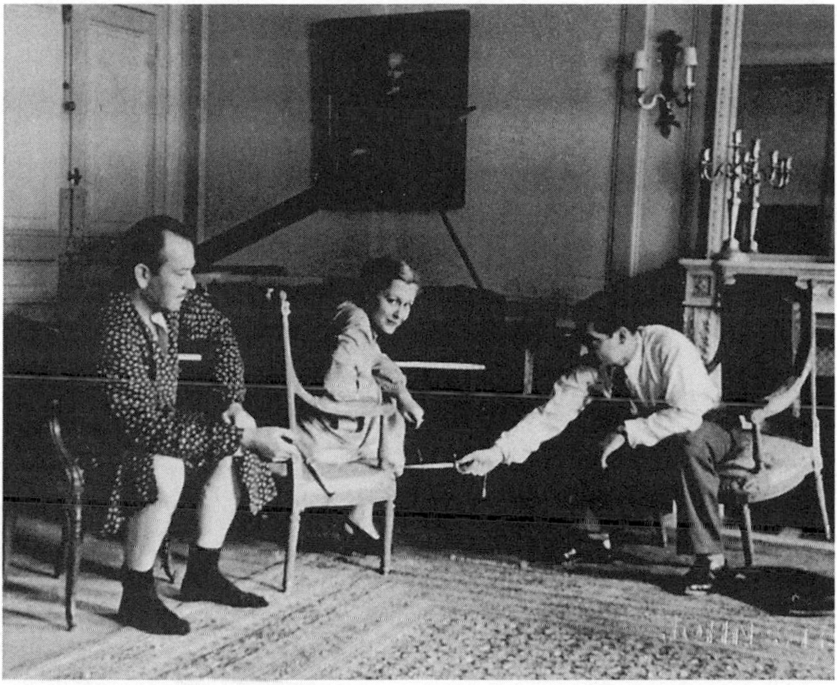

Capa with John Steinbeck and his wife Gwyn in a Paris hotel in 1947, just a few days before crossing the Iron Curtain.

Back in action. A newsreel cameraman captures Capa photographing the wounded from Dien Bien Phu, Indo-China, May 1954.

-BEIO

'She could talk of nothing else.' 'Julita' Friedmann at the grave of her favourite son in upstate New York.

OPPOSITE: 'He asked me to take his camera.' The last photograph of Capa alive, taken by friend and colleague Michel Descamps.

‘The man who invented himself’.
André Friedmann, alias Robert Capa, 19

thing is no good to me,' said Capa. 'These aren't action pictures.'[5]

When the group reached the Ebro late that afternoon, they discovered that two of their rowers had deserted. The swirling waters were so powerful that the remaining men were not strong enough to keep the loaded boat on course. Midway across the river, one rake-thin peasant lost control of his oar and the boat suddenly lurched downstream towards the jagged spine of the bombed Mora Bridge. Hemingway reacted instinctively, grabbing an oar and pulling hard to regain control of the boat. It took them several minutes to row the boat to safety. Capa took 'action pictures' all the way.[6] That night, Lister's men evacuated their bridgehead. The Battle of the Ebro was lost. At least 16,500 men had been slain in the Republic's last, four-month-long battle.

The following night, a group of do-or-die Republicans crossed the Segre River, a tributary of the mighty Ebro, determined to stall Franco's advance one last time. Capa joined them in the small town of Fraga, south-west of Lérida. They were armed with ancient 1901 Russian rifles, dressed in motley uniforms; clay was slapped on to their helmets to help camouflage them against the dry, stony terrain. Suddenly, a deafening explosion shook the ground. One of the soldiers staggered into the open, stunned by the blast. With one shutter release, Capa then froze the Spanish Civil War to far greater effect than he had with 'The Falling Soldier': this time, the image was undeniably real – a young Spaniard stumbling in terror as earth and rock rained down. 'The focus and exposure of this picture were correct,' *Picture Post* later assured its readers. 'As our photographer clicked the shutter, a shell burst twenty yards away, and the earth shook with the explosion . . . you can almost smell the powder in this picture.'[7] Capa's most moving photograph showed a bandaged man, lying on a stretcher, mumbling his last words to a comrade who scribbles a final message to a loved one. 'A comrade listens, tries to catch his meaning, jots his words down.'[8]

Picture Post captioned another notable picture: 'The Attack Begins: A Man Is Shot: He Falls.'[9] It is remarkable that this picture has never been discussed, given the enormous attention focused on the contentious 'Falling Soldier', for it actually shows a man who has been hit falling to the ground. 'In spite of the cigarette between his lips, this man has just been hit,' *Picture Post* declared. 'The bullet has struck him in the stomach and doubled him up. He drops, still holding his rifle. He is one of the worst casualties.'

Capa's story for *Picture Post*, magnificently laid out by Stefan Lorant, confirmed his status as the most courageous photographer to cover the Spanish Civil War. Lorant in fact paid him the highest compliment of his career. 'In the following pages you see a series of pictures of the Spanish War,' the magazine announced. 'Regular readers of *Picture Post* know that we do not lightly praise the work we publish. We present these pictures as simply the finest pictures of front-line action ever taken.' When Capa opened the magazine's 3 December 1938 issue, he saw a full-page picture (which appears on the jacket of this book) of himself holding up an Eyemo camera, captioned 'The Greatest War-Photographer in the World: Robert Capa'.

Capa's coverage of fighting on the Segre River was the closest any photographer had ever come to war's chaos and carnage, and was so evocative that many of *Picture Post*'s readers must have wondered whether he had a death wish.

As Franco's forces swept through the last strongholds of the Republic in Catalonia and along the Mediterranean coast they murdered and tortured tens of thousands of their fellow Spaniards. In early January 1939, Capa returned to Barcelona to cover the desperate flight of hundreds of thousands of terrified Republicans. On 15 January, he again witnessed a horrific attack on columns of refugees, this time heading for Barcelona. Thousands died as Hitler's and Mussolini's planes, which now had total command of the skies, strafed mostly women and children. Capa discovered one old woman walking in a daze around an overturned cart. 'She couldn't make out what happened,' he told *Picture Post*. 'She just walked blindly round and round her cart.' Her entire family had been cut down.[10]

When Capa returned to Barcelona, he found the city in total chaos. Martial law had been declared to prevent total panic. More than a million refugees, living on a daily ration of a few ounces of bread, crowded the streets. Potato skins had replaced tobacco. The city of a once-romantic people's revolution was exhausted beyond resistance.

For several hellish nights, the 'last ditchers' at the Hotel Majestic, including Herbert Matthews, Martha Gellhorn and O'Dowd Gallagher, lived on their nerves, trying to type heart-rending stories as Heinkels swooped down, in forty-seven raids within four days. Mingled with explosions were the pistol shots of different Marxist and anarchist factions, once united in fighting fascism, now assassinating each other. After several other correspondents had abandoned the city, Capa and Gellhorn huddled together in her hotel room, shaking from the cold as shells dropped incessantly nearby.

At 1 a.m. on 25 January, the reporter Georges Soria of *L'Humanité* rushed into the Majestic with news that Franco's troops were crossing, unopposed, the Llobregat River, a few miles away. Around 2.30 a.m., Herbert Matthews found Capa sleeping like a baby in his room, despite the continued bombing. He shook Capa awake and hustled him into an unreliable Belgian Minerva car, 'Old Minnie'. At first light, they found themselves on a road clogged with some of the 400,000 refugees who would eventually escape Spain. Orphaned girls hugged rag dolls. Old men in tears clutched handkerchiefs full of soil from towns they would never see again. It took thirteen hours to drive the hundred miles to Figueres, twenty miles from the French border.[11]

Figueres was swamped with a hysterical, starving exodus. Fights broke out on pavements between emaciated refugees looking for a doorway to sleep in. Children screamed for lost families and stale bread. Trucks loaded with 600 masterpieces – Goyas, El Grecos and Velázquezes – stood under armed guard before being evacuated into France. 'This place is like a tomb,' a *Times* correspondent told Ilya Ehrenburg of the Soviet newspaper *Izvestia*, who replied: 'This is a tomb not only of the Spanish Republic but also of European democracy.'[12] In one street, Capa came across a young girl lying on a few bags. 'She's a pretty little girl,' he reported, 'but she must be very tired, for she doesn't play with the other children. She hardly moves; only her big dark eyes follow all my movements. It's not easy always to stand aside and be unable to do anything except record the sufferings around one.'[13]

When Franco's troops entered Barcelona on 26 January they met only sporadic resistance. As Franco's Moors marched down the Ramblas, people emerged nervously from underground stations and made the fascist salute, some carrying hastily acquired photographs of Franco. Within days, 10,000 political suspects were butchered in a culling which even an Italian fascist commander admitted was a 'very drastic purge'.[14]

In Figueres, meanwhile, Vincent Sheean frantically searched everywhere for his friend Capa – a marked man among the Insurgents because of his new-found fame. Sheean finally found him in a makeshift press office where he had made a bed from now useless boxes of propaganda leaflets; he snored on his bed of paper promises louder than Sheean had heard anyone before.

On 28 January, Capa crossed into France, exhausted and depressed. One of his final images was among his most moving – it showed a long line of defeated Republicans crossing into France, guided by a lone French policeman, and carrying a few possessions as they shivered in the bitter winter winds. By the time Capa got to Paris he could barely function, so overwhelming was his sense of defeat. Even the high praise of *Life*'s Wilson Hicks failed to lift Capa's deep depression. 'We here were greatly concerned about you as Franco's troops neared Barcelona and during the capture,' he wrote on 31 January. '*Life* has been well pleased with your pictures from both China and Spain. I know your modesty will not lessen when I tell you that you are the No. 1 war photographer today.'[15]

Several weeks later, as war clouds gathered over Europe, Capa returned to the Spanish border, this time to cover the appalling conditions in many refugee camps. (Now that the war was all but over, these refugees were a political embarrassment to the French and also a significant cost.) In Argelès-sur-Mer he discovered 60,000 Spaniards, many sleeping in holes in the ground, a few protected from the bitter winds and freezing temperatures by flimsy shacks. There were no cooking arrangements and no sanitation, 'only barbed wire to keep them in,' he wrote, 'and brutal Senegalese troops to keep them in order.'[16] For sport, many mounted and armed French guards beat up dying men who had fought Franco for three years. One night in

February seventeen had died of exposure and were buried where they lay.

In other camps, a further 175,000 Spanish men, soldiers and civilians, lived in equally deplorable conditions, abandoned by the other Western powers to the callous French authorities. In the village of Bram, near Carcasonne, Capa photographed a former professor of international law, lying sick in a bed of straw in a freezing hospital. 'He is an old man, and he took no part in politics,' *Picture Post*'s caption read. 'But he wrote articles on justice and the rights of nations for a foreign review, and there is no place for such as he in Franco's Spain.' Outside, in the late winter light, Capa walked along rows of crosses. 'On the white crosses are names once celebrated in Spanish art and literature,' reported *Picture Post*. 'And the line of crosses grows steadily longer.'[17]

On 28 March 1939, the Insurgents seized Madrid. The 'Passionate War' was finally over. At least 300,000 people had died, more than half of them civilians. In the coming years, 300,000 of the vanquished languished in Franco's prisons. Perhaps as many as 100,000 people were executed.

Betrayal followed defeat when, on 23 August 1939, Germany and the Soviet Union signed a non-aggression pact. Anti-fascists the world over felt they had been stabbed in the back; the surviving European democracies, especially France, feared that war was now inevitable. As a prominent Jewish émigré who now contributed regularly to *Ce Soir*, a communist publication, Capa may have begun to worry that he would be among the first to be rounded up should France's right-wing government decide to exact widespread revenge on the treacherous 'reds'.

At 6 a.m. on 1 September 1939, a Wehrmacht force of 1.5 million troops swept into Poland, practising a form of warfare it had perfected in Spain: blitzkrieg, or 'lightning war'. Two days later, France and Britain were at war with Germany. By October, Robert Capa was fleeing yet again, this time aboard a ship headed for America.

9 Splendid Isolation

'Never in the field of human conflict was so much
owed by so many to so few.'

WINSTON CHURCHILL, 1940

Within days of arriving in New York, Capa was enjoying the city's nightlife, playing poker with friends he'd made in Spain, and joining Julia and his brother Cornell, who had both emigrated in 1938, for traditional Hungarian dinners at their Upper West Side apartment. If he was going to stay in Manhattan, he needed to get work, and fast, and a few weeks after landing he took the lift to the 31st Floor at 9 Rockefeller Center, where he met *Life* picture editor Edward Thompson, a gruff, no-nonsense operator.

'I understood only a little of what [Capa] said,' Thompson later recalled. 'I tried – not entirely successfully – to find assignments for Capa.'[1] But it quickly became apparent that he was no perfect match for Henry Luce's profit-driven corporation, or for America, which he soon viewed as a temporary refuge, and a soulless one at that. Its isolationist outlook and puritan values began to grate on him within months. Compared to Europeans, the Americans didn't know how lucky they were. And they didn't know a damn thing about food and wine. Not long after starting to work for *Life*, Thompson recalled, Capa 'astounded an accompanying reporter, Don Burke, by making a scene in a railroad dining car because there was no vintage wine.'[2]

Late that autumn, Capa met the young writer Irwin Shaw, a handsome and athletic Brooklyn-reared Jew who became a close friend. 'I first met Bob Capa with a pretty girl in a bar in Greenwich Village. It was not the last time I was to meet him in a bar or with a pretty girl. Just returned from Spain, he was already famous, and I recognized him immediately: the thick-lashed dark eyes, poetic and streetwise, like the eyes of a Neapolitan urchin, the curled, sardonic mouth with the eternal cigarette plastered to the lower lip.'[3]

Shaw was struck by how Capa was 'already famous' yet penniless – 'a condition that, because of the hazards of his trade and his lust for gambling, was almost chronic with him. He was also in danger of being deported to his native Hungary, a country that he memorialized in accent, a musical deformation of speech in all languages, which was dubbed "Capanese" by his friends.'[4]

Around this time, Capa also met a young man from Chicago, John Morris, who was working as an assistant on *Life*'s picture desk. Morris remembers taking Capa skating in the Rockefeller plaza rink one lunchtime that winter. 'Capa grabbed Bobby Rock, a *Life* secretary, and it was quickly obvious he didn't know how to skate. She dragged him round and damn if they didn't take a spectacular spill right in front of the plate-glass window of a restaurant. I was just behind them and I saw three top *Life* editors, sitting at lunch, roaring with laughter.'

Capa's immigration status was not so funny. 'Capa had a "Nansen" passport, named after Fridtjof Nansen of the League of Nations,' recalled Edward Thompson, 'a document issued to "stateless" people. The Hungarian quota for immigration to the United States was backed up for a couple of dozen years, so a begrimed, taped-together document – "If it was clean it would look fake," said Capa – was his shaky basis for being around.'

Capa was forced to take drastic action before his visa expired in early 1940. There was only one thing for it – he would have to get married. On 27 March he attended a party with John Fernhout, who had divorced Eva Besnyö and remarried Polly Korchein, a spunky American dancer. Polly introduced him to Toni Sorel, a striking, dark-haired New Yorker. At another party several days later, a tipsy Capa and Sorel agreed to get hitched the next day in a 'quickie ceremony' in

Maryland, the nearest place that allowed such unions – several hours' drive south of Manhattan.[5]

When Capa sobered up the next morning, he realized he had neither the money nor a car to get to Maryland. But in the *Life* offices he'd heard that two photographers were also planning to marry – Otto and Hansel Mieth. The couple had left Germany in the 1920s, busked their way from Budapest to Vienna and then arrived in America, where Hansel became a citizen, and then a *Life* staff photographer in 1937. By 1940, they needed to marry in order for Otto, who had entered the US illegally, to avoid deportation back to Nazi Germany. Hansel later remembered the day well.

Capa burst into *Life*'s editorial offices and found Otto sitting behind a light-box near her. 'How about you and us getting married?' he asked them. 'Let's make it a double . . . I got to leave the country tomorrow. They didn't extend my visa. I'm Hungarian, a Jew. The Hitlerites are in Hungary . . . I made this bargain with this girl. She would marry me for a year's dancing lessons.'

That afternoon they collected Toni Sorel, and Otto drove them all to Maryland in heavy rain. They arrived in Elkton just fifteen minutes before a marriage licence office closed. When Capa and Otto rushed inside, the clerk delivered bad news – the law had been changed. A three-day waiting period was now required before a licence could be issued. They begged him to make an exception but he refused. Depressed, they returned to the car and started back for New York.

As they reached the outskirts of Elkton, Otto saw a car in the rear-view mirror. Two men signalled frantically for him to stop. He slowed down. The men explained that there was a loophole in the law, and then asked to talk to Otto and Capa alone. From the car, Hansel and Sorel saw Otto shaking his head emphatically and turn away, only to be pulled back by Capa. Then Otto took out a billfold and handed over several banknotes. When Otto and Capa returned to the car, Otto explained that if they got a doctor's written testimony that they were pregnant, they could marry straight away. Hansel and Sorel both refused. Capa begged them to reconsider, while the two local men waited impatiently for the couples to follow.

Finally, the women were persuaded. A local doctor didn't even look at the women as he typed out official documentation of their pregnancy. Otto peeled off a few more banknotes. Then they found themselves before an old man, the marriage 'minister'. Both couples were married but when the time came to pay the minister, Otto didn't have enough money left, so Hansel and Sorel rifled through their purses for the required amount. Marriage papers in hand, the four newly-weds stood in the rain outside the marriage bureau.

'This calls for a drink,' said Capa.

But they were all out of money, so they climbed back into the car and headed for home. Otto and Hansel sat up front, Sorel and Capa in the back seat. After a few miles, Hansel heard Sorel slap Capa across the cheek – he'd made a clumsy pass at her. Sorel sat in tears, hunched in one corner. As they neared the Lincoln Tunnel between Newark and Manhattan, she asked to be dropped off. She said goodbye, her voice cracking with emotion. Capa asked to be dropped off at the Bedford Hotel. He got out of the car and, without saying a word, walked off into the night.[6]

'See, Capa was a strange human being,' Hansel Mieth later wrote. 'He acted, as if life was a joke, and at the same time, he took life very seriously. He was made up of many people, some very good, some not so good. He was our friend, and still, he told us stories, that did not hold up under clear light. He was an adventurous character, but many times he cried on my shoulder. He was a made-up person, mostly by himself.'[7]

Sorel later claimed she had been doing Capa a favour when she married him.[8] But according to Georgia Brown, a close friend of the Mieths, she had fallen in love with him. Ed Thompson also believed the marriage meant more to her than it did to Capa. 'Capa considered the marriage temporary,' he recalled. 'Toni, sadly, did not, and was always wistfully asking me for news of Bob whenever I chanced to encounter her.'[9]

To gain legal status after marrying, Capa and Otto needed to leave the country for six months and then re-enter. *Life* took this into account and within weeks conveniently found Capa work in Mexico, while Otto went to Cuba.

Capa arrived in Mexico City in late April, checked into the Hotel Montejo, and made contact with the veteran Latin American expert Holland McCombs, bureau chief of *Time-Life* in Mexico, who explained the volatile political situation over drinks at several of the city's nightspots.[10] As *Life* reported in one of Capa's first photo-essays from Mexico, 'Nazi agents are hard at work throughout Latin America, stirring up hatred of Britain, France and particularly of the US. In Mexico they are working hand in glove with Communists, taking advantage of Mexico's approaching Presidential election on July 7th.'[11]

When Capa wasn't getting drunk on hot buttered rums in the Montejo bar, he wandered the streets, covering the election campaigns of the left-wing General Manuel Ávila Camacho and the more middle-class, right-wing General Juan Andreu Almazán. He arrived at dawn on election day at a central polling station where Ávila Camacho was due to vote. The atmosphere fizzed with the promise of violence: a bizarre election rule in Mexico stated that the first men to arrive at the polling stations took charge of the voting for the remainder of the day, and shooting began as soon as the booths opened.

For several hours, Capa worked without a break, dodging bullets as police and rival supporters shot indiscriminately into the crowds. He photographed the first man to be killed that morning, the wounded being carried into ambulances, the stripped victim of a bombing, and a 'dying newsboy', called Felix Rodriguez, splattered in blood, death overtaking him, a stone he was about to throw still in his hands.[12] According to *Life*'s report on 22 July, this 'free' election for President, the first in thirty years, was far less violent than expected, with only one hundred killings reported by the end of polling.

On 8 July, both candidates declared victory. Election officials announced that the official result would not be declared until 1 September, when Mexico's parliament reconvened. Tensions and temperatures in the capital rose throughout August, as both candidates' supporters murmured about insurrection and a rigged vote.

When Capa checked into the *Life* bureau, he found in the pages of the magazine ever more disturbing reports from Europe. France and Belgium had fallen within weeks to Hitler's blitzkrieg. The Battle of Britain raged above England's summer fields and only the young pilots of the RAF separated Hitler from the total domination of Europe. In London on 20 August, Churchill spoke to the defiant British people, paying tribute to the flyers who were winning the first great battle against Hitler.

On the same day that Churchill made his famous speech, Capa was with many other reporters outside a Mexico City hospital where the subject of his first story – Leon Trotsky – lay dying. That afternoon, Trotsky had been stabbed in the head with an ice pick. Before losing consciousness in an ambulance taking him to the hospital, he had whispered: 'I am sure of victory . . . Go forward.'[13] Already sentenced to death by a 'treason tribunal' in Moscow, Trotsky died the next day. On 27 August his body disappeared into a crematorium's flames. Outside, Capa photographed his widow as she was carried, fainting, to a nearby car.

On 10 October 1940, Capa returned to America via Laredo, Texas, having been granted resident status. The election season was nearing its climax, and he arrived back in New York in time to cover several speeches by candidates Wendell Wilkie and President Franklin D. Roosevelt. Under pressure from the isolationists, Roosevelt fought a tough campaign that hinged on a promise to keep America out of the war.* When America went to the polls, Capa was in Sun Valley, Idaho, on a ten-day assignment covering the country's most intriguing literary couple: Hemingway and Martha Gellhorn. For several days, Capa photographed the 'great American at work and play' with Gellhorn: shooting pheasant, hunting, and dancing together at a nearby Trail Creek Cabin, two miles from Hemingway's ranch.[14]

Hemingway was at the zenith of his success. His novel of the Spanish Civil War, *For Whom the Bell Tolls*, was selling at the phenomenal rate of

* Roosevelt won an unprecedented third term on 5 November.

50,000 copies a week, and had been optioned by Paramount for a record $100,000: *Life* would soon run a special feature using many of Capa's Spanish pictures to promote the movie.

One of Capa's photographs of the 'happy couple' showed Hemingway proudly holding up a freshly killed cock pheasant. 'Over his shoulder', a caption explained, 'is a leather hunting bag bought for him in Finland by Miss Gellhorn when she was covering the Russo-Finnish war.' To get another picture of Hemingway looking suitably macho, Capa waded out into marshland and snapped the writer slugging from a bottle of Scotch. The image did not appear in Presbyterian Luce's magazine, but in a rare picture by a second photographer, Capa can be seen focusing his camera, up to his waist in freezing muck.

Another assignment was even more enjoyable – photographing Calumet City, Illinois, a 'sin city' for the tens of thousands of workers in local factories. *Life* reported that the town had 'no railroad station, no Protestant church, no traffic lights, no central telephone system, 308 night clubs and seven policemen. Its ratio of one bar for every 46 persons is [the] highest in the US.'[15] Capa stayed late into the night to record strippers unzipping their skirts and old drunken couples propping each other up in dive bars.

It was around this time, on the train to Chicago, that Capa chatted with a twenty-eight-year-old black porter who said he'd love one day to be a photographer. The porter was called Gordon Parks and he went on to a long career with *Life* before directing the classic 1970s movie *Shaft*. 'Bob Capa came aboard,' he recalled, 'hoping to sleep the next four hundred miles back to Chicago, only to be kept awake by my constant barrage of questions . . . [Capa] said, "See you in Europe someday," when he stepped wearily off the car several hours later.'[16]

Europe was very much on Capa's mind by 1941. He had seen much of North America but found his work for *Life* frustrating. Whenever he glanced at the front cover of the *New York Times*, his assignments seemed trivial and irrelevant. He had also come to resent *Life*'s management: in 1941, all but one of the magazine's photographers – namely Margaret Bourke-White – were treated as 'snappers', one rung up from the compositors, but several floors below the true players – the advertising salesmen.

When Capa learned that Vincent Sheean's wife Dinah needed photographs for a book on the London Blitz, he jumped at the chance to get back to Europe. But when he arrived in London in July, he discovered that the mass bombing was over. Undeterred, he concentrated on showing the resilience of one working-class family, the Gibbs, as they went about their daily lives. Sheean's book, *The Battle of Waterloo Road*, was published to mediocre reviews in late 1941. Capa had done his best, but the subject matter was by then old news. As a record of the Blitz it looked and read like a tender postscript to the real thing. The book failed, above all, because it included not one passage or picture depicting any real drama.

By October 1941, Capa was back in New York, anxious to find a lengthier assignment covering the war itself, rather than dreary streets where the Nazis had left plenty of heartbreak and damage, but nothing meriting a headline. Moscow was under threat from four panzer divisions, each consisting of 5,000 tanks, and Capa applied for a Russian visa. But his application was rejected.[17] On 6 December 1941, history finally ended Capa's 'phony war', as well as America's isolation. That morning, the Japanese bombed Pearl Harbor. By New Year 1942, Uncle Sam was finally at war with the Axis powers: Italy, Germany and Japan.

10 Muddling Through

'He spoke of the English with affection, as of equals; he told jokes about their unexcited way of muddling through.'

MARTHA GELLHORN, *Till Death Do Us Part*

One morning in early 1942, Capa awoke in a bare studio apartment on the top floor of a five-storey brownstone at 60 West Ninth Street in New York. When he picked up his mail, he found an encouraging letter from *Collier's* magazine – they wanted him to go to England, and then prepare to cover an Allied landing in France or North Africa. Even better – there was a cheque for $1,500 enclosed as an advance, or so he later claimed. But a letter from the Department of Justice spelt disaster: he had been classified as a potential enemy alien. He could possibly be interned. At the very least, he would be barred from taking photographs in public; if he so much as pulled out a Leica in Central Park, he could be arrested.[1]

In his 1947 memoir, *Slightly Out of Focus*, Capa also explained how he was able to cover the Second World War as a 'potential enemy alien', the only photographer to do so. After asking the editor of *Collier's* to pull some strings, he visited the British Embassy in Washington. Capa took a sympathetic official out to lunch, treating him to dozens of oysters and a bottle of Montrachet 1921. The official indicated that special arrangements might be made for him.* While

*Capa may indeed have charmed his way to war as he later claimed. But some sections of *Slightly Out of Focus* are unreliable and a few are completely fabricated. In fact, Capa intended his memoir to be a movie, and never claimed it was a straight account of what he

waiting to hear back from the embassy, Capa stayed in Washington with Myron Davis, a twenty-three-year-old *Life* photographer, and his young wife. Davis remembers Capa commandeering his bathroom and 'soaking in the tub for an hour or two reading his books'. One morning, Capa forgot to lock the door. When he refused to get out of the bath, Davis grabbed his Rolleiflex and began to photograph him in the nude. Capa was not amused. 'It was the only way I could get Bob out of my bathtub,' Davis says, whose pictures show Capa reading a Simenon novel, looking suitably bleary-eyed. To this day, he believes Capa's morning ritual was necessary to 'convert himself from a Friedmann into a Capa'.

Finally, Capa received an official letter from the British Embassy that would serve as a temporary travel document. He returned to New York, packed and then had one last night out on the town. He later claimed that he lost his advance from *Collier's* at poker and had to borrow the $5 cab fare to get him to a ship in Brooklyn. Julia waited in the cab while Capa collected several permits allowing him to leave America. He left his teary-eyed mother behind on the dock, waving goodbye. He then went below to stow his kit bags and poured himself a celebratory drink – at long last he was a war correspondent again.

Capa's ship was part of a convoy, and his journey across the Atlantic promised to be a good story in itself. By 1942, the Battle of the Atlantic was at a crucial stage, with huge losses in freight caused by rapacious U-boats. Between Capa and safety were 3,000 miles of cruel seas, infested with 'wolf-packs' totalling more than 140 U-boats. There was no more perilous time to be crossing to Britain.

The next day, Capa introduced himself to Commodore Magee, who was in overall command of the convoy. Magee had served on the famous Dover Patrol during the Great War, and had been retired for eight years before rejoining the service in 1939. 'Now, don't expect any

experienced from 1942 to 1945. Upon publication in 1947, *Slightly Out of Focus*'s dust-jacket blurb even included a few cautionary words from the author. 'Writing the truth being obviously so difficult, I have in the interests of it allowed myself to go sometimes slightly beyond and slightly this side of it. All events and persons in this book are accidental and have something to do with the truth.'

scoops for your blasted photography on this trip!' he warned Capa. 'Our job is not to fight, but to run and dodge. We'd rather have a hundred freighters safe in port than a hundred Victoria Crosses any day.'[2]

Several days into the crossing, an alarm sounded. A wolf-pack had been detected thirty miles away. Capa pulled his cameras out and was just in time to photograph sailors emerging from an engine-room and running to their boat stations. On deck, he saw a destroyer creating a protective smokescreen; black clouds belched from the ship as it cruised through the convoy. Soon he could not even make out officers a few yards from him, let alone another of the convoy's twenty-odd ships. At dusk, the sea erupted from the explosion of depth charges. Nerve-racking hours passed before welcoming British destroyers joined the convoy and began to escort it to safety.

Capa reached London in mid-May. Quentin Reynolds, the *Collier's* correspondent assigned to cover stories with him, arrived a week later. A boozy 220-pound Brooklyn-born extrovert, he quickly warmed to Capa as they toured London's pubs. 'The spirit of London,' Capa wrote, 'just after the blitz but before the full American invasion of England, was open and inviting.'[3] One night they met Lieutenant Richard Llewellyn, the author of *How Green Was My Valley*, a memoir of growing up in a Welsh mining community. The film of his book had won the Best Picture Academy Award in 1941. 'Just how green is your valley?' Reynolds asked him. 'Go and see for yourself,' the author replied. 'See if I over-painted the picture. See how those men and women live – these people who are cutting coal – these people who are engaged in one of the most vital war industries.'[4]

Capa and Reynolds took Llewellyn's advice. In early June they took a train to Wales and then drove to the village of Gilfach Goch, in an area between Cardiff and the Brecon Beacons known as the 'Lost Valley'.[5] Grey soot frosted the streets and hillsides and poisoned the grass. The Great Depression of the thirties still lingered. Many of the shops were boarded up and most families were struggling to put food on the table. Capa photographed children running down an empty street, behind them steep terraces of miners' cottages leading towards a grey horizon – a view little changed today. One of his pictures, showing a miner returning to the surface after a long day, was selected as one of the best pictures of 1942 by *US Camera* magazine. Other images showed men emerging from a pit, blinking in the hot sun on pay-day, their teeth shining white against their blackened faces.

Capa's next assignment was to photograph pioneering techniques in plastic surgery, a branch of medicine that was developing rapidly in response to the injuries of war. On a warm July day, in a London operating theatre, Capa watched Dr Thomas Pomfret Kilner prepare to operate on a young Pole. In autumn 1939 a German rifle butt had smashed the Pole's face and obliterated his nose, and Capa's brief was to photograph Kilner as he constructed a new one. Stomach churning, he saw Kilner reach for a scalpel, open the nose and begin to remove pieces of smashed bone and cartilage. Under the gas and ether, the Pole slept like a baby. Not one facial muscle twitched. Then one of Kilner's assistant surgeons nudged Reynolds, chuckled and pointed to Capa, whose 'usually ruddy face was now a pale gray'. Reynolds and Kilner helped Capa into an anteroom. Capa moaned: 'I'm blacking out.'

Kilner sent for a large glass of brandy. Good brandy was then very scarce in London, Reynolds recalled, and it seemed ridiculous to waste it on an 'unconscious man', so he drank it himself. When Capa came to, Reynolds told him he'd poured a good shot of superior cognac down his throat to revive him. 'Must have been good!' Capa replied. 'I never felt it go down.'[6]

It was around this time that one afternoon in *Life*'s darkroom on Dean Street in Soho, Capa met the dashing *Yank* magazine photographer Sergeant Slim Aarons. Aarons had just photographed Winston Churchill at Downing Street. He recalls that Churchill 'was loaded, absolutely loaded', and he had duly snapped Britain's inspirational leader looking much the worse for wear. 'I had this great scoop. But when I got to the *Life* lab, they developed it and the picture was ruined. What could I do? I couldn't kill anyone. Capa was there, and he said, "Come on, I'll make you feel better." So he took me to a club in Mayfair. Within five minutes, he had seven girls around him. We had a wonderful time, and ran around town that night. Everywhere he went, Capa knew somebody.'

At a party the previous summer, Capa had met several other foreign correspondents in London, including *Life*'s Mary Welsh, a petite blonde who shortly afterwards began an affair with Ernest Hemingway. In autumn 1942, Capa renewed his friendship with Welsh and others, and attended parties thrown by the American society hostess Pamela Churchill. Red-haired, voluptuous and sexually omnivorous, Pamela was then married to Randolph Churchill, the Prime Minister's only son. When Randolph wasn't around, Pamela had the time of her life, hosting riotous gatherings as well as bedding top generals, both American and British, and the famous American broadcaster Edward R. Murrow. She also found time to drink and joke with Capa at a Soho bar called the White Tower. Several decades later, she would still laugh at the memory of the Capa she met in wartime London. She believed he had changed his name to avoid anti-Semitism and because it caused important people to mistake him for the director Frank Capra.

When Capa wasn't chatting up London society girls or drinking with Churchill's daughter-in-law, he spent his nights with tarts who lurked in the shadows around Shepherd's Market, a short stroll from the Dorchester Hotel. On one occasion, Pamela Churchill recalled, Capa was politely asked to leave because the manager was 'tired of the constant parade of young women' he took up to his room.[7] Like Bara, Martha Gellhorn's fictional version of him, he 'clung to tarts because he liked them . . . they were as unattached as he was.'[8]

By early August, several weeks after arriving in Britain, Capa had still not been given credentials to cover military operations outside Britain. Unable to leave the country, he missed out on what would have been his first major story of the war – the Allies' attempt to open up a beachhead in Western Europe. On 19 August, Reynolds reported without Capa on an amphibious landing in the French Channel port of Dieppe. The landing rapidly turned into a bloody disaster. Six thousand commandos, mainly Canadian, landed under ferocious fire from the Germans. Within hours, more than half were killed, wounded, or taken prisoner.

On 8 September 1942, the Washington and London high commands agreed to begin American day bombing of German cities, coordinated with the RAF's massive night raids. While Reynolds wrote censored reports about Dieppe, Capa visited an American air base in Chelveston, outside London. The base was already home to the crews of forty-eight Flying Fortresses – the famous B-17 bombers, fitted with pairs of Browning 0.5in machine guns in powered turrets that allowed tight formations to spit out unprecedented quantities of anti-aircraft fire. Such ferocious armament was vital: by autumn 1942, the B-17s needed every protection they could muster against the flocks of Bf-109 Messerschmitts greeting them every mission over the Third Reich.

But Capa's luck still hadn't turned. Bad weather kept the crews grounded for several days. While waiting to scramble, he practised several new forms of poker: the 'manly art of self-destruction'. 'I was losing my expense account quite freely,' he recalled. 'Games lasted until early in the morning.'[9] Finally, after countless hands of 'spit-in-the-ocean' and 'red dog', he joined a tense briefing at five thirty one morning. A young colonel stood up and pointed to a large map on a wall. 'You will, of course, have heard about this target before,' he said. 'It is St Nazaire. The RAF have bombed it many times before, but it is more important now than ever before, since it is from St Nazaire that the Nazi U-boats go out to attack the convoys.'[10]

The crews returned to their mess room to wait for the final call. Suddenly, there was a ripple of excitement. The beloved American comedian Bob Hope could be heard cracking jokes. For a few moments, the mission was forgotten as the American flyers crowded around a small radio set. But then came the long-awaited announcement: 'To your planes.' As aircrews scrambled, Capa rushed to a control tower where he photographed the bomb-laden Fortresses lumbering into the air. He counted twenty-four planes taking off. Six hours later, only seventeen returned. One was forced to make a crash-landing: its landing gear had been shot away during the raid, and several of the crew had been killed or wounded.

Capa ran towards the plane as it slid to a halt on the turf runway. He saw a hatch open. A mutilated young soldier was quickly handed to waiting medics. Two corpses followed. The last man to leave the crippled Fortress was the pilot, bleeding from a gash on his forehead. Instinctively, Capa moved closer to get a shot. The traumatized pilot turned on him angrily. So this was what Capa had been waiting for? Images of his dead and bloodied buddies?

Capa wrote in *Slightly Out of Focus* that he snapped his camera shut, left the airfield without saying another word and on the train back to London vowed he would no longer be an 'undertaker'. If he had to attend funerals, then he would also have to take part in the 'procession'. From now on, he would have to join such men on possibly fatal missions. Combatants would only tolerate his presence if he experienced war alongside them. Capa added that the roll of film he took of the dead and wounded flyers would 'show people the real aspect of war'. But his pictures of the wounded airmen were too gory for any magazine.

That wasn't the end of Capa's ill-fated story. His pictures had, he later told a radio interviewer, 'somehow [gone] through the censors without any kind of censorship. [*Illustrated*] wanted to put a picture on its cover of a young man in the nose of a bomber. Unfortunately, there was a little black thing and it turned out to be a secret bombsight.'

'The little black thing' was the top-secret Norden bombsight, so accurate, it was claimed, that it allowed bombardiers to 'drop a bomb in a pickle barrel'.[11] By the time the photograph was spotted by censors, *Illustrated* had printed 400,000 issues. Len Spooner, the editor, was forced to replace the cover shot at the last moment at great expense.[12] Fortunately he did not bear a grudge, and over the coming years he and Capa became good friends. He greatly admired Capa as a news photographer, and soon showcased his talents with generous spreads. When Capa was finally accredited in early 1943 to cover the war in North Africa, Spooner eagerly agreed to consider whatever stories he could send him.

Before leaving for Africa, Capa dined with Vincent Sheean and his wife Dinah, then accompanied them on a visit to Dinah's sister Blossom, who lived near Reading. Blossom was married to a successful aircraft manufacturer, Frederick Miles. Capa enjoyed the Mileses' witty, unpretentious company and decided to visit them again one weekend. To his delight, this time he discovered another houseguest: a strawberry blonde called Elaine Justin.[13]

Elaine had an infectious sense of humour and a superb figure; she was twenty-five years old, and was looking for romance. Her marriage to John Justin, a handsome RAF pilot, was already over, or so she later claimed. Struck by her beautiful hair, Capa was soon calling her 'Pinky' and ladling on the charm. At one point during his stay, Capa was awoken from a nap to find 'Pinky' standing beside a gramophone in the living room, wearing a tight black dress. As they danced the rumba and drank champagne, she quickly succumbed to his charms; she would later say she fell in love with him that very weekend. For the rest of the war, whenever he returned to London, she would be waiting for him, often with a chilled bottle of champagne and the keys to a London penthouse where they would make intense love.

A spring evening in 1943: dressed in a specially tailored correspondent's uniform, Capa downed a last bottle of champagne and then kissed a tearful Pinky goodbye at Euston station. Pinky sang a few lines from her favourite song, '*J'Attendrai*', and then Capa stepped aboard the 7.30 p.m. train to Glasgow, where he would join a troopship bound for North Africa. At long last, he was headed back to the front lines.

11 The Desert

> 'There are only four essentials – clothes, food, cigarettes, and whatever portion of safety you can manage to arrange for yourself . . . No letters, no obligations, no worries – what more could a man ask?'
>
> ERNIE PYLE, North Africa, 1943 [1]

The Scottish division aboard Capa's troopship knew that the war in Africa was entering a decisive stage. As reinforcements, they would be entering the front lines to relieve men who had battled in the hellish desert temperatures for month after month. A large offensive was rumoured to be imminent.

By the time the troopship docked in Algiers, the Scots had got used to the exotic Hungarian in their midst, wearing his bespoke uniform and mangling his English in an accent as thick as any private's from the Gorbals. As for Capa, he had resigned himself to dealing with yet more red tape from public relations officers when he landed. It would probably be weeks before he finally got to record the war, already three and a half years old.

He was surprised, however, to find that no one wanted to examine his papers, question his accent or take away his cameras – quite the opposite. A public relations officer briskly assigned him a jeep and told him he had better get a move on if he wanted to catch up with the war, several hundred miles away in the hilly interior of Tunisia.

For the next day and night, he crossed terrain that reminded him powerfully of the arid interior of Spain, though the temperatures were much higher than he'd endured even in China: away from the coast, it sometimes topped 140 degrees in the shade. As his jeep bounced along tank-rutted roads, he basked in the sunshine, admiring the rambling hills covered in citrus groves and lush valleys.

Capa finally arrived in the Tunisian town of Gafsa and was billeted to an abandoned Arab schoolhouse. That night, he dreamed he would be the only photographer to record Field Marshal Irwin Rommel's capture. But when he awoke he could barely open his eyes: his exposed upper face was covered with insect bites. Later that morning, in a hastily erected press camp in Gafsa, he was briefed on the war in Africa.

In November 1942, while he had been gallivanting in London, British, French and American troops had landed in North Africa and quickly secured the Allies' first major victory against Hitler. Now the desert war was in its final stage. American General George Patton's 2nd Corps was fighting the Italians and Germans, advancing from the west while Montgomery chased Rommel across southern Tunisia.*

Among Capa's fellow correspondents was the remarkable American Ernie Pyle, a rake-thin, gnomelike man, beloved for his simple but elegant reports on the grind and horror of the average GI's war. Meek though he looked, Pyle didn't pull his punches in print. One of his first reports from Africa had been a fierce condemnation of America's refusal to dislodge collaborationist officials in Vichy French Africa. 'We have left in office most of the small fry officials put there by the Germans before we came,' Pyle wrote. 'We are permitting Fascist societies to continue to exist.'[2]

In late March 1943, Capa set out for the Tunisian town of El Guetar. Several weeks earlier, the Axis had counter-attacked and forced the American troops back through a high mountain gorge called the Kasserine Pass on the Algeria–Tunisia border. Now Patton's 2nd Corps was stalled near El Guetar, meeting unexpectedly bitter resistance from Italian infantry. En route, Capa ordered his driver to stop the jeep and went to relieve himself beside a cactus. To his horror,

* The tide was also turning against the Axis on the Eastern Front. On 31 January 1943, in Stalingrad, General Chuikov's Red Army had forced Field Marshal von Paulus to surrender with what was left of Hitler's Sixth Army after a horrendous siege which cost the Wehrmacht 300,000 men and ended Hitler's eastward advance.

he spotted a small wooden sign: '*Achtung! Minen!*'[3] – he'd wandered into a German minefield. He ordered his driver to fetch help. A few hours later, a mine-disposal team arrived along with a *Life* photographer, Eliot Elisofon, who took several pictures of Capa frozen to the spot.

The incident prompted raucous laughter in the press camp but later that night, Capa wrote, the hilarity turned to terror: the Germans bombed the camp. Several tents were blown away and the entire press corps were left rattled, except for Capa who claimed that he slept through the whole raid. The next morning, he learned that the situation in El Guetar was increasingly precarious. The Americans were faltering, so much so that General Eisenhower ordered his West Point classmate, Major General Omar Bradley, to the town to bolster American morale.

Capa arrived to find the Americans dug in on a ridge of hills overlooking a strategically important pass. One morning, he joined GIs in front-line foxholes as they cooked up C-rations. Then, just as he was tucking into a tin of beans, a shell whistled overhead, and he dived for cover, spilling beans and meat all over his impeccably tailored uniform. As the Americans engaged fifty tanks and two German infantry regiments, he watched from a front-line trench. Three American generals arrived later that afternoon for a 'grandstand seat to cheer the team': Patton himself, the Texan Brigadier General Terry Allen and Teddy Roosevelt, who commanded the 1st Division. 'After every hit on a German tank,' Capa wrote, 'Patton bubbled with delight under his three-star helmet.'[4]

For three days, Capa photographed the battle for El Guetar, barely sleeping and enduring constant bombardment. 'All [Capa's shots] are front-line pictures,' *Collier's* announced on 19 June 1943. 'Many were taken at considerable risk; on one of the three days, Mr. Capa had to seek shelter from German dive bombers thirteen times, and spent several hours crouched with his cameras in slit trenches and dug-outs.'[5]

'I got a lot of dirt in my lenses that day,' Capa told *Collier's*, 'and was very scared in my stomach.'[6]

Each evening, after covering the battle, Capa knocked back bottles of Algerian wine with his fellow correspondents. When they boasted about how gorgeous their girlfriends and wives were back in America, Capa mentioned Pinky, but when he described the colour of her hair, his colleagues laughed in disbelief. 'They said that pink women didn't exist,' he recalled, 'and that I ought to have the decency to lie honorably about blondes, brunettes, and redheads like everyone else. I had no snapshots to prove my claim.'[7]

The Battle of El Guetar rumbled on for another three weeks. According to *Collier's*, Italian troops fled so fast that GIs found plates of spaghetti and meat balls, still warm, on tables in their officers' quarters. As the Allies mopped up what remained of the Afrika Korps and the Italian army, squeezing them towards the Mediterranean ports of Tunis and Bizerte, Capa decided to join the 301st Bomber Group, with which he'd learned to play 'red-dog poker' back in England.

The 301st was now based in Constantine in northern Algeria. In early May, Capa again found himself playing poker and losing heavily for several days while bad weather grounded the crews. Finally he joined the crew of a Lieutenant Jay, who had won heavily in a long poker game the previous night; he reasoned Jay would want to protect his winnings and would bring him back safely, in a B-17 bomber nicknamed 'the Goon'.*

For several days, Capa joined the Goon's crew on bombing raids over the harbour of Bizerte, still held by the Germans. The oxygen pumping through his facemask cured his hangovers, and the coolness at 20,000 feet was a very pleasant change from the exhausting heat on the ground. Several times, Capa claimed, the Goon came under attack from 'ack-ack' (anti-aircraft) guns. Once the silver dots of German fighters plunged down from the endlessly blue skies and spat machine-gun bullets into the Goon's fuselage. The plane flew so low on another sortie that he was able to photograph its rippling shadow on the Mediterranean a hundred feet below.

*Accompanying a bomber crew was a bold gamble, for American flyers suffered the worst casualties among the Allies throughout the war. According to some estimates, barely one in four men survived the requisite amount of missions before they could return home, usually between thirty and thirty-five bombing raids.

When the Goon landed back in Constantine after one mission, Capa learned that the British First Army had liberated Tunis on 7 May and the Americans had just taken Bizerte. The most ambitious pincer movement in the history of war, reaching from the Nile to the Atlantic across thousands of miles of inhospitable desert, had ended in tumultuous victory.*

Capa and several other correspondents celebrated with an all-night binge in Tunis; the booze came courtesy of a raid on a captured warehouse. Every new Allied victory was invariably followed by terrible hangovers amongst the press corps who, unlike the troops, could drink themselves stupid whenever the opportunity arose.

Knowing he might not get another chance to relax for several months, Capa obtained a four-week permit from the British Consulate in Algiers allowing him to return to England. He arrived in London in early June 1943 and checked into the Savoy, which remained his favourite London hotel until his death. One evening, he sat drinking with a *Chicago Tribune* correspondent in the crowded bar. Unknown to him, John Steinbeck, the author of *The Grapes of Wrath* (1939), was in earshot. He had just arrived in London on assignment for the *New York Herald Tribune*.[8]

'Capa, you have absolutely no integrity!' snorted the *Chicago Tribune* man. This outburst intrigued Steinbeck. 'I was fascinated that anybody could get so low that a *Chicago Tribune* man could say such a thing. I investigated Capa, and I found out it was perfectly true.'†

Life magazine now had an enlarged office operation on Dean Street, and when he wasn't at the pub next door, the Bath House, Capa flirted with many of the female staff. One of the correspondents, Mary Welsh, was present for one of his tipsy afternoon visits: 'One could almost hear the upswing in female heartbeats around the office.'[9] Working for *Life*

* The Germans and Italians had lost 349,206 in dead and prisoners. Il Duce's dream of a new Roman Empire had ended in rout in the very deserts where Scipio Africanus had defeated Hannibal's Carthaginians at Zema. The Americans, after a shaky start, had proved their mettle. The British, having engaged Rommel for three years in France and North Africa, were rightfully jubilant, and Montgomery was a national hero.

†Steinbeck never explained why Capa lacked integrity, but it made for a good anecdote.

had its perks: attractive secretaries who didn't mind having their bottoms pinched, healthy expense accounts and preferential treatment by the Allies' increasingly formidable Public Relations Organization, now numbering several hundred officers under strict orders to ensure morale-boosting coverage of the war. And for those who needed to take a break from wartime London, the magazine provided a weekend retreat, soon dubbed 'Time Out', and based on a country estate near High Wycombe in Buckinghamshire.

It was often difficult to find a bed at 'Time Out'. Mary Welsh recalled one weekend when 'Time Out' was so crowded that she ended up sharing a bed with Capa and Pinky, 'a sweet-natured, pretty, strawberry-blond girl . . . whom everybody liked and who frequently came for weekends at Time Out.' Though they were given the best bedroom, the threesome spent a miserable night, 'little Pinky on the right, Capa breathing softly but furiously in the middle, [Welsh] hanging over the left edge until [her] right side atrophied.'[10]

Capa's holiday ended in early July with a cable from *Collier's*: 'REGRET HAVE TO RECALL YOU TO NEW YORK'.[11] To his horror, he learned that his contract would expire on 19 July. He had a fortnight to find another employer or be out of the war, but immediately contacted *Life*'s New York office asking to be hired once again.[12] Early in July, he boarded a plane for North Africa in the hope that *Life* would arrange accreditation. Now very much taken with Pinky – he carried her picture in his wallet – Capa sat in the rattling plane as it flew south, back to Algiers and an uncertain future.

In Algiers, he discovered that the Allies were about to invade Sicily, a prelude to a broader assault on mainland Italy. Here was his chance at an exclusive. If he could somehow find a way to join the first American troops to land on Italian soil, *Life* would probably offer him another contract. At last, his luck began to turn: in the Algiers press camp, he met a photographer assigned to jump with the 82nd Airborne Division into the area east of Ponte Olivo. The photographer had a bad case of 'C-ration diarrhoea' and when Capa volunteered to take his place, he quickly agreed.[13]

Capa rushed to an improvised airfield near Kairouan, in the

Tunisian desert, where he managed to track down a contact from London, a public relations officer who introduced him to Major General Matthew Ridgway, commander of the 82nd Airborne Division. Ridgway had seen Capa's work and admired his chutzpah. Not knowing that Capa's accreditation was about to run out, he agreed to the cocky Hungarian joining the 82nd Airborne's invasion of Sicily.[14]

But as it turned out, Capa did not join the first wave of troops to land in Sicily, and it was not until after the Americans had established a beachhead that he found himself beside eighteen young paratroopers in a shaking plane. He had not managed to accompany the invaders, but was allowed to photograph reinforcements being dropped behind enemy lines. As they crossed the Mediterranean, several men vomited from nerves and airsickness. He photographed their grim, determined faces. 'I wouldn't have your job for anything,' one told him. 'Too damn dangerous.'[15] Capa had not done any parachute training and was therefore barred from jumping. After the jump light turned from green to red, he was left feeling terribly alone, determined that next time he too would leap from the hatch into the darkness of enemy territory.

'From then on,' recalled General James M. Gavin of the 82nd Airborne, '[Capa] kept mumbling in Capa-language about wanting to jump. We finally got around to it in England when he took the requisite five training jumps. Then he kept after us to make a combat jump. Since we could not predict the exact date of our next combat jump it meant that he would have to wait around with us and sweat it out. This was not to his liking. Torn between idling around Leicestershire and the flesh pots of Soho, he displayed an understandable leaning to the latter . . . He was a good guy to have around. His conversation wasn't limited to subject "A", or how to take pictures. He had had a lot of practical combat experience, and he knew more about judging combat troops and how to fight than most so-called experts.'[16]

Capa still hadn't heard from *Life* as the July deadline neared. On the 19th, sure enough, *Collier's* instructed him to leave the front lines and return immediately to New York. Taking the biggest gamble of his career, he ignored the instructions. As long as he could stay a step ahead of the Army Public Relations officials, he stood a chance of staying in the war – if *Life* decided to hire him before *Collier's* alerted the Public Relations Office in Algiers. After boarding a supply ship bound for Sicily, Capa landed in the small port of Licata and then made contact with the US 1st Division as it fought its way across the island. Many of its senior officers had come across him in Africa and had no reason as yet to suspect that he was the only American correspondent now in the front lines without accreditation – a court-martial offence.

Capa's subsequent coverage of the 1st Division provided the definitive images of the Americans' battle for Sicily: a twenty-one-day race, with the enemy, Capa noted, always a few miles in the lead. On one isolated road, he photographed the 1st Division's Brigadier General Theodore Roosevelt, grinning and leaning on a walking stick beside a ragged Sicilian who pointed in the direction of the retreating Germans. Another image showed a beaming medical corpsman of the US Seventh Army getting his battered boots shined in newly liberated Palermo, a beautiful Italian woman looking fondly on.

The Americans' costliest battle in Sicily began in early August 1943 outside the staunchly defended hilltop town of Troina. The Germans had dug in so deeply and created such an impregnable ring of defences that the Allies had no choice but to rely on artillery and air bombardment to dislodge them. One day Capa lay in a foxhole and watched German shellbursts creep up a hillside towards him. A few days later, he flew in a small Piper Cub – a 'flying jeep' – to photograph the devastated town.

On 6 August 1943, the day Troina was captured, Capa entered the town with his old colleague from Spain, Herbert Matthews, still working for the *New York Times*. 'Bob Capa, best and bravest of all war photographers,' recalled Matthews, 'was there to remind me of Spain.' They accompanied several mine-detector squads and found 'a town of horror, alive with weeping, hysterical men, women and children who had stayed there through two terrible days of bombing and shelling, seeing their loved ones killed or wounded, their houses destroyed and whatever was left pillaged ruthlessly by departing Nazis.'[17]

In the town centre, Capa ran into Roosevelt, who had good news.

He'd heard that Capa was now officially working for *Life*.[18] Capa was overjoyed, and celebrated late into the night. He was back in the war, working on contract for the top magazine in America, with the best access to units on every Allied front line.[19]

After sweating off a bad bout of malaria, he returned to Algiers. Only the narrow Straits of Messina now lay between the Allies and the tip of the toe of Italy. The city was bustling with thousands of military personnel and hundreds of correspondents awaiting the invasion of mainland Europe.

At the official hotel for the press, the Aletti, every room was taken. Capa eventually found some space on the floor of Room 140 among the bedrolls of the most distinguished group of war correspondents ever to sleep cheek by jowl: A. J. Liebling of the *New Yorker*, John Steinbeck, Jack Belden of *Time and Life*, and *Scripps-Howard* correspondent Ernie Pyle. Steinbeck described the group as a 'ruffian gang, gallant and gay'.[20] Their room resembled 'a set for a Maxim Gorki play', needing only 'water dripping from the walls to make it perfect, that and the screams of the tortured in some sub cellar'.[21] The wallpaper had been loosened by bomb blasts. There were no windows or mirrors.

After two days, Capa was ordered to report to General Ridgway of the 82nd Airborne, who apparently told him he would be having dinner that night in Rome. The plan was for American paratroops to occupy the city. Capa was thrilled: he would be first to get pictures of victorious Americans liberating Rome, birthplace of Patton's idols – the great Roman generals. It would be one of the biggest scoops of the war. While his fellow photographers would be taking unexciting pictures, he would be holed up in the finest hotel in Italy, 'calling the bartender by his first name'.[22]

A few days later, however, Capa was told that the invasion had been cancelled. On closer inspection, the Italian plan to disarm the German anti-aircraft defences in Rome and hand over the city was unrealistic. Capa was bitterly disappointed. He wouldn't get to liberate the best hotels and bars in the Eternal City after all.

12 It's a Tough War

'The war is like an actress who is getting old. It is less and less photogenic and more and more dangerous.'

ROBERT CAPA, *Life* magazine, 1944

Capa set foot in Europe, after five years' absence, at the small port of Paestum in September 1943, two weeks after the first American troops. He then headed towards the northern sector of the American beach-head, around the Chiunzi Pass, the last major geographic barrier before Naples. He had missed out on the invasion itself but now had the chance to be the first photographer to record the liberation of the first major European city.

The troops most likely to reach the city before any other were a squad of daring American commandos known as Rangers. Capa found them under heavy fire from Germans well dug in on the plain of Vesuvius. With the elegant *Life* correspondent Will Lang, a tall and pencil-moustached Chicago native, Capa made his way to a farmhouse doubling as an observation post, dubbed 'Fort Schuster' after the doctor in charge of its first aid station. When Capa entered, the first thing he saw was a large table in the centre of the room, used for emergency operations on wounded men. Several medics were preparing mangled soldiers for a trip down the pass to the full military hospital in Maiori. According to Lang, they were offered whiskey to steady their nerves. They soon discovered why. Day and night, shells rained down on the position, which was surrounded, in Lang's words, by 'steep pinnacles of dark rock shrouded by mist'.

'This is the place for fighting,' Capa told Lang as they surveyed the scene. 'It reminds me of Spain.'[1]

One morning, Capa watched twenty-one-year-old Captain O'Brien attempt to locate nearby German mortars. O'Brien wore a Silver Star pinned to his chest, and when he drove out into the open, sure enough the Germans opened up, revealing their positions; Capa used his longest lens and managed to get thirty-six shots of the action. The next day, he accompanied American troops as they reconnoitred a nearby village suspected of harbouring German artillery units. Suddenly, the unit came under fire. Then the ground started to shake. Mortar shells whistled in several directions. The furthest Capa dared lift his head from the ground in order to photograph was three inches. He had two choices: be frightened lying on his back or on his stomach. Finally, the shelling stopped and Capa scrambled back to Fort Schuster.

After several nerve-racking days there, Capa accompanied the 82nd Airborne on their final push into Naples. Just before entering the city on 1 October, Capa photographed British tank crews slicking up – washing and shaving in the shadow of a bombed-out building before driving into the Piazza de Torre Annunziata where, according to *Life*, the Germans had fought a 'ferocious delaying action'.[2] 'The first ride through a captured town gives you an initial feeling of elation,' Capa told *Illustrated.* 'But soon your heart is gripped with pity.'[3] He saw bodies strewn in every via and piazza. The retreating Germans had terrorized Naples in a five-day orgy of looting and indiscriminate killing, prompted by revenge for Italy's surrender to the Allies on 8 September. Hospitals had been targeted to destroy their food stocks. Water mains and sewers were dynamited.

On 2 October, Capa entered a school to be greeted by what he later described as the 'sweet, sickly smell of flowers and the dead'. Before him lay twenty coffins, 'not well enough covered with flowers and too small to hide the dirty little feet of children – children old enough to fight the Germans and be killed, but just a little too old to fit into children's coffins.' Their black-clad mothers screamed in mourning a few feet from the lens. 'Those were my truest pictures of victory,' he wrote, 'the ones I took at that simple schoolhouse funeral.'[4]

Also in Naples in the days following its liberation was the film director John Huston, who had met Capa before the war, at a New Year's Eve party in New York. He was there preparing to make a documentary film, *The Battle of San Pietro*, which became the finest portrait of American combat in the Second World War. One afternoon, he and Capa were walking down a street when an air-raid siren sounded. They ducked into a doorway to escape shell fragments from anti-aircraft fire. Suddenly, they saw a hearse – 'a great ebony affair drawn by a span of black horses' – thunder around a corner. 'The air-raid sirens were wailing,' Huston wrote, 'the guns were booming, and just as the hearse passed us, the back doors flew open and it began to eject coffins. The coffins burst open as they hit the cobblestones and the street was littered with corpses, slowly unfolding from their cramped positions. It was grotesquely funny. What could we do but laugh?'[5]

On 7 October, Capa witnessed 'one of the greatest horrors of the war', in the words of *Life* magazine.[6] That afternoon, Allied soldiers and Italian civilians crowded Naples' ornate post office, built in 1933 by Mussolini's fascist architects. Suddenly, a delayed-action mine, left by the Germans when they evacuated the city, exploded in the basement. 'There was a sudden overwhelming roar and then shattered window glass clanked and tinkled all over the furniture,' Lang cabled *Life* that evening. 'It was dark; huge masses of black smoke blotted the light from the room. From the street below a woman screamed in short, labored breaths. A wild dissonant chorus of pain pierced up through the gloom . . . Here and there were misshapen bodies and parts of bodies sprawled on the street and sidewalk. It was unreal, and even blood was black.'[7] One of Capa's images showed an Italian, his scorched arms held out helplessly and his face and clothes badly charred, calling for help.

As Capa and Lang wandered through the rubble, stepping over mangled limbs and headless bodies, they came across an American soldier 'so black he could be distinguished only by his leggings'. The soldier wandered in a daze towards several exhausted Red Cross medics, clutching his bleeding forehead. 'Those sonsabitches,' he blurted. 'Those goddam dirty sonsabitches.'[8]

*

'Bob always paced himself superbly,' says John Morris, *Life*'s London bureau picture editor from 1943 to 1945. 'He knew how to conserve his energy and his film.' After his harrowing experience in Naples, Capa joined Herbert Matthews on a visit to the nearby island of Capri. On 12 October, the pair interviewed the remarkable anti-fascist philosopher Benedetto Groce. When the Allied armies attacked Salerno in early September, they'd discovered that Groce, seventy-seven years old and the 'greatest anti-fascist still living in Italy', had been arrested by the Germans. A handful of daring British troops then parachuted behind enemy lines and spirited him to safety on Capri. Groce told Matthews that Italy had suffered 'the disease of fascism' but could now walk among the 'infected nations' with immunity. However, he suspected that Nazism might be a 'natural and suitable expression of the German temperament'.[9]

Capa was so taken by Capri's ancient charms that he returned to the island a week later to celebrate his thirtieth birthday on 22 October. A fellow *Life* photographer, the Englishman George Rodger, accompanied him. In a photograph taken at this time, the pair look like archetypal dashing war photographers: their hair slicked back, immaculate uniforms, cameras dangling from their necks, cigarettes between their fingers. Capa had been so taken by Rodger's cravat that he had started wearing one. 'From what George told me later,' recalls Rodger's widow, Jinx, 'he had never known Bob quite as relaxed and happy as during those few days [on Capri].'

On 21 October, Rodger wrote in his diary: 'Bob and I took a fishing boat to Capri at 1pm and arrived at 3.30 . . . We got rooms at the Morgano Hotel where Morgano himself made sure we were well looked after.' The following day, Capa's birthday, they 'strolled through the quaint little town and did some shopping after which Bob and I lunched with Graziella [an attractive Italian aristocrat and according to Jinx Rodger 'another of his lady conquests'] in her magnificent villa on the far side of the island. It is very beautiful and looks more like a stage set than anything real.'[10]

The following day, Rodger and Capa ate at a black-market restaurant and 'lazed all day . . . It is impossible to do anything but relax for there is such an air of tranquillity and nobody ever speaks about the war.' Soon Capa was calling Rodger 'old goat', a playful reference to the Englishman's body odour after weeks in the front lines. 'Listen, old goat, today doesn't matter and tomorrow doesn't matter,' he told him one day. 'It's the end of the game that counts and how many chips you've got in your pocket – if you're still playing.'[11]

In Capri, they also shared their gripes about *Life* magazine. 'That was when we first started talking about a future brotherhood,' Rodger recalled. 'We were not very happy [with *Life*] . . . The object of this brotherhood was that we should be free of all sort of editorial bias and that we would work on stories we wanted to work on and have somebody do all the dogs body work.'[12]

On their last day in Capri, Capa and Rodger 'sailed around the island in an Italian schooner towing two rowing boats behind, which we used to explore the grottos.' The water in one grotto was the 'electric blue of a butterfly's wing'. That night, Rodger wrote ominously in his diary: 'Tomorrow, we return to Naples. Bob goes to the front.' Before parting, they promised to reunite in Paris one day. Whoever arrived first would book the other a room in the Lancaster Hotel.

In Naples, Capa packed his camera bag with new film and reluctantly returned to the front lines. 'The war is like an actress who is getting old,' he told *Life*. 'It is less and less photogenic and more and more dangerous.'[13] The Allied advance up the spine of Italy had already become a costly slog, so slow and fatal that Churchill and Eisenhower now worried that invading Italy – Europe's 'soft underbelly' in Churchill's words – might have been a disastrous mistake.

For two weeks that autumn, Capa climbed with the American 504th Regiment into the mountains north of Naples. Winter was fast approaching and as temperatures plunged the body count soared. Each new mountain was better defended than the last by crack German troops. The scenes he witnessed reminded him of stories he'd heard about the attrition of the First World War. The country had been turned into a vast, mountainous no-man's-land. Trees were charred skeletons. The higher he climbed, the more dead he found on the hillsides. Young Americans lay in pieces in field and ravine. 'Their blood was dry and rusty,' he recalled, 'blending with the color of the late autumn leaves.'[14]

Capa's photographs expressed better than words the awful truth of the Italian campaign. Early in 1944, *Life* ran his coverage of the winter advance around Monte Pantano in a story headlined: 'It's a Tough War'. 'With the troops of the Fifth Army during the battle for the Liri valley . . . was *Life* photographer Robert Capa. His pictures, printed here, are grim and unsentimental, but they tell something of what war is like in Italy.' Capa's shots included a wounded American tended by a medic and four pictures of dead soldiers covered by blankets. 'All that can be seen of this dead American,' read one caption below the most graphic picture of death yet to appear in *Life*, 'are his legs, one shoulder, part of a hand.'[15]

Readers in America were shocked by Capa's images. 'We need stories like "It's a Tough War" to slap us in the face,' wrote one civilian to *Life*'s editor, 'and keep us awake to realities.' A soldier wrote: '[Capa's] pictures clearly portray the bitterness and grimness of the battles to be fought before we reach Berlin and Tokyo. It also brings home the realization of [our] responsibilities in doing all [we] can to support the boys with bonds and work on the home front.'[16]

In late December, Capa joined a platoon from the American 45th Division whose mission it was to attack a small village called Venafro, near Monte Cassino. As he set out in the pre-dawn blackness, fear gripped him. His boots felt heavier after each step. The first rays of sunshine heralded death. German artillery spotters found their range and shells soon forced every man to lie face down in the frozen mud. Later that morning, Capa found himself pinned down between a private and a sergeant. Trembling with terror, he was hit three times by shrapnel. Mercifully, the shards didn't pierce his uniform. Suddenly, the private beside him was killed and the sergeant wounded, Capa noted, 'just badly enough for a Purple Heart'.[17] A few hours later, a badly shaken Capa made it back to the American lines.

Depressed and suffering from battle fatigue, he returned to Naples in early 1944. The streets were filled with military police and black-marketeers. The daughters of Naples strolled on the Via Roma in flimsy floral-printed frocks looking for bubble-gum-chewing Yankees with pockets full of Lucky Strikes and nylons. Mount Vesuvius, Capa noted, had put on 'its greatest show in a hundred years'[18] and soot and smoke covered the entire city. Capa learned that he would soon be recalled to London to prepare for the long-expected invasion of France but first he would have to complete one more mission in Italy – an amphibious landing at Anzio, twenty-six miles from Rome.

The Anzio landings became one of the most controversial operations of the war in Italy. Code-named Shingle, the planned invasion was an audacious attempt to outflank the Germans, who had halted the Allied advance towards Rome in bitter fighting around the monastery of Monte Cassino. By landing in Anzio, the Allies hoped to break the stalemate at Cassino and strike quickly towards Rome.

On 22 January, Capa jumped out of an assault barge and waded forty yards to the Anzio beach. He and the men beside him were amazed by the lack of German resistance; only 13 of the 36,000 men who came ashore with him were killed. As far as the press corps was concerned, the near court-martial of *Yank* photographer Sergeant Slim Aarons was the most exciting incident during the invasion. To Aarons' lasting gratitude, Capa and several other veteran reporters saved him from a court martial when they heard that MPs were going to arrest him for joining the invasion without proper accreditation. To make matters worse, he had commandeered a jeep. 'Capa and all the other great correspondents, Lang, Pyle, all the guys from *Life*,' recalls Aarons, 'told the army boys they had to be kidding. "You're gonna court-martial these guys for going on an invasion?" The army guys calmed down . . . when they realized they were outnumbered, and the press would make them look like fools.'

Save for the Aarons episode, the whole mission had been a huge anticlimax, with no heroic tales of bravery to report. 'At 9.30 [the next morning],' Capa reported for *Illustrated* magazine, 'the first enemy planes arrived and the first artillery shell landed in the town. But we met little serious opposition . . . until we had advanced five miles into the flat, closely-settled farmland beyond the town, where we had to pay heavily for every yard gained. For the first time in the Italian campaign the Germans were bringing up two men to every one of ours. Then we knew we weren't going to stroll quietly into Rome. Soon waves of German bombers started plastering Anzio, and they kept up their attacks almost to the hour.'[19] It was the heaviest bombing yet endured by American forces in the Second World War.

Capa and his fellow correspondents took cover in the basement of a seaside villa. They soon learned that the invasion forces had advanced ten miles inland towards the Alban Hills, and then had ground to a brutal halt. Field Marshal Kesselring had thrown six divisions, including the elite Hermann Goering Panzer Division, at the invaders. The Allies were now trapped on a sea-level wedge of land, ten miles long and ten miles deep. The American commander, Major General John P. Lucas, had ordered no retreat. Then the Germans had opened fire.

Among Capa's colleagues hunkering down in the beachfront villa were Ernie Pyle, the cartoonist Bill Mauldin, Will Lang and Aarons. Shells whizzed overhead day and night. Aarons remembers long, sleepless nights when the correspondents killed time by playing poker. A British officer, Jeffrey Keating, organized the games, setting strict rules, creating a casino atmosphere in the cramped basement. 'We played open poker, seven card stud, always dealer's choice,' remembers Aarons. 'What else was there to do? Go dancing? . . . The Brits bet with pounds, the French with francs, and we dealt in dollars . . . We didn't talk about how we felt, fear or whatever, just how to get wine and food, and about the Red Cross nurses.'

By day, Capa and Aarons patrolled Anzio and its hospital tents, holed by shrapnel, trying to exchange bread for wine and flirting with nurses. But the nurses could afford no more than a few minutes of weary small talk before returning to the thousands of casualties soon crowding the town of Anzio itself. 'It wasn't as if any of us were going to get a date,' stresses Aarons, a self-described 'brave coward'. 'We were in the middle of a battle that raged twenty-four hours a day.' Aarons and Capa also made several visits to a 'secret' crack unit of the

American Special Forces: 'daredevils in baggy pants' who raided German positions. 'They did all the dirty jobs – engaging the Germans in close combat,' recalls Aarons. Capa was fascinated by this elite unit of throat-slitters: they snapped terrified German youths' spines by night and shot cattle for breakfast steaks when they returned before dawn to their own lines. They were the kind of men, recalled Bill Mauldin, 'who called their officers by their first names if they felt like it . . . A couple of them were rumoured to have been former bodyguards for Chicago gangsters.'[20]

Back in the basement of the press villa, the stakes in Keating's professional games got higher as the shelling intensified through February. But now a fateful silence descended on the correspondents during rare lulls. Nerves were jagged, tempers frayed, and some veteran reporters began to pray. In late February, Capa received orders to return to Naples and then London. As soon as he could, he sailed from Anzio aboard a hospital ship – 'the one man unhurt among the boatload of badly wounded'.[21] He left behind Aarons and Pyle, who would both be injured on 17 March when a stick of 500lb bombs landed just thirty feet from the villa.*

Again, Capa left the front badly shaken. He was relieved to be leaving Italy's 'tough war', but he also knew that in a few months he might have to face his greatest test of nerve in a decade of front-line action. Word among the press camp was that the Allies were preparing for the most ambitious invasion in history, code-named 'Overlord'.

* Anzio was attacked mercilessly for another three months. Not until the summer of 1944, after the fall of Monte Cassino, was the US 5th Army able to dislodge the Germans from the Alban Hills and free the shell-shocked Anzio forces to begin their advance on Rome.

13 The Longest Day

> 'Omaha Beach was a nightmare. Even now [thirty years later] it brings pain to recall what happened there on June 6, 1944. I have returned many times to honor the valiant men who died on that beach. They should never be forgotten. Nor should those who lived to carry the day by the slimmest of margins. Every man who set foot on Omaha Beach that day was a hero.'
>
> GENERAL OMAR BRADLEY[1]

Capa arrived in England in early April 1944. Who knew how long it would be until the call came to go into action again? A few weeks? Maybe a month? In the meantime, he was determined to live it up, if only to forget the horrors of Italy. When he took a stroll in the streets and parks nearby, he found himself surrounded by American officers and other Allied personnel. In the Underground, people were on edge. Something big was about to happen. London had 'invasion fever'. Every drink, every seduction, every good meal was to be savoured, and Capa spent several days with Pinky, drinking her booze ration and making love.

Nothing made for better sex than not knowing if you would see your lover again. 'A woman only had to look at you twice on a tube, and you knew you were laid,' recalls Warren Trabant, who served with American counter-intelligence and later befriended Capa in Paris. The scenes and sounds of Hyde Park and Green Park at dusk and after dark shocked many a callow young officer. One young Canadian who toured the same streets as Capa said the area sounded like a battlefield of sex.

Of the 175,000 men who saw action on D-Day, Capa was one of a handful who chose their destiny. Given the option of going in with a regiment's staff or with the first waves of assault troops, he staked his life on the latter. Knowing he'd chosen the riskiest but by far the most important assignment of his career, he soon found that sex with Pinky was not enough to distract him from his impending gamble with death. Many of his fellow correspondents, including Ernie Pyle, began to drink themselves to sleep. 'All the time fear lay blackly upon our consciousness,' Pyle wrote. 'It bore down on your heart like an all-consuming weight.'[2] Capa chose to play poker instead.

By the time the horse-chestnut blossoms in Hyde Park were over in early May, Capa was losing heavily to a remarkable group of American writers and film-makers. He didn't bet against matchstick hustlers if he could help it, preferring serious players who could bluff convincingly and preferably call with a witty rejoinder to every royal flush or pair of a kind. That spring, his opponents were no less than the writer Irwin Shaw, the Pulitzer-winning playwright William Saroyan, and the Hollywood directors George Stevens and Irving Reis, who all belonged to a section of the US Army Signal Corps that made propaganda films.[3]

'London before D Day,' wrote Shaw, 'was a time of revelry for Capa, an occupation for which he had a highly developed taste. When he was not touring the pubs, he was the host for intense poker games, during which, in the middle of almost nightly bombings by the Luftwaffe, it was considered very bad form indeed to hesitate before placing a bet or to move away from the table, no matter how close the hits or how loud the anti-aircraft fire.'[4] All those present at Capa's card table fondly recalled Pinky as a wonderful hostess. After a particularly close explosion, she would smile sweetly, a glitter in her eye, and mix several more cocktails to keep everyone's chin up.

Saroyan knew how to bluff but annoyed Stevens because he didn't seem to care whether he won or lost. Stevens, who as a colonel held the highest rank, was a superb player – 'deadpan and cold'. Saroyan, a private who loathed army life as much as Shaw, was a 'no-good gambler, wild, reckless',[5] and later described Capa as 'a poker player whose side-line was picture-taking, a business he loathed.' Capa never dropped out, however high the stakes became, and never won in Saroyan's presence. 'I kept figuring out his expenses,' Saroyan reminisced, 'and together they came to enough to start a shoestring moving picture studio.'[6]

'If Capa was making money out of the war, the poker games made it certain that when peace came he would not be a rich man,' Shaw recalled. 'He did not take losing to heart, though. When he came up with a pair against three of a kind or was caught with a four flush, the most he would say would be "Je ne suis pas heureux", a favorite line from the opera *Pelléas et Mélisande* that he used on other, more dangerous occasions.'[7]

By mid-May, London's best bars and restaurants were jammed with senior American officers and increasingly jittery correspondents, among them Slim Aarons, Ernie Pyle and George Rodger, who had returned from Italy to await D-Day. One evening, Capa found Ernest Hemingway in the bar of the Dorchester Hotel, and the pair hit the town until the early hours. At first, he hadn't recognized 'Papa', with his thick beard covering a nasty case of sunburn. 'Papa's got troubles,' he told Hemingway's brother, Leicester, the following day. 'That bloody beard scares off all the girls.'[8]

On 22 May, all correspondents accredited to cover the invasion gathered in the theatre of a military club in central London. General Eisenhower, Allied supreme commander for the expedition, walked to a podium. 'Ike' said that Capa and his colleagues were in effect an arm of the military, crucial to winning the war. 'I've been informed by the newspapers that an operation is pending,' he added, to peals of laughter. 'Our countries fight best when our people are best informed. You will be allowed to report everything possible, consistent, of course, with military security. I will never tell you anything false . . . I have no doubt as to the outcome of the future but I have no illusions as to the magnitude of the task . . . It will be no basket of roses.'[9]

On 24 May, Capa held an extravagant party. For all he knew, it might be his last. It seemed to guests, including John Morris and Capa's poker partners, that everyone who mattered in the press corps had been invited, including Ernest Hemingway, now reporting for

Collier's. Leicester Hemingway was as impressed as every other guest by the quantities of black-market booze Capa had found to steady everyone's pre-invasion nerves: 'Capa was a master at organizing, scrounging, and liberating.'[10] The huge punch bowl that dominated the room was a 'ten gallon glass jug borrowed from an atomic research laboratory, and it was full of fresh peaches floating around in spirits'.[11]

By three in the morning, the booze had finally run out and people began to leave. Ernest Hemingway left just after four with a Dr Peter Dorer, who had offered to drive him back to the Dorchester. Around seven, Capa woke Leicester. 'Papa had an accident right after they left this morning.'

'Is he badly hurt?' asked Leicester.

'Not bad, just cut. He's in the hospital right near here.'

They rushed to St George's Hospital in Knightsbridge. Ernest lay in bed; a bandage 'ran like a halo around his head' below a serious scalp wound. 'What happened?' asked Leicester.

'Hit a water tank right down the block,' replied his brother. '[Dorer's] legs are bad. I'm the lucky one.'[12]

Before Capa left Papa to have his head stitched up, he took a hilarious picture of Pinky laughing as she lifted the revered author's hospital robe, exposing his lily-white buttocks. This shot did not make it into the pages of *Life* magazine, but one of Hemingway with the bandage wrapped around his head did.*

Not long after Hemingway's accident, Capa was called to a meeting at the Allied forces' Public Relations Division. He was told to pack his bags and to provide details of a last will, if he had one, and of his blood type. He should not leave his hotel for more than an hour at a time. Knowing that D-Day was now imminent, he decided to do some last-minute invasion shopping. His main purchases were a new Burberry

*A reporter had earlier visited the hospital and been told that Hemingway had been killed. In Italy, *Stars and Stripes* carried a report that he had died in an accident caused by the London blackout. The crash was not fatal but it was one of several serious blows to his head that may have contributed to his final breakdown in 1960, when he picked up a silver-inlaid 12-gauge double-barrelled Richardson shotgun and blew his brains out.

army overcoat and a silver flask. A photograph of *Life*'s D-Day photographers, shortly after this shopping spree, shows him, hands deep in his coat pockets, a cigarette stub stuck between his lips. Capa ignores the camera altogether and only Frank Scherschel – assigned to the USAAF – manages a smile. Bob Landry, the only *Life* photographer other than Capa assigned to go in with American assault troops, doesn't even hide his apprehension.

Capa started to pack. In the 125lb of baggage he was allowed to take on the invasion he stowed brandy and a fresh supply of condoms. In Italy, he had noticed how many troops used army issue rubbers to keep ammunition dry, and had started a trend among photographers when he used his to protect his film and cameras. On 28 May, the very day that Pinky was to visit him and say goodbye and good luck, he was woken early by a public relations officer, and told he had to leave immediately. The long wait was finally over.

Capa joined several thousand troops in one of the many camps specially set up on the south coast. He later recalled that once he had passed through gates, he felt as if he was already halfway across the English Channel. All contact with the outside world stopped; there was only one way out – on a truck full of soldiers bound for the beaches of France. Inside his camp, he joined men of the 116th Infantry, 2nd Battalion. He would go in with the first wave, scheduled to hit Omaha Beach at precisely 6.30 a.m., an hour after low tide.

Capa and the men of the 116th Infantry sat in silence as intelligence officers explained the specifics of their role in Operation Overlord. Special amphibious tanks designed to break through the German beach defences, thereby clearing 'escape' channels from the beach, would land first. The first troops ashore would include crack assault teams, toughened after months of intensive training, and armed with every powerful new weapon available: .30in machine guns, bazookas and flame-throwers. Demolition teams assigned to major obstacles on each section of the beach would leave flags as signals to coxswains who would then guide several waves of landing craft on to the beach. Two hours after H-Hour – the moment at which the first troops would hit the beach – Omaha would be secured.

The Germans had long expected an Allied landing in northern France. If it succeeded, their eventual defeat was inevitable. And so, given the enormity of the threat, Hitler had appointed his most brilliant general, the maverick Desert Fox – Erwin Rommel. 'The war will be won or lost on the beaches,' Rommel had declared upon first visiting the beaches in January 1944. 'We'll have only one chance to stop the enemy and that's while he's in the water, struggling to get ashore. The first twenty-four hours of the invasion will be decisive . . . For the Allies, as well as Germany, it will be the longest day.'[13]

Capa would be landing on one of the most heavily defended beaches in history. Rommel had immediately ordered the placement of ingenious and lethal obstacles along the entire coastline. A waist-high stake with a mine attached to it, and covered by water at high tide, was Rommel's own invention. Huge iron crosses covered with limpet mines were scattered across beaches to stop amphibious vehicles and tanks. To hinder the landing of gliders, tall stakes ('Rommel's asparagus') were planted in fields a few miles inland.

After being briefed, Capa and the men of the 116th Infantry exchanged their dollar bills for invasion currency: flimsy franc notes. Each man then received a small book with German and French phrases that, Capa noted, 'promised cigarettes, hot baths, and all sorts of comforts, all in exchange for the simple act of unconditional surrender. Indeed, the booklet made for promising reading.'[14]

On 4 June, in Weymouth, Capa boarded a transport ship, the *Samuel Chase*, part of the largest armada ever assembled. Other than Capa, almost three million Allied soldiers, sailors and airmen were now ready for the attack on Fortress Europe. The actual landings would involve 176,475 men, 20,111 vehicles, 1,500 tanks and 12,000 planes. '[This] mighty host was tense as a coiled spring,' recalled General Eisenhower, 'and indeed that is exactly what it was – a great human spring coiled for the moment when its energy should be released and it would vault the English Channel in the greatest amphibious assault ever attempted.'[15]

Capa crossed the Channel after dark on 5 June.[16] Captain Oscar Rich, an artillery observer for the 5th Field Artillery Battalion of the 1st Division, was among his shipmates. Rich recalled examining a 'foam rubber map of the Calvados coastline', set up on a table in the *Samuel Chase*'s gymnasium, which Capa photographed. The mock-up was the most detailed Rich had ever seen. 'Trees were there, the trails, the roads, the houses, the beach obstacles – everything was there . . . Everything was to scale – it was actually like being in an airplane, about 500 feet above the beach and looking at the beach and seeing the whole thing in true perspective.'[17]

After studying his allotted section of the beach, Easy Red, Capa joined the groups of gamblers shooting craps on the swaying deck and playing intense games of poker.* Oscar Rich and *New York Times* correspondent Don Whitehead were among his opponents as the *Chase* slowly chugged across the choppy Channel. 'I was on this nice, clean ship with the 116th Infantry,' Capa told *Life*'s Charles Wertenbaker three days later. 'And she is a nice, clean ship. The food is good and we played poker most of the night, and once I filled an inside straight, but I had four nines against me, which was not unusual.'[18]

Thousands of dollars were staked on some dice games as men crouched around blankets and, between sharpening daggers and bayonets, kissed small fortunes goodbye. 'It didn't matter whether you won or lost, it was just a way to pass the time,' recalls Sergeant Roy Stevens of Company A, 116th Infantry, 29th Division. 'You knew you probably weren't gonna get a chance to win your money back anyway.'

Capa's game was interrupted by a stern command over a loudspeaker at 2 a.m. The men were to go to their assembly points. Capa's fellow gamblers, Rich among them, sealed their winnings in water-resistant money belts and went to the positions. H-Hour, for which many had trained since 1942, was nigh. At 3 a.m., Capa sat down to a

*There were in all eight sectors on Omaha: Charlie, Dog Green, Dog White, Dog Red, Easy Green, Easy Red, Fox Green, and Fox Red. All were murderous.

last breakfast of pancakes, sausages, eggs and coffee. Few men actually ate the superb meal, served by upbeat orderlies in starched white uniforms. Capa then joined 2,000 men gathered on deck at 4 a.m. They waited for dawn in total silence; it seemed that whatever each man was thinking formed part of some communal prayer.

Around ten miles from the beach, Capa climbed into a swaying barge with thirty other men. The barge was then lowered into rough waters. His companions were mostly ten years younger – their faces numb, waxy, expressionless. Older men in their mid-twenties who had landed in Africa and in Italy barked quick instructions to those who had never even visited the seaside, who had graduated from high school only the summer before. At all cost, they should keep their heads below the gunwales. Once the Germans opened fire, anything above it stood a good chance of being blown to pieces.

Loudhailers sounded again: 'Fight to get your troops ashore . . . and if you've got any strength left, fight to save yourselves . . . Away all boats! . . . Our Father, which art in Heaven, hallowed be thy name . . .'[19] At 5.50 a.m., warships began to pound the American beaches. The battleships *Texas* and *Arkansas* fired more than 600 shells at a single German battery on Omaha. The men nearing the beach, some bailing water frantically with their helmets, looked up at the heavy salvos flying over their heads and cheered. Then the skies filled with aircraft and the throbbing hum of B-26 bombers joined the constant thunder of exploding shells. Meanwhile, in Capa's landing craft, as in all those in the first wave, men momentarily relaxed a little. Finally crucial air cover had arrived to pepper the beach with friendly craters, knock out batteries and leave the Germans stunned and confused. Now they stood a fighting chance.

A few miles from the beach, already exhausted men – having gone without sleep for over twenty-four hours – started to collapse with acute seasickness. 'Some of the boys were politely puking into paper bags and I saw that this was a civilized invasion,' Capa recalled. 'We waited for the [special assault teams] to go in and then I saw the first landing boats coming back and the black coxswain of one boat is holding his thumb in the air and it looked like a pushover. We hear something popping around our boat, but nobody paid any attention.'[20]

Capa crouched down in vomit and seawater as artillery fire from German shore emplacements found the range of his landing craft. He pulled out one of his two Contax cameras from a waterproof oilskin. Despite the overcast sky, there was just enough light to take fast-action pictures. Then his craft's door lowered and men in front of Capa leaped into waist-deep water with their rifles above their heads. 'My beautiful France looked sordid and uninviting,' he recalled, '[but] a German machine gun, spitting bullets around the barge, fully spoiled my return.'[21] Hundreds of men died in the first few minutes on Easy Red, mere yards from him. 'I saw men falling,' he told Wertenbaker, 'and I had to push past their bodies, which I did politely.'[22]

There were no bomb craters to offer cover, and the gently sloping cliffs along most of the beach, which was shaped like a long open pincer, made for a perfect shooting gallery. To make matters worse, the Germans had only the previous day been training on Omaha itself to repel an amphibious attack. The garrison normally numbering a score of men had swelled into the hundreds, and now manned formidable defences: eight concrete bunkers with guns of 75mm and 88mm calibre, thirty-five pillboxes, four batteries of artillery, eighteen anti-tank guns, six mortar pits, forty rocket-launching sites, and at least eighty-five machine-gun nests.

Typically, Capa later joked about his first harrowing moments on Omaha. 'I was going in very elegant with my [Burberry] raincoat on my left hand,' he told Wertenbaker. 'At a moment I had a feeling I would not need that raincoat. I let go of it and it floated away and I hid behind some tanks that were firing on the beach. After twenty minutes I suddenly realize that this is not a good place to be. The tanks were a certain amount of cover from small arms fire, but they were what the Germans are shooting shells at.'[23]

The German mortars were so accurate, says first-wave survivor Lieutenant Ray Nance, that 'they could land one right on your head if they spotted you.' As shells exploded around Capa and the shallows became clogged with corpses, he found himself repeating words he'd learned in Spain. '*Es una cosa muy seria,*' he muttered. '*Es una cosa muy seria.*' ('This is a very serious business.')

Men dared not lift their heads above the dead ground of the beach in case they were shot. 'The slant of the beach gave us some protection, so long as we lay flat, from the machine gun and rifle bullets,' Capa recalled, 'but the tide pushed us up against barbed wire, and the guns were enjoying open season.' For several minutes, he lay with his entire body pressed as close to the sand as possible, gripped by a debilitating fear, far greater than any he had experienced in Italy: 'I had it bad. The empty camera trembled in my hands. It was a new kind of fear shaking my body from toe to hair, and twisting my face.'

Capa unclipped his entrenching tool and tried to dig a foxhole but he hit shingle almost immediately and threw it away. Suddenly, he noticed that the men around him were motionless – 'only the dead on the waterline rolled with the waves.'[24] He knew that the only way to overcome the terror was to take pictures, get the job done as quickly as possible, and get the hell off the beach. He later told Wertenbaker that he spent ninety minutes taking pictures until he had used all his film. Then he saw a landing craft fifty yards out at sea.

A group of medics, with red crosses daubed on their helmets, jumped out of it. A machine gun snarled. Several of the medics died instantly. Capa stood up and without making a conscious decision ran for the boat. Soon he was wading through blood-red water. The cold seas came up to his chest and then waves were slapping his face. He held his cameras above his head. He knew he was running away.

On the landing craft, LCI 94, nineteen-year-old motor machinist Charles Jarreau was struggling to lift wounded aboard when he spotted Capa.* 'Poor fellow, he was there in the water, holding his cameras up

* Jarreau was a keen amateur photographer and took many pictures from the LCI that day, rolls of film in one pocket, a rosary in another. His captain, a wily merchant mariner, had stowed a large supply of J&B Scotch aboard the boat to fortify the crew. 'Essentially, we drank most of the day,' recalled Jarreau. 'Didn't have any food, but I drank all day and didn't get the least bit intoxicated. It had absolutely no effect.' Jarreau survived the war and fathered eleven children. D-Day, he always insisted, was his and America's finest hour, as dearly valued in his memory as the day in 1947 when he slipped a wedding ring on to his wife Audrey's finger.

to try to keep them dry, trying to catch his breath.'[25] As soon as Capa had clambered aboard LCI 94, he started to change his film. Then he felt 'a slight shock' and found himself covered with feathers. 'What is this?' he thought. 'Is somebody killing chickens?'[26] He looked up and saw that the 150 foot boat had taken a direct hit from an 88mm shell.* Pieces of body littered the blood-splattered craft. 'The feathers were the stuffing from the kapok jackets of the men who were blown up. The skipper [a thirty-two-year-old nicknamed 'Popeye'] was crying because his assistant had been blown all over him and he was a mess.'[27]

The landing craft was listing badly but somehow managed to slowly pull away from Omaha Beach. Capa went down below, dried his hands, changed the film in his cameras and returned to the open deck. All around him, he found dead and moaning men. A few hundred yards from the beach, he looked back and took a last shot of 'Bloody Omaha', shrouded in smoke. It was littered with the enormous waste of war: burnt-out tanks and smashed landing craft; Bibles floating in red-hued rock-pools; a lone guitar off Easy Red; and countless bodies of young Americans.

Although *Life* had bagged two of the four slots assigned to photographers covering the American ground assault, it had to pool photographs with three wire services: AP (Associated Press); Planet News, a London affiliate of Acme, the picture subsidiary of United Press; and Keystone. It was twenty-seven-year-old John Morris' job to get live action shots of the D-Day landings – the most important story of the century – to *Life* magazine in New York. 'Capa was the acknowledged professional,' he recalls, 'the star who everyone was looking to.'

Morris knew that the pictures would need to reach New York by Saturday evening, 10 June, to be included in *Life*'s 19 June issue. To meet his deadline (and keep his job), he would need to send original prints in a pouch that would leave by motorcycle courier at 9 a.m.

*According to a report in *Life*, LCI 94 took three hits from the German shore batteries of 88mm guns.

exactly, British Double Summer Time, on Thursday 8 June.* A motorcycle courier would then take the pouch to a plane waiting at Heathrow, which would transfer it to another at Prestwick in Scotland. After a couple of fuel stops, the pouch would arrive in Washington and then be hand-carried to New York on the Saturday.[28]

Morris arrived at *Life*'s Dean Street offices early on 6 June and waited for news to arrive from his crew of six D-Day photographers. By midday, he had resigned himself to a long wait. Meanwhile, Capa was in the middle of the English Channel, talking to Charles Jarreau. He looked stunned by what he'd seen – grey-faced and still in shock, and told Jarreau he was 'really grateful'[29] to get off the beach. After changing his film again, he photographed the first American wounded to be taken off Omaha in the LCI.† He then put down his cameras and helped lift several stretchers of wounded men aboard the *Samuel Chase*. Only six hours before, he had clambered down into a landing craft from the *Chase*'s immaculate decks. Now it was 'no longer nice and clean. Even the cooks that made such good food were helping to hoist the wounded.'[30]

Once he was safely aboard the *Samuel Chase*, Capa collapsed with exhaustion. The ship was nearing the English coast when he woke up naked beneath a coarse blanket with a note around his neck: 'Exhaustion case. No dog tags.'[31] Beside him in a bunk was a survivor of the amphibious tank regiment that had landed before the first wave of troops. His and ten other tanks had sunk in the heavy seas off Omaha. The young man despairingly told Capa that he himself was a coward and that he should have stayed back on the beach. Capa reassured him that he was no coward. He was blameless. It was he who was the coward, Capa insisted, not the young soldier.

* Morris had rehearsed the route from *Life*'s offices to the censor and then to the pouch hand-off many times; he had even driven the route in a two-door Austin through London to ensure he could make the pouch in time. To speed up the delivery, he would sprint the last fifty yards across Grosvenor Square.

† One picture showed a medic, two bars on his large navy helmet, preparing to give a transfusion to a crewman hit by fragments of an 88mm. The helmet belonged to Jarreau. 'You can see Charles' number on it,' insists his widow, Audrey. 'Charles had lent it to the medic who had lost his own when the boat got hit.'

Early on 7 June, the *Samuel Chase* docked at Weymouth. Reporters surrounded Capa, eager to get a first-hand account of the invasion. Also waiting on the dockside was *Life*'s David Scherman. 'David took a wonderful picture of Bob trying to smile as he arrived,' recalls his widow, Rosemarie. 'It was such an extraordinary coincidence that they'd meet like that.'

Capa later claimed that when he stepped on to dry land he was offered a plane to whisk him to London so that he could make a radio broadcast about the invasion. Instead, he put his film in a courier's pouch, changed into clean, dry clothes and found the first boat returning to the beachhead.

In London that morning, Morris woke to discover that Bert Brandt of Acme had returned to London with a 'FIRST PICTURE!'[32] The image showed troops landing, but none of the heart-rending drama and bloodshed of Omaha. Where the hell was Capa? The hours passed with excruciating slowness. By late afternoon, Morris and his staff were thoroughly downhearted. *Life*'s darkroom staff – the chief, Braddy Bradshaw, four young assistants and a photographer, Hans Wild – had been waiting to go into action for well over twenty-four hours. 'Nothing came in except background stuff – real crap – from official sources: the Signal Corps, the Navy, the British,' recalls Morris. 'It was all the preliminary stuff. There was nothing of the real thing.'[33]

About 6.30 p.m., Morris got a call from Weymouth: 'Capa's film is on the way. You should get it within an hour or two.' He called E. K. Butler of AP, the pool editor, who had been pestering him continually for an image that would show actual combat. 'All I want is pictures,' snapped Butler, 'not promises!' At last, at 9 p.m. on 7 June, a courier arrived with the precious package. 'It was a small packet,' recalls Morris. 'There were four rolls of 35 millimetre film, and some 120 [millimetre rolls], maybe half a dozen, and a short handwritten note from Capa which said simply "John all the action's in the thirty-five millimeter." Capa added that he'd had a rough day and was returning to the beach.'

Life's darkroom staff went to work, hoping to beat the next morning's 9 a.m. deadline. Hans Wild called Morris as soon as the

35mm had been exposed. Capa had done a superb job under terrible conditions and with only limited light. 'I need contacts,' Morris ordered. 'Rush, rush, rush, rush!' A few minutes later, one of the assistants, Dennis Banks, leapt up a flight of stairs and ran into Morris' office. He was in tears. 'They're ruined,' he blurted. 'Ruined! Capa's films are all ruined!'

'What do you mean?' asked Morris.

'You were in such a hurry,' replied Banks, 'I put it in a drying cabinet and closed the doors.'

It was normal procedure to put film in a wooden locker with a heating coil at the base. But with the doors closed, the heat had become so intense that it had melted the film's emulsion. Morris ran down to the darkroom with Dennis. He held up the four rolls, one at a time. Three were useless, just a brown sludge in frame after frame. 'I couldn't see anything,' Morris recalls. 'Just grey mud. But on the fourth there were eleven frames that could be printed, and I printed every single one of them. By now, they've determined that two of them were not really worth printing anyway – so there are nine that survive to this day, which is okay. There was a certain amount of repetition, but there were half a dozen good pictures in there.'

As midnight fast approached, Morris ordered his staff to make four proof prints of every single surviving negative. As soon as the prints had been made, around 3.30 a.m., he headed for the censor's office through London's blacked-out and deserted streets. He had several hundred photographs other than Capa's 'grainy' images of men cowering in the surf of Omaha. The minutes felt like hours as he waited for the censor to clear the photographs. All Capa's pictures passed. By 1944, he knew very well what would and would not pass. He would not bother to waste film on scenes the American public could not be trusted to stomach.* With less than an hour to go before the pouch deadline, there was a snag. The censor had to seal envelopes with a tape that had 'Approved by Censor' printed on it. 'But, at the crucial moment when the censor was to seal the envelopes, the Scotch tape stuck. We couldn't

* Pictures showing dead men's faces, expressions of defeat, and severe battle fatigue were unlikely to get past censors.

get the damned thing to work.' Finally, the envelope was taped, but by now it was around twenty to nine. 'I got to Grosvenor Square at one minute of nine. Down in the basement the courier was literally about to padlock the pouch when I found him.'

'Hold it!' cried Morris.

He handed over his precious packages. He'd made the deadline with only seconds to spare.

Capa's pictures appeared in *Life* on 19 June across seven pages beside perhaps the magazine's most famously understated strap-line: 'THE FATEFUL BATTLE FOR EUROPE IS JOINED BY SEA AND AIR.' *Life* informed its astonished readers: 'The picture above and those on the next six pages were taken by *Life* photographer Robert Capa who went in with the first wave of troops. Although the first reports of landings indicated little opposition, his pictures show how violent the battle was and how strong the German defenses.'

Morris says Capa never discussed the ruined film with him, and has written that he appeared to 'take the news of melted emulsions well'. Capa had taken seventy-nine pictures, according to Charles Wertenbaker: 'the only complete photographic record of the worst hours of the invasion.'[34] Although blurred, Capa's images had captured for posterity something of the crazed first moments of the invasion. They were indeed great pictures – in Capa's own words, 'a cut out of the whole event which will show more of the real truth of the affair to some one who was not there than the whole scene.'[35]

The only man who has been identified in Capa's pictures is Edward K. Regan, of Company K of the 116th Infantry, who died in 1998. Capa's photograph of the eighteen-year-old soldier has been published thousands of times and remains the definitive image of the first minutes of 'Bloody Omaha'. For Regan, the photograph would always mark 'an important rite of passage . . . the transition from adolescence to manhood.'[36]

Regan remembered spending the previous night sick with fear. His landing craft ran aground on a sandbank about twenty yards from the shore, and he came under heavy fire as soon as the ramp was lowered. For the rest of his life he was haunted by the memory of struggling to keep his head above water and get his feet on terra firma, weighed down by a 66lb pack on his back and with dead comrades bobbing in the bloody surf around him.

'When I ran out of steam, I dropped down on the sand to catch my breath. The water came up to my nose. That was when the photo was taken.'

Back in America, his mother cut out the picture from *Life* with tears in her eyes. When he returned to Virginia in 1945, she held up the cutting. 'Look, that's you, isn't it?' she said.

'Yep, that's me,' he replied. 'And I'm very proud of it.'

14 The Bocage

> 'There was a linnet singing in a wrecked house in Nehou; the shell that had blown the house apart had not even scratched its cage. There were the odd positions of the slain cattle . . . some leaning against trees and fences, and one standing on all four legs, swaying slightly in the wind . . . There were the rambler roses still clinging to the walls of shattered farmhouses, and the smell of flowers when the other smells were gone.'
>
> CHARLES WERTENBAKER, *Invasion!*

Capa landed back on Omaha Beach on 8 June, D+2. Before heading for the press camp inland at Bayeux, he paused to photograph the beach once again. Macabre flotsam and jetsam crowded the high-water line: rifles, body parts, scattered kit and many a Bible. Near Easy Red, Capa found local fishermen gazing solemnly at rows of covered corpses. Elsewhere, he watched captured Germans, who had fired on him forty-eight hours before, digging temporary graves. That afternoon, an American priest held a funeral service on the beach. In a rare newsreel located by the film-maker Patrick Jeudy, Capa is clean-shaven and looking extremely fit as he moves quickly but unobtrusively around praying combat troops and newspaper correspondents.

He arrived in Bayeux, five miles inland, by evening. The Germans had abandoned the town and left little damage. Capa photographed British officers ambling down a well-kept main street. Behind them was a dress shop, its window displaying three mannequins in summer frocks. 'This moderate opulence,' reported *Life*, 'is typical of Bayeux. Its German commandant kept looting and labor conscription to a minimum.'[1]

Life did not mention that collaboration had been widespread and Resistance activities negligible. The French in this prosperous Norman town had had a very good war. So much so that children at first greeted their new occupiers with Nazi salutes. Elsewhere, some newly liberated Frenchmen were less than pleased to see the Americans and British. The D-Day bombardment had killed thousands of Normans, some of them not as innocent as others.

Later that evening, Capa found his press colleagues sitting in a barn around flickering candles drinking a bottle of Calvados. They were holding a wake in his honour. He later claimed that a sergeant had reported seeing his corpse floating in the shallows on Omaha. Because he had been missing from the front line for forty-eight hours, he had been announced officially dead. He wrote that censors had even approved his obituary.[2]

That night, in a hotel called the Lion d'Or, Capa and his colleagues apparently polished off several more bottles of Calvados to celebrate his return from the dead. Among those at this celebratory wake were Ernie Pyle and Charles Wertenbaker, the imposing new head of *Time and Life*'s European staff. The next day, Capa teamed with them to report on the Allied advance on Cherbourg, a vital Channel port and 'the first great objective of the invasion'.[3] Before returning to the front lines, each man tucked into a good steak, shaved, took a hot bath, and changed his clothes. It might be weeks before they'd do the same again.

By D+9, the three correspondents were in the thick of the fighting. 'From June 15 to June 27,' Wertenbaker recalled, 'nearly every day we were with a battalion or a company in action.'[4] The men who had survived D-Day were losing yet more friends and brothers as they crept from steep hedgerow to hedgerow, most of which were booby-trapped and mined. They were lucky if they advanced two hedgerows each day: the *bocage* – Normandy's ancient patchwork of small fields separated by steep embankments and thick undergrowth – gave defenders a distinct advantage. 'There were, on average, fourteen hedgerows to the kilometer in Normandy,' the historian Stephen Ambrose has pointed out. 'The enervating, costly process of gearing up for an attack, making the attack, carrying the attack home, mopping up after the attack, took half a day or more. And at the end of the action, there was the next hedgerow, fifty to a hundred meters or so away.'[5]

At any moment, recalls Sergeant Roy Stevens of the 116th Infantry, his friends would be picked off by a sniper or disappear in a mass of blood and flesh as they stepped on a mine. Stevens himself was badly wounded when a comrade triggered a mine a few yards in front of him. Others lost their nerve, committed suicide or shot themselves in the foot. It was the quiet ones, who had been mocked in training camp, who often showed themselves as ruthless killers. Ruthless or not, most men discovered to their relief that they were not cowards: they did not break down when terror gripped them. When they entered a new town or village, they were often forced to clear every street, sometimes house by house.

Wertenbaker and Capa spent day after day cowering behind hedgerows, ducking into buildings, and running for cover as the Germans fought a fierce defensive action. Unlike their attackers, many of the Germans were hardened veterans from Africa, the Russian front and Italy. Experience had taught them, as it had taught Capa, how to lie as tightly balled as possible under shellfire, and how to endure days of constant stress without sleep and adequate nourishment. At the very last moment, when they could either put their Mausers to their head or unfurl a white flag, most opted to live. 'They fight, not to the last German, but to the first American,' Capa told Wertenbaker contemptuously one day.[6]

In the articles accompanying Capa's pictures of the American advance up the Cotentin peninsula, *Life* magazine made no mention of the Germans' superior combat readiness, nor of their formidable armament. Capa quickly came to recognize every sound of every weapon, as did any GI who experienced the nightmare maze of the bocage. The Wehrmacht's MG42 machine guns fired at 1,200 rounds per minute. Among the concert of other fatal noises, they sounded as if a giant piece of fabric was being torn close to one's ear. The German 88mm guns, by far the best artillery of the war, fired shells at head height down lanes at nearly three times the speed of sound – flesh and blood targets never heard them coming. The German *Panzerfaust* was vastly superior to the American equivalent, the bazooka. Its sudden 'whoooosh' echoed in the fevered sleep of many American tank crews. Then there was the most terrifying sound of all – the wail of 'Moaning Minnies', the bombs fired almost simultaneously by a Nebelwerfer, which the 'Krauts' nicknamed 'Stukas on Wheels' because the sirens with which the shells were equipped, like Stukas, 'had an effect on those who heard them often more penetrating than their explosive power'.[7]

After several days of slogging north through the deadly *bocage*, Capa and Pyle decided one evening they couldn't take another meal of C-rations and would go in search of some real food. They persuaded a mess sergeant to put together a package of mess supplies and then drove to the small village of Les Pieux, where Capa walked into the sole restaurant. He returned after a few minutes and gestured for Pyle and their driver, Private Cogan, to follow him inside, into a packed room with low ceilings and sloping floors. The restaurant's proprietress sat them at a long table. Capa had struck a bargain with her: the box of canned supplies in exchange for dinner. They ate magnificently as Capa talked passionately with several locals. '[The Frenchmen] didn't have much bad to say about the Germans,' Pyle reported. When they left the restaurant, Cogan was ecstatic. At just nineteen, he'd wolfed down his first great French meal.

On 26 June, Capa joined Pyle and Wertenbaker as an American battalion of the 9th Division entered a suburb of Cherbourg.[8] At one street corner, Capa found several German prisoners as well as Russian conscripts accompanied by their wives, who were hysterical with fear: the Germans had told their husbands that the Americans didn't take prisoners. It was the best way to keep them fighting.

In the distance, Cherbourg harbour was ablaze. As the battalion advanced towards the town centre, Capa heard intense fighting in nearby streets: the hack-hack-hack of MG42 machine guns and lonely single Luger pistol shots. Sniper fire crackled. 20mm shells soon whined overhead. The battalion's immediate objective was a hospital where German troops had captured over a hundred wounded Americans. Suddenly, a young lieutenant, wearing sunglasses despite the overcast weather, approached Capa and his colleagues. 'Our company is starting in a few minutes to go up this road and clean out a strongpoint,' he said. 'It's about half a mile from here. There are probably snipers in some of the houses along the way. Do you want to go with us?'

Pyle didn't want to go but couldn't refuse the invitation. It would have been cowardly. Wertenbaker nodded calmly. Capa looked eager. They moved forward, Capa checking his cameras, until they were at the front of a column. The lieutenant introduced himself as Orion Shockley of Jefferson City, Missouri. He'd been named after Mark Twain's brother. One of his fellow officers had arrived with the company just three hours before, and was so new to combat that he now ducked when 'outgoing mail' (American shells) flew overhead. By contrast, the men under his command had been in combat since 14 June. They had snatched a few hours' sleep in damp cellars and hastily dug foxholes. Their uniforms were slick with dirt and sweat, their expressions numbed, for each one now knew he'd either die or be taken home on a stretcher – the only two ways out of the hell of Normandy. By war's end, the 9th Division had spent 264 days in combat, suffering 33,864 casualties, more than any other infantry division in Europe. The turnover in troops was a staggering 240 per cent.

'Why don't you tell the folks back home what this is like?' a soldier asked, anger in his voice. 'All they hear about is victories and a lot of glory stuff. They don't know that for every hundred yards we advance somebody gets killed. Why don't you tell them how tough this life is?' Pyle told the exhausted GI that he tried to tell America how tough the war was in every one of his columns.

It started to rain. Soon, Capa was soaked to the bone. Shockley explained to Capa how his men were going to wipe out machine-gun positions and pillboxes at the end of a street. 'We don't know what we'll run into,' he said, 'and I don't want to stick you right out in front, so why don't you come along with me?' Capa nodded. Suddenly, there was a loud 'thwack-thwack' of bullets passing just above his head. He crouched down behind a high wall near a crossroads. To advance any further, he would have to brave open ground under fire. Shockley ordered his men forward while Capa watched. 'Spread it out now!' he yelled, knowing that men bunched together would be easy targets. 'Do you want to draw fire on yourselves? Don't bunch up like that. Keep five yards apart. Spread it out, dammit!'

Pyle was struck by the utter vulnerability of the men as they carried out Shockley's orders: 'They were really the hunters, but they looked like the hunted. They weren't warriors. They were American boys who by mere chance of fate had wound up with guns in their hands, sneaking up a death-laden street in a strange and shattered city in a faraway country in a driving rain. They were afraid but it was beyond their power to quit. They had no choice.'

Word came down the line that German troops were two hundred yards ahead, near their objective – the hospital full of wounded Americans. Fifty yards from the hospital, an American tank opened up with its 75mm gun. Windows shattered as the street shook from the blast. Then the tank took a direct hit, flames ripping from its underbelly. The crew scampered out and ran for cover. A few minutes later, a group of Germans appeared ahead, an officer leading them, waving a Red Cross flag on a stick. They were carrying two stretchers with wounded. Capa jumped over some wreckage, ran towards the surrendering Germans, lifted his Leica and photographed them several times. He then told them in German to follow him back to the American lines.

When Capa finally arrived at the hospital, he discovered more than 200 bandaged men from the 82nd Airborne Division, and was told that the hospital's basement had a supply of the very best wine and brandy. But when he got to the basement, he found 'every soldier of the 47th Infantry [Regiment] already had his arms, jacket, and pockets bulging with precious bottles'. He needed a drink badly, and begged one soldier for some booze. The soldier laughed: 'Only if you're Ernie Pyle.'[9] So Capa asked another soldier for a bottle for Pyle, and was quickly given one. For the one and only Ernie Pyle, most GIs would willingly give whatever booty they'd liberated. By this stage of the war, the Scripps-Howard correspondent was sometimes mobbed by GIs, much to his embarrassment. Wherever he went, soldiers asked him to sign franc notes and rifle stocks. 'Each day brought new invitations,' Pyle's biographer

James Tobin has written, 'from soldiers ranging from privates to generals yearning to have Pyle's recognition bestowed upon their units.'[10]

Later that afternoon of 26 June, Capa witnessed the surrender of General von Schlieben, the German commander of Cherbourg. Refusing to let his picture be taken, von Schlieben told his aide in German that he was bored with the American press. Capa replied in German that he was bored with photographing defeated German officers. Outraged at his insolence, von Schlieben turned on him furiously. Capa was waiting, finger poised above his Leica's shutter release, and got the perfect picture of angry defeat.

By the time Cherbourg fell, the Americans in Normandy had suffered heavy losses. Two-thirds of the 40,000 Allied casualties in the first two weeks after D-Day were American. The mounting death toll as the Germans fought to defend every field and town began to bear heavily on any of those who witnessed it. On 30 June, after spending five days with Capa and the 9th Division, Pyle wrote to a friend: 'This hedge to hedge stuff is a type of warfare we've never run into before, and I've seen more dead Germans than ever in my life. Americans too, but not nearly so many as the Germans. One day I'll think I'm getting hardened to dead people, dead young people in vast numbers, and then next day I'll realize I'm not and never could be.'[11]

Capa and Wertenbaker were also overtaken by 'the ghastliness of it all'.[12] As they travelled back towards the press camp in Bayeux after the fall of Cherbourg one afternoon, Wertenbaker reflected bitterly on how some politicians saw war as a grandiose game:

> War is loneliness, and alone man may be a creature of dignity. But war's fear and filth so destroy this dignity that he loses even the chance of dignified death. Death in battle is seldom the clean, unexpected bullet that kills a man before fear has distorted his face . . . It is usually a shell or a bomb or a spray of machine-gun bullets coming closer to living creatures huddled on the earth in terror, and when death has passed there is no dignity left in the pieces of bloody pulp in the dirt.[13]

As their jeep bounced through the deadly *bocage*, with Capa looking like a Mongolian bandit because of his heavy beard, their spirits did, however, lift for a few moments. As they crossed a bridge to Isigny under shellfire, they looked up at a fighter plane skimming the underbelly of a lone cloud in the clear sky. 'The French sky,' said Capa, 'it is lovely.' Wertenbaker looked up, and then nodded in admiration. 'I think it's the loveliest in the world,' added Capa.[14]

Capa returned to London with Wertenbaker in mid-July. Only then did he discover the fate of his D-Day photos.[15] *Life* initially lied to him, saying that his pictures had been destroyed because water had seeped into his Contaxes. When he saw a copy of *Life* magazine, he was so upset, according to Irwin Shaw, that he 'no longer was much interested in photographing the war'.[16] He became even more bitterly resentful when he discovered in *Life*'s 19 June issue an explanation for his spoilt pictures: 'Immense excitement of moment made Photographer Capa move his camera and blur picture.'*

When Capa returned to the war in late July, he discovered that more than 300 members of the press corps, including Steinbeck and Hemingway, were vying for pole position in the race to Paris: the city's liberation was the next great story. 'Papa' was busy waging his own private war, advancing with a unit of the 4th Infantry Division, whose senior officers he had befriended. According to Capa, he had his own cook, a driver/photographer, and his very own ration of Scotch. Hemingway's companions, whom he dubbed 'irregulars', were public relations officers but under Papa's influence had become a 'bunch of bloodthirsty Indians'. Barred from carrying a weapon, as were all war correspondents, Hemingway had made sure his personal platoon carried 'every weapon imaginable' – both German and American.[17]

In early August, Hemingway invited Capa to join him as he and his band of 'irregulars' advanced towards Paris. Capa accepted, sensing a story in the making, with Hemingway his main focus. According to the

* Despite his anger and disillusionment, Capa did not seek revenge. According to some accounts, he even threatened to leave the magazine if the darkroom assistant responsible for the disaster was fired.

American journalist Peter Hamill, one afternoon Hemingway was riding beside Capa in a jeep when a German fighter appeared and began strafing the road. Capa and the driver dived beneath the vehicle for cover but Hemingway remained erect in his seat, ignoring the bullets. When the plane passed over, Capa crawled from beneath the jeep and ordered the driver to head back to a command post so he could fly some film back to London.

'What?' shouted Hemingway. 'Go back? I'm not going to retreat because of Henry Luce!'[18]

Early on 5 August, Hemingway sent a captured Mercedes field-car to pick up Capa for another jaunt. With Colonel Charles 'Buck' Lanham, he had decided he was going 'to take' the village of St-Pois, and wanted Capa along to record the action yet again. When he held up a map and outlined his plan of attack, Capa this time advised 'Papa' against the foolhardy and unnecessary action, telling him that he should obey a simple rule – always go forward behind as many soldiers as possible, and never take 'lonely shortcuts through no-man's-land'.[19]

Hemingway looked at him with disdain, implying he was a coward. Capa reluctantly agreed to go along, but only if he could follow at a safe distance behind. Hemingway set off, riding in a motorcycle sidecar. Capa followed in the Mercedes. Suddenly, Hemingway again came under fire as the motorcycle rounded a corner. In the distance stood a panzer. The motorcycle's driver slammed on the brakes and Hemingway was thrown into a shallow ditch where he was soon pinned down. 'Get back, goddammit!' Hemingway snapped. But Capa apparently stayed where he was. 'Get back, goddammit, I said.'[20] Still he refused to budge. When the Germans finally withdrew, a furious Hemingway confronted him, and for several days neither spoke to each other. According to several biographers, Hemingway never quite forgave Capa for this incident, and their friendship remained strained until Capa's death.*

* There were several other reasons why the two saw little of each other in coming years. As his marriage to Martha Gellhorn failed, Hemingway's affection for Capa became tinged with envy. Gellhorn had never hidden her enormous affection, if not love, for Capa, and Papa knew that she confided in him, and that he sided with her. On one occasion, Capa

Hemingway's son John heard what happened that day from both Capa and his father: 'Capa said that he finally did go back and the only reason he stayed at first was so he could help Papa. But Papa always swore that the reason Capa didn't go back was because he wanted to be there to get the story and pictures of Papa getting it from the machine-gun.'[21]

After the aborted attack on St-Pois, Hemingway and Capa went their separate ways. There was only provision for one snapper in Hemingway's private army and after St-Pois it wasn't going to be Capa, who seemed overly keen to record Papa's death rather than his mock-heroic exploits.

Capa made his way to Mont St-Michel to rendezvous with John Morris; he had reluctantly agreed to give his young editor a taste of life on the front lines. 'The day I arrived,' recalls Morris, 'Capa suggested we take a walk down a long street [through the centre of the town]. He knew how to get acquainted with people very fast. As we walked along he saw a young girl, tickled her under the chin and asked who her boyfriend was. A few minutes later, we passed a little café where men were playing chess and he said, "Why don't you move this [piece]?" He was brilliant at getting a rapport started . . . It was also that day that a farmer approached him and asked if he could do anything to help. Bob said yes – "Buy us dinner." '

Morris and Capa visited nearby St-Malo a few days later. As the pair approached the city, they came across a special unit of American soldiers engaged in 'psychological warfare'. Morris thought their activities would make a good story, and persuaded a sceptical Capa to follow the men to the front lines where, over loudhailers, they urged German troops to surrender. When Morris asked their driver what usually happened after making such entreaties, the driver said pointedly: 'We get the hell out of here.' Morris soon saw why: mortar rounds started to land nearby.

---

even scolded Hemingway for wanting to marry every woman he fell for. Over the years, Hemingway became increasin^gly bitter, later telling a mutual friend, the writer Peter Viertel, that Capa 'could never satisfy any of his women, which is why he kept flying from one continent to the other.' (Viertel, *Dangerous Friends*)

'This really isn't very healthy,' said Capa.

They took cover in the cellar of a farmhouse. 'Bob was very practical and calm [under fire], not excitable,' recalls Morris. 'He had a good sense of self-preservation. He'd been through a lot by then.'

Later that day, a group of German prisoners passed the farmhouse. Morris asked Capa 'to go over and ask them how they reacted' to the psychological warfare team's appeals. Capa talked to one after another of the men and then returned to Morris: 'None of them heard.'

After bidding his over-zealous boss farewell, Capa decided to reunite with Charles Wertenbaker. On 18 August, the pair entered the cathedral city of Chartres. As they reached the city's prefecture, they heard the angry shouts of a French crowd: '*Salope! Salope!*' (Whore! Whore!) Wertenbaker described the scene in *Invasion!*: 'The patriots were bringing in women collaborators, old ones who had helped the Germans or operated black markets and younger blowsy ones who had sold themselves to the Germans. They were lined against a wall, some with their hair already clipped close to the skull, and in the center of the courtyard was a pile of gray and blond hair. In a corner of the courtyard a woman and a boy were selling red wine by the glass.'[22]

Capa ran ahead of the rabble as it taunted a woman who carried her German lover's baby through the cobbled streets. 'It is cruel and unnecessary,' a young female Resistance worker commented. 'They are soldiers' women and tomorrow they will be sleeping with the Americans.'[23] Walking backwards, Capa photographed the shaven-headed woman several times as hundreds of her compatriots jeered and shouted obscenities. The image remains one of his most famous pictures, a vivid record of France's complicity with Nazism and the subsequent bitterness of those who had not apparently collaborated.

On 23 August, Capa and Wertenbaker learned that the first troops to enter Paris would be General Leclerc's French 2nd Armoured Division, but Leclerc had stated that he wanted only the French press with him and had moved his division closer to Paris without informing any of the American correspondents. On the 24th, Capa and Wertenbaker caught up with Leclerc's tanks in Étampes. That afternoon, 'the clouds blew away and the sun shone through a pale blue sky. The tall lovely bending trees that lined the roads and fields stood dark against the sunset.'[24] That night, they laid out their bedrolls beside Route National 20. 'From beneath the Big Dipper came occasional flashes of light and then the sound of artillery in the distance. The French tanks were dark blurry shapes beneath the trees.'[25] The blacked-out city of light was only a few miles away.

15 Victory

'It was the most unforgettable day in the world.'

Robert Capa, *Slightly Out of Focus*

Dawn, 25 August 1944: the sun seemed to rise in a rush. Capa didn't bother to brush his teeth. At nine o'clock, the driver of his and Wertenbaker's jeep manoeuvred just behind Leclerc's armoured car and drove fast towards the Porte d'Orléans. Suddenly, a dense crowd swarmed around them, waving flags and bouquets of flowers. Women climbed aboard their jeep and kissed them passionately. '*Vive De Gaulle*,' they cried. '*Vive Leclerc.*' Others shouted over and over again: '*Merci, merci, merci!*'

Capa and Wertenbaker passed through the Porte d'Orléans at precisely 9.40 a.m. They had beaten Hemingway's army to the gates of Paris. Now women held their children up to be kissed and cried out again: '*Merci, merci, merci!*' After five years, Capa was back in the only city he would ever consider home. It was the most joyous day of his life.

All the bottled-up emotions of the last few years soon flooded out. 'Bob Capa and I rode into Paris with eyes that would not stay dry,' Wertenbaker recalled. 'We were no more ashamed of it than were the people who wept as they embraced us.'[1]

They left their jeep near the Boulevard des Invalides and walked towards the Quai d'Orsay, where the Germans were still putting up a spirited resistance. A bearded priest in a steel helmet ran past them, rushing to reach a fatally wounded French marine and give him the last sacrament. At one street corner, Capa came across a crowd gathered around a German officer kneeling in the street, praying for his life. Several Resistance workers wanted to shoot the German there and then but suddenly three French marines arrived and took him prisoner.

Then fighting broke out. The Germans still held the Ministry of Foreign Affairs and several other key buildings.[2] By evening most of the Germans left in Paris had surrendered. As darkness fell and the sound of gunfire faded into the distance, the city of light was again lit up for the first time in four years, and the Tricolour and the Stars and Stripes were raised side by side over the Eiffel Tower. All night, Parisians sang the 'Marseillaise' from their windows.

The next afternoon, beneath azure-blue skies, Capa photographed General de Gaulle as he walked in a victory procession from the Arc de Triomphe to Notre Dame. Capa's photographs show him breaking into a rare smile during his greatest moment of glory. But the victory parade was cut short in the Place de l'Hôtel-de-Ville: several maverick German snipers, perhaps ignorant of the order to surrender, opened up on the crowd. Thousands of Parisians were soon huddled together on bloodstained pavements. A beautiful, lone woman wearing sunglasses, utterly fearless, stood tall, too proud to cower any more. In nearby streets, Resistance fighters quickly located the snipers and returned fire with machine guns and automatic rifles. In one street, Capa found an elegant businessman in a double-breasted pinstripe, lying on his back, firing a carbine: behind him, bullet holes scarred the door of a restaurant.

A few hours later, the last of the snipers had been eliminated and Capa joined Wertenbaker at the Hôtel Scribe, whose bar quickly became the watering hole of the international press corps. *Life* artist Floyd Davis later captured the bar scene wonderfully. In his painting, Capa looks like a swarthy bandit as he surveys his colleagues: Wertenbaker, resembling a distinguished general; the *New Yorker* writer Janet Flanner with her perpetual cigarette; eye-patched broadcaster William Shirer; a barrel-chested Hemingway; and a grim-looking John Steinbeck.

John Morris vividly recalls editing Capa's photographs of the liberation. 'At the time, I remember not being too impressed – I was disappointed by them . . . It was easy to edit his [pictures], not difficult to follow his line of thought. He didn't go in for crazy angles. He was pretty much an eye-level photographer. You might say that was a weakness – he wasn't fluid enough in his approach to subject matter.' Looking back almost sixty years later, however, Morris says he would 'love to see those contact sheets [of the liberation story] again.' Capa was the most unaffected of photographers, surprisingly limited in his technical range, but he nevertheless had an uncanny ability to focus his camera at exactly the right moment. His images of Paris that joyous day remain the definitive record of liberation – the happiest day in his life, and arguably in the history of Paris.

In the first heady days after liberation, Capa shared many a bottle of champagne with Morris, as well as George Rodger, Mary Welsh, Slim Aarons and William Saroyan. But he chose not to stay at the Scribe, opting for the Lancaster instead. To his surprise, he found that George Rodger had arrived an hour before and reserved him a room, just as he had promised in Italy.

One night, Capa and Hemingway forgot their squabble in St-Pois and dined on black-market food at the Lancaster. The next evening, the writer Marcel Duhamel, Hemingway's translator, took Capa and Hemingway's band of 'irregulars' to a small restaurant on the Rue de Seine where Pablo Picasso often ate. As they sat down to dinner, Capa spotted Picasso at a table nearby. Old friends, Hemingway and Picasso embraced each other, and then talked late into the night at Capa's table, knocking back vintage after vintage and feasting on fresh lamb.

The following morning, according to Leicester Hemingway, Capa visited Picasso at his two-storey studio on the Rue St-Augustin on the Left Bank: from eleven to one each morning, Picasso held an 'open house' for fellow artists and friends. Capa photographed him wearing a striped T-shirt, his left arm around what *Life* described as a 'grotesque figure' made from 'wire, metal, ox skulls and all kinds of junk'.[3] Although the Nazis had declared Picasso a 'degenerate' painter, they had left him largely unmolested during the occupation.

For several days, Capa rediscovered other corners of Paris, and met up with his closest friends from before the war: Cartier-Bresson, Chim and Pierre Gassmann. At a party held by the editor of French *Vogue* the three drank champagne, toasting the liberation of their beloved city, and shared war stories. Cartier-Bresson had spent three years in a prisoner-of-war camp. He had escaped on his third attempt and joined the Resistance in Paris, posing as his alter ego, an absent-minded Buddhist painter. Chim had spent the war in the US Army, assigned to photo-interpretation of aerial intelligence. By 1944, he was a lieutenant and an American citizen. He learned shortly afterwards that his parents and most of his relatives had died in 1942 in the Warsaw ghetto.

After the elation of liberation, most Parisians resumed their grim struggle to find food and other essentials. Capa was woken at the Lancaster by calls from old acquaintances in search of food, coffee, American cigarettes or anything else the legendary scrounger could rustle up. At the top of Capa's list of people he actually wanted to help were his only relatives in Paris – Béla and Szeren Fischer, and their sixteen-year-old daughter Suzy Marquis.

The Fischers had suffered terribly during the occupation. In the weeks before liberation, Suzy had walked miles each day to try to find a few raw onions to feed her family. On the day Capa arrived in Paris, she had tried to get word to him at the Scribe Hotel but without luck. Then, a few days later, she saw a young GI pull up in a jeep outside her home. The grinning soldier was soon lugging a huge duffel bag crammed with food into her parents' living room. 'We couldn't believe it,' recalls Suzy, who still prizes the bag. 'It was stuffed with everything we'd dreamed of for years – flour, fresh butter. The American gave me a watch and some stockings, said the bag was from Bob. We just sat and stared for hours at all the food. We were just stunned.'

In early September, Capa was delighted to hear that he'd been assigned to stay in Paris for several more weeks. He had no desire to continue photographing the war now that he was back in the only city he considered home. 'There would never again be pictures of doughboys like those in the deserts of North Africa or the mountains of Italy, never again an invasion to surpass that of the Normandy beach; never a liberation to equal Paris.'[4] Later that month, Bill Graffis, an American public relations officer, invited him to leave Paris to do a story on the Resistance in southern France – the Maquis. He later explained Capa's reaction:

> People say that the Happy Hungarian lacked fear of any assignment during the war. Don't get me wrong. I think Capa has a plethora of guts, but on his part it was always a beautiful demonstration of bravery. As an officer in the 82nd Airborne, I once asked Capa to go on a small troop carrier re-supply mission to the Maquis. He refused, stating, 'To your pilots and the Maquis, the mission is important. To my editor it means only one or two pictures at most. To Capa, it is not worth the trouble of such a small affair to get his beautiful head blown off, without benefit at least, of a four-page spread. I refuse, my old.' [sic] I'll ride with you on the statement that Capa was probably the greatest photographer of World War II, just because he was smart enough to weigh the risk to himself against magazine space. Moreover, Capa is one of the most truly liberal and democratic gentlemen I have ever had the pleasure to know. Capa will chase any woman, regardless of race, color, creed, height, age, weight, marital status or nationality.[5]

It was not until late October that the 'truly liberal' Capa left Paris, headed for Toulouse, where he made contact with the Spanish Civil War veterans of the Unión Nacional Española. On 22 October Spanish Republicans had invaded Spain but had quickly been brutally repulsed by Franco's army. In a bare hospital, Capa took several wrenching pictures of these last brave survivors of the Loyalist cause. Several had lost limbs to frostbite, while most of their comrades had died trying to cross the Pyrenees back into France.

Back in Paris, he ran into Martha Gellhorn at the Lancaster. She was planning to have dinner with Papa and ask him for a divorce. But when she arrived at the restaurant, she found him with a group of his 'irregular' soldier friends. Apparently he had insulted her throughout dinner, and Capa found her still crying at four the next morning. He told her that Mary Welsh was having an affair with Papa, and if she didn't believe him, she should call the Ritz and ask for her. Gellhorn called and asked to be put through to Welsh. Hemingway picked up the phone. Capa then told her to ask Hemingway for a divorce. After swearing at her for several seconds, Papa agreed to her request. Why Capa was in Gellhorn's room at 4 a.m. has yet to be explained.[6]

Capa also had problems on the woman front. Pinky was demanding that he make a commitment to her. She wanted to divorce her husband and marry him. If he didn't propose to her, she would run off with the first eligible man she met. Mustering all his charm, Capa asked her to wait for the war to end. But Pinky said she was tired of waiting. She was getting older, and she feared he would no longer want her when she lost the sheen of youth. He was fearless in war, she added, but terrified of falling in love.[7]

Capa returned to Paris not knowing if Pinky would be faithful to him. A few weeks later, he was called back to action. In early December, near the German border in the Saar valley, he joined the US 95th Division as it pushed the last deadly miles towards the Third Reich. The men he encountered were tragically young and unprepared for the bitter winter fighting on Germany's borders. They were doomed 'replacements', with minimal training and no experience of combat. They had not even been given orientation lectures on what to expect, and they died like flies in the first frost. In some battles, more than 50 per cent became casualties within three days in the front line. Veterans, by then defined as men who had survived a month in combat, would often not bother to ask the replacement's name. They didn't want to know the next man to die. It only reminded them of their own inevitable fate.*

In his memoirs, Capa made no mention of such slaughter. In *Slightly Out of Focus*, he only ever hinted at the war's true horrors. Humour substituted for candour. Irony masked criticism of bad tactics. As a non-combatant, painfully aware that he could choose when to risk his life and when to cower in a foxhole, he had no right, he later told friends,

*According to nineteen-year-old Private Ken Russell of the 82nd Airborne, the replacements Capa photographed were 'all the good boys with the strength of a mule and the ignorance of old maids. We pitied the scared, shy eager youngsters who were awe-struck around us old boys. In the first battle they usually died in heaps.' (Ambrose, *Citizen Soldiers*.)

to do anything but smile at misfortune, shrug at loss, and move on to the next battle or poker game.*

In the Saar valley that December, Capa came across increasingly surreal scenes. In one sector, he discovered a new weapon: artificial fog that made it impossible to see more than a couple of yards. The men laying down the fog were black soldiers, and they braved constant fire. One told Capa he believed the 88mm shells were speaking to him, warning him he wouldn't return to Alabama.

The shelling intensified the further Capa advanced and so he decided to hole up in a cellar – he couldn't take photographs in any case because of the artificial fog. As shells whizzed overhead, he read an old copy of *War and Peace* by torchlight. The sound effects, he wrote, 'were made to order'.[8] After five days reading Tolstoy's classic, he heard a disturbing radio bulletin. The Germans had launched a massive counter-attack against the Allies. The Wehrmacht had regrouped and fresh panzer divisions were driving fast across Belgium towards Antwerp via Liège and Bastogne in the Ardennes. The push towards Germany was gravely endangered, with a 'bulge' in the Allied front now growing toward the River Meuse. Capa immediately returned to Paris.

The legendary Battle of the Bulge began on 16 December as three German divisions neared the road junction of Bastogne in south-east Belgium. Before the Germans arrived, however, the 101st Airborne Division, under Brigadier General Anthony C. McAuliffe, entered Bastogne and secured it. But the Germans quickly surrounded the 101st

* The cartoonist Bill Mauldin was one of many who later delighted in recounting stories about Capa's apparent nonchalance in the face of horror. One day, he claimed, Capa invited him to cross a river under German surveillance. He refused the offer and 'soon Capa returned with a bloody leg. Crossing with a couple of riflemen, he had encountered a German soldier, apparently dazed by the shelling, in an attitude of surrender. As soon as the trio was close, the German had lifted his hands a little higher and released a US grenade from his armpit, killing one American and wounding Capa and himself. The surviving American had shot the culprit, tossed Bob his first-aid kit, and gone on. Meanwhile, the photographer had gotten the whole episode on film. He hadn't even bothered to open the kit, although he was bleeding badly.' All Capa could now focus on was how to get his film back to London. (Mauldin, *The Brass Ring.*)

Airborne. When Lieutenant General Heinrich von Luttwitz then demanded his surrender, McAuliffe famously replied: 'Nuts!'

Capa left Paris just before Christmas to cover the relief of Bastogne by General Patton's forces. On the frigid drive north, he was stopped regularly and questioned by paranoid MPs who had been told to arrest anyone who seemed remotely suspicious: the Germans had dropped paratroops and commandos in US uniform behind Allied lines to occupy road junctions and cause chaos. Capa's thick accent did not go down well. 'They insisted on asking me a lot of very foolish and very embarrassing questions,' he recalled. '"What is the capital of Nebraska?" . . . "Who won the last World Series?" . . . I was arrested a number of times, each time being delayed by many hours.'[9]

On 23 December, temperatures plunged to well below freezing. Mud soon turned to stone. Foxholes became refrigerators. As in Italy, men started to die from exposure and frostbite. His hands frozen, his eyes streaming from the cold, Capa pushed forward with a tank unit assigned to relieve the 101st in Bastogne. The lone photographer on the drive to save the division, he could not keep his hand on his frozen shutter for 'more than a split second'.[10] Like the men he photographed, Capa was soon pilfering anything he could find to keep himself warm.

It was around this time that Capa ran into the young American reporter Andy Rooney, today a celebrated author and broadcaster.

Rooney remembered him talking to a public relations officer, Ken Koyen, with Patton's 4th Armored Division: '[He] was wearing a fur coat he'd appropriated from a Wehrmacht supply dump. If there were fashions in war, that coat would have been featured in the Sunday paper style section that week because every American soldier wanted one. The fur was on the inside, the skin on the outside. They were not only warm but very trendy, and Capa liked trendy. Koyen warned Capa that the front was no place for an American to be wearing any article of German army clothing but Capa couldn't be persuaded to take it off.'[11]

Five miles from Bastogne, dressed in his modish overcoat, Capa stopped to photograph men crossing a snow-covered field. Suddenly, a GI 150 yards away raised his machine gun. 'Take it easy!' Capa yelled.

The GI heard Capa's accent, saw his coat, and began to shoot. Capa considered his options. If he ran for it, he'd be killed. If he dived for cover, the bullets would find him quickly too. So he threw up his hands and yelled '*Kamerad!*' Two GIs approached, guns trained on him. Noticing the three expensive German cameras dangling from Capa's neck, they broke into broad grins. Then they saw his press pass. 'I should have shot the bastard before,' one of them swore.[12]

On Christmas Eve 1944, Capa stood with several shivering tank crewmen under a clear sky filled with blazing stars and sang 'Silent Night'. Suddenly, a German flare lit up the sky and they returned to their tanks and pressed on towards Bastogne. 'Capa traveled with the tanks as they fought German paratroopers on the road to Bastogne,' *Life* reported on 15 January 1945, beside pictures of frozen Americans crossing white fields as flocks of transport planes circled Bastogne. 'On the sixth [day], Lieut. Colonel Creighton Abrams, commander of the leading tank battalion, said, "We are going in to join those people now!" On the day after Christmas a sudden three-mile thrust lifted the siege of Bastogne.'

After several weeks' rest, which included a rejuvenating visit to the Alps for some skiing, Capa received orders to report to the US 17th Airborne Division's headquarters for a planned parachute jump over the Rhine. Before joining the outfit, he returned to Toulouse where his old friend Pierre Gassmann found him 'beaming' with delight as he photographed a congress of the exiled Spanish Socialist Party. At Capa's side was Henri Cartier-Bresson.

One afternoon, a speaker praised Capa as the first man to show the world the heroic resistance of the Spanish people in the face of fascism. At a hotel that evening, he discussed with Gassmann the idea of setting up a cooperative photographic agency. He also planned to involve Chim and Cartier-Bresson. According to Gassmann, he had first imagined such an agency in 1935 when a picture of his showing the Paris stock market had been bought and captioned by the Nazi *Müncher Illustrierte Presse* to show how French Jews planned to destabilize the French franc.[13]

In late March, in the vicinity of the French city of Arras, Capa finally joined a group of young American paratroopers belonging to the 17th Airborne Division who had shaved their heads into 'Mohican' cuts in a bonding ritual before they dropped into Germany unannounced. While waiting for the jump, he apparently arranged for a special delivery of whiskey to steady his nerves.

'Capa appeared at the base public relations office and announced he wanted whiskey,' recalled John Hersey. 'The public relations officer said that whiskey was not permitted on the base for twenty-four hours before a mission. Capa asked to use the phone. The PRO threatened to pull the phone out of the wall if Capa reached for it; the base was under a blanket of absolute secrecy. Capa left. A few minutes later he returned and said casually, "I found a telephone." A couple of hours later the chief public relations officer from the headquarters of Lieutenant General Lewis Brereton landed at the field; his errand was to unload a case of whiskey for Capa. A couple of hours after that, a silver plane circled the field and landed, and General Brereton himself stepped out, brushed past the nervous commanding officer of the base, greeted Capa, and asked him if he'd got the whiskey alright.'[14]

On 24 March, Capa sat beside thirty 'Mohicans' as a plane taxied down a runway and then flew low over grey, frozen landscape. Knowing that the 'end of darkness always brought the beginning of death',[15] he checked that his cameras were properly strapped to his legs and that his 'flask [of Brereton's whiskey] was in [his] breast pocket over [his] heart'.[16] 10 a.m. The light flashed green. 10.25 a.m. A red light.

Capa stood up, held on to his parachute release wire, shuffled down the plane, reached the hatch and jumped. Forty seconds later, having dropped just 600 feet, he landed then detached his pack, rolled up his parachute, and followed troops as they advanced under fire towards hedgerows and farmhouses occupied by Germans. His pictures showed a bleak landscape draped with silk chutes. In one shot, several paratroopers hung from branches – their parachutes canopied in the bare treetops, their bodies riddled twenty times with German machine-gun bullets.

By 11 a.m., Capa had two rolls. He lit his first cigarette. His films now contained many more deeply affecting images, such as a medic propping up the head of a young paratrooper as his life ebbed away, his parachute draped across barbed wire in the background. At 11.30 a.m., he took his first swig from his flask. Allied forces had secured the east bank of the Rhine.

Much later, Capa told his friend Pierre Gassmann about the parachute jump. He insists, 'Capa never enjoyed danger. He tolerated it – it was part of his business. He knew how to survive – he was a good soldier, and he had a way of laughing about things that was healthy. He told me that after landing he had to open his pack and pull out a new pair of underwear because he'd filled his pants. He said the really terrible thing was changing your pants under fire.'

As the Allies advanced through the heart of Germany in April 1945, they discovered a charnel house of suffering and horror. On the 15th the British liberated Belsen. Though Capa could have joined reporters such as Edward Murrow, Martha Gellhorn and George Rodger in recording the liberation of other camps, he chose not to. 'The [camps] were swarming with photographers,' he explained, 'and every new picture of horror served only to diminish the total effect. Now, for a short day, everyone will see what happened to those poor devils in those camps; tomorrow, very few will care what happens to them in the future.'[17]

There was one story Capa did want to cover – the liberation of Leipzig. In a radio report, Edward Murrow described what 'strategic bombing' had done to Gerda's home town: 'The shelling had caused no fire. There was nothing left to burn. It was merely a dusty, uneven desert.'[18] Amid the desolation, Capa exposed his last rolls of the war. On 18 April 1945, as Germans surrendered in tens of thousands throughout the remnants of the Third Reich, he joined the US 2nd Infantry Division as it approached the Zeppelin Bridge over the Weisse Elster Canal. He explained in a 1947 radio interview how he then came to take the most poignant photograph of his career:

> It was obvious that the war was just about over, because we knew the Russians were already in Berlin [sic] and that we had to stop shortly after taking Leipzig. We got into Leipzig after a fight, and just had to cross one more bridge. The Germans put up some resistance so we couldn't cross. There was a big apartment building which overlooked the bridge. So I figured, 'I'm going to get up on the last floor and maybe I'll get a nice picture of Leipzig in the last minute of the fight.' I got in a nice bourgeois apartment where there was a nice young man on the balcony – a young sergeant who was [setting up] a heavy machine-gun. I took a picture of him. But, God, the war was over. Who wanted to see one more picture of somebody shooting? We had been doing that same picture now for four years and everybody wanted something different, and by the time this picture would have reached New York probably the headline would be 'peace'. So it made no sense whatsoever. But he looked so clean-cut like it was the first day of the war and he was very earnest. So I said, 'All right, this will be my last picture of the war.' And I put my camera up and took a portrait shot of him and while I shot my portrait of him he was killed by a sniper. It was a very clean and somehow a very beautiful death, and I think that's what I remember most from this war.

'And that was the last – you think – probably the last man killed during the official war?' asked Capa's interviewer.

'That's right,' Capa replied. 'I'm sure that there were many last men who were killed. But he was the last man maybe in our sector.'

'It was certainly a picture of the uselessness of the war,' said Capa's interviewer.

'Very much so,' agreed Capa. 'It was certainly a picture to remember because I knew that the day after, people will begin to forget.'[19]

Capa did not tell his interviewer what happened after he took his shot of the 'last man'. In his next frame, the man lay slumped on the floor, blood gushing from his neck, a bullet between his eyes. For long seconds, he shot the pool of blood as it seeped towards him. According to *Life*, the 'other members of the platoon [then] decided to find where the fatal shot had come from. Stealthily they single-filed on to the cobblestone street and surrounded Germans barricaded in several abandoned streetcars. They fired a few warning shots. Presently two Germans came out with their hands up shouting, "Kamerad!" The Americans, feeling no elation, took them away.'[20]

In Leipzig that evening, Capa was woken with the news that America's finest Second World War reporter, his good friend, Ernie Pyle, had finally run out of luck. The previous day, around 10 a.m., he had been shot through the temple, just below his helmet, by a Japanese machine gunner on the ten-square-mile Pacific island of Ie Shima. Capa sat in silence, getting blind drunk. He had slept beside Pyle in Africa, shared his flask with him in times of terror and jubilation in Italy and on the killing fields of the Cherbourg peninsula. Like tens of millions of Americans, he'd read Pyle's column to find tenderness and humour amid what Steinbeck had called 'the crazy hysterical mess'[21] of the Second World War.

While so very different in so many respects, as craftsmen in the trade of journalism Capa and Pyle had set the standard for both reporters and photographers to this day. After Pyle, his biographer James Tobin has written, 'no war correspondent could pretend to have gotten the real story without having moved extensively among the front-line soldiers who actually fought.'[22] The same, if not more so, had been true of Capa: Pyle hadn't had to stick his head above a parapet, day after day, to do his job.

Loss always provokes introspection. At some point in every war photographer's career, there comes a time of profound self-awareness. The fog of denial is swept away, either by loss of nerve or by the equally common realization of the ever-narrowing odds of making it through the next battle. Perhaps for the first time since Gerda's death, Capa now started to take stock of his own life. He had played hand after hand and survived to join every new game. But how much further could he push his luck?

There was more bad news, this time from Pinky. She had fallen in love with a public relations officer called Chuck Romine, whom Capa disguised in his memoirs as Captain Chris Scott. Eventually, she divorced her husband and married him.

*

VICTORY

7 May 1945, 2.41 a.m., Central European Time: General Alfred Jodl, seated at a plain wood table in a grimy school building in Reims, signed the official German surrender. The following day, Victory in Europe was declared. Since Gerda's death, Capa had been sustained by the camaraderie of soldiering, the necessity of only living in the moment, thinking only of the next bed, meal, bottle of booze or woman. But now, as champagne corks popped around the world, all that too had gone. 'Capa was a gambler and a great performer,' says his friend and colleague Slim Aarons. 'His stage was war. But what if he couldn't go to war anymore?'

16 'Here's Looking At You, Kid'

'I'm only interested in two kinds of people, those who can entertain me and those who can advance my career.'

INGRID BERGMAN[1]

6 June 1945: the French paparazzi call her name, reaching for her as she steps out of a limousine and walks up the steps to the Ritz Hotel. In an old newsreel, her hair lifts in a gentle breeze as she waves to her admirers. Before disappearing into the hotel, Ingrid Bergman turns and smiles for their bulky Speed Graphic cameras. She had not been to Europe since 1937 and her obvious delight at being back shows in numerous photographs. Paris made her feel as if she was 'starting to live all over again'.[2]

As she swooped through the lobby, entourage in tow, she passed Capa and his poker-playing friend from New York, the writer Irwin Shaw. She had been billeted at the Ritz with other performers in a show that was touring US bases around Europe. Her arrival in Paris had already electrified the press corps, who sent fevered wires from the basement of the Hôtel Scribe. The fuss over her actual arrival at the hotel had caused jealous fellow 'troop-booster' Marlene Dietrich to greet her one morning in the lobby with the famous put-down: 'Ah, now you're coming – when the war's over!'[3]

'The very afternoon I arrived,' Bergman wrote in her autobiography, 'I found a note pushed under my bedroom door. I found it very funny.'

SUBJECT: Dinner. 6.6.45. Paris. France.
TO: Miss Ingrid Bergman

Part 1. This is a community effort. The community consists of Bob Capa and Irwin Shaw.
2. We were planning on sending you flowers with this note inviting you to dinner this evening – but after consultation we discovered it was possible to pay for the flowers or the dinner, or the dinner or the flowers, not both. We took a vote and dinner won by a close margin.
3. It was suggested that if you did not care for dinner, flowers might be sent. No decision has been reached on this so far.
4. Besides flowers we have lots of doubtful qualities.
5. If we write much more we will have no conversation left, as our supply of charm is limited.
6. We will call you at 6.15.
7. We do not sleep.[4]

When Shaw and Capa rang her room at six fifteen that evening, she agreed to meet them in the Ritz's basement bar. Capa and Shaw were already well oiled by the time she arrived at 6.30 p.m., as promised, wearing a beautiful haute couture gown and a red flower in her hair. Both men rushed over to greet her, amazed that she had actually come down to see them rather than some important general. She had accepted the invitation, as she later explained, because she would rather dine out than sit in a hotel room 'staring at a vase of flowers'.[5]

'You said you were going to take me out to dinner,' she told them – sounding to Capa like 'a school kid' on a mischievous dare. 'I hope you have enough money, because I'm very hungry.'[6] They took a cab to the celebrated nightspot Fouquet's, and Capa ordered the best champagne. All eyes turned to their table as Bergman laughed merrily, obviously enjoying herself. Before Capa, giggling and knocking back flute after flute, was a pin-up with Allied soldiers, and the ultimate catch for a womanizer of his legendary prowess. But surely he didn't stand a chance?

Ingrid Bergman, thirty-one years old, was married to a handsome young Swedish dentist, Petter Lindstrom, and had a daughter, Pia. Having starred in the wildly popular *Casablanca* (1942), she won an Oscar for best actress in 1944 for her performance in *Gaslight*, and was the biggest female box-office draw of 1945. At the zenith of her career, she could choose – if she wanted to be unfaithful – any man she wanted. Capa did not yet know that her marriage was almost over: Lindstrom had become more of a manager than a true husband, and she was already thinking about divorce.

After Fouquet's, the group went to Maxim's for dinner. Again, heads turned. With their cash running low, Capa and Shaw took Bergman on to a small nightclub in Montmartre and danced the night away. Capa quickly discovered that the real Bergman was nothing like the pure, virginal image that had been so carefully constructed by Hollywood producer David Selznick. Indeed, in real life, she was far from being an innocent 'Swedish milkmaid'[7] – her Hollywood image. She drank copiously, told bawdy jokes and, it seemed, as Capa held her close on the dance floor, as if she wouldn't take much coaxing into bed.

When Capa and Shaw ran out of money, Bergman pulled out her purse and kept the booze flowing, and in the early hours, she and Capa ambled along the banks of the Seine. Unfortunately, she had to leave for a United Services Overseas (USO) show the next day: they parted, both hoping they would see each other again.

Bergman shared her first impressions of Capa with her publicity manager, Joe Steele: 'Capa is wonderful and crazy and has a beautiful mind.'[8] She had met Capa at his best, and in the most seductive of cities imaginable. 'From her first meeting with Capa,' writes Donald Spoto, Bergman's most recent biographer, 'Ingrid was desperately addicted to [Capa's] presence . . . he was the kind of man she had known only in movie scripts but who had now sprung magically to life.'[9] They had much in common. Both had collaborated with the construction of their personas: polishing one's legend was good for business. They shared modest European origins and had endured tragedy. And neither had cause to trust in lasting love.

In mid-July 1945, Bergman arrived with the USO tour in Bavaria, where the celebrated harmonica player Larry Adler joined the troupe of entertainers, which also included Martha Tilton and Jack Benny. While not conventionally handsome, Adler was a charismatic, brilliant musician with a wonderfully pithy sense of humour. Within days, Bergman was spending much of her time with him. '[He was] so romantic, so much fun to be with,' she wrote, 'and his simple but wonderful music wrapped you up in warmth.'[10]

Throughout her time in Europe, Bergman acted as a 'Kindernatur',[11] as her Aunt Mutti had called her – a natural child of the moment. Unsure whether she would ever see Capa again, she was soon sleeping with Adler. 'Ingrid was stunningly beautiful,' he recalls. 'You could sit and look at her for hours. It was like looking at a great painting. She was also absolutely unconscious of her stardom.'*

While Bergman pursued her affair with Adler, Capa did his first post-war assignment for *Life*. It was perhaps the most tasteless story of his career. On 13 August 1945, readers opened the magazine to find several pictures of Aryan babies. Capa had visited a German chateau in Hohenhorst, *Life* explained, which housed a 'Nazi establishment known as a *Lebensborn*'. In the dormitory, Capa found dozens of illegitimate babies. '[These] Nazi bastards at Hohenhorst are children of SS men encouraged by Heinrich Himmler to father "super babies." Grown pig-fat under the care and overstuffing of Nazi nurses, they now pose for the Allies a problem yet to be solved.'†

From Hohenhorst, he went to Berlin to photograph the city's appalling devastation. Allied bombing had killed at least 800,000 German civilians by 1945, with Berlin the most frequent target: 95 per cent of the city's centre had been destroyed, and in the rest of Berlin only one

* 'Why do people say to me I'm beautiful?' Bergman asked him early in their affair. 'In Stockholm, everybody looks like me.'

'I've played Stockholm,' he replied. 'Nobody looks like you.'

Adler says that unlike many of the actresses recruited to the USO tour, she genuinely cared about the ordinary fighting men. 'She would wander among the soldiers and take their names after shows and then call their parents back in the States,' recalls Adler. 'She refused to eat with the officers. She always ate with the enlisted men. She never acted like a star.'

† One of Capa's nine pictures, spread over a full page, showed babies eating from large bowls of porridge. The caption read: 'The Hohenhorst bastards of Himmler's men are blue-eyed, flaxen-haired and pig-fat. They must eat porridge whether they want to or not.'

house in four was habitable.* He soon discovered that he had arrived in Berlin at the same time as Adler and Bergman with the USO tour; Bergman was delighted when he made contact, but did not tell him that she was already seeing Adler.

'Ingrid juggled Capa and me around,' Adler says. 'I remember the three of us had dinner one night, and things got uncomfortable, so I left. And then Ingrid came to my room later to apologize. She didn't know which of us she wanted, and neither of us knew which one of us she really wanted. But it didn't make Capa and I mad at each other – not at all. We remained good friends.'

On several occasions, Bergman accompanied Capa through the streets of Berlin, disguised in a *Casablanca*-style raincoat and head-scarf. She may even have been with him when he photographed a massive black market in the Tiergarten. American-style capitalism had already taken deep root amid the ruins of the Third Reich: Berliners bartered with 'wide-eyed' Red Army soldiers desperate for trinkets of Western decadence – Mickey Mouse watches that cost $3.95 in the States now sold for up to $500 each. Capa photographed a Russian officer completing a deal for a bottle of wine, another testing out an accordion, and a bloody-nosed man being led away from the vast open-air black market after being arrested for carrying a gun and not showing papers.

Bergman was deeply shocked by Berlin's devastation. It was hard to believe how little remained of the city she remembered. In the late Thirties she had worked for the Nazi film studio UFA, starring in *The Four Companions*, and had spent several months in Berlin, seemingly oblivious to the political repression around her. In her memoirs, she understandably played down her work for Goebbels' propaganda studio. There is no reason to believe she mentioned it to Capa either. '[Bergman] would never discuss the picture she made in Germany with me,' says Adler, who remained a close friend until she died of cancer in London in 1982. 'I think she was rather ashamed of it.'

One afternoon Capa spotted a bathtub lying in the skeleton of a

* Capa's pictures of Berlin, showing what war had cost Germany's civilian population, did not appear in *Life* magazine.

house. What a scoop! Imagine! Ingrid Bergman photographed in the bathtub for the first time! He snapped away but in his haste to develop the shots the film was ruined. However, the moment was not lost. Another photographer, Carl Goodwin, happened to be with them that afternoon. His picture shows Bergman in her headscarf and raincoat disguise looking joyously carefree.

After ten days in Berlin, Adler left to rejoin his family in America, and Capa and Bergman returned to Paris. For several weeks they were inseparable. They sipped champagne again at Fouquet's, toured Notre Dame, and one night were seen holding hands in a corner of the Ritz bar, obviously infatuated with each other. It was in Paris, Bergman later wrote, that she fell in love with him.* Over several weeks, she got under the skin of a man who dreamed in 'dangerous pictures'[12] and was haunted by images of death, and particularly by the words of the pilot who had accused him of being a heartless vulture at Chelveston airfield back in 1942. 'The scar that insult left on Capa's self-esteem remained with him for the rest of his life.'[13]

Bergman also quickly realized that Capa had a 'gambler's sense of priorities', a polite way of saying he'd drop anything and anyone for a flutter on the horses at Longchamps or a big-pot poker game in the photographers' locker room at *Life*'s Paris office. 'He was intensely aware that he had but one short life to live,' she stressed, 'and that he should not leak it away conforming to a set of standards which did not amuse him.'[14] Profligate, passionate, impulsive, Capa brought an immense vitality to Bergman's life, energizing her and inspiring her to be less concerned about the future and more inclined to focus on enjoying the moment.

* Capa may have wondered why she had fallen so hard for him. If he had looked in one of her precious scrapbooks, he would have discovered one powerful reason. He looked very similar to her deceased father, Justus Bergman, a Bohemian, spendthrift studio photographer, who died when she was just thirteen, ten years after the death of her mother. Bergman often said that her father had been her 'best friend' throughout childhood. He had taken away her fear of the camera, photographed her in silly costumes and poses and even filmed her, aged three, placing flowers on her mother's grave. It had been her first starring role.

On 14 August, five days after the bombing of Nagasaki, Paris celebrated V-J Day – victory over Japan. Bergman was with Capa in a jeep as he photographed an ecstatic crowd on the Champs-Elysées. She had seen newsreels of liberation celebrations at premieres, including scenes of women embracing and kissing Allied troops, and told Capa: 'I'm going to throw myself at somebody and kiss him.'

'Which one?'

'Him – over there.'

She jumped out of the jeep, threw herself at a soldier and kissed him on the mouth. The amazed GI kissed her right back.[15]

As autumn approached, Bergman talked of divorcing Petter. Capa told her not to do anything rash on his account. He wasn't sure what lay in store for him. He was, after all, an unemployed war photographer, and he needed to work out what he would do with his life. He was as smitten with Bergman as she was with him. But now, as with Pinky, he had to confront once again what, since Gerda's death, he feared most – true intimacy with a woman. Would falling in love end once more in rejection, as it had with Gerda and then Pinky?

Was it worth the gamble? He had famously quipped: 'If your pictures aren't good enough, you're not close enough.'[16] But with women, getting too close could hurt him one hell of a lot more than the 'million-dollar wound' GIs had joked about in the war – an injury severe enough to warrant return to the US.

Used to men falling at her feet, Bergman was upset by Capa's rather blithe reaction. Later describing herself as part Bohemian, part prude, she had traditional expectations of where love between two adults should lead: marriage and a family. Yet she refused to give up hope of Capa becoming what she now wanted – the next Mr Ingrid Bergman. Why not come to Hollywood? He could direct, write up his stories. Irwin Shaw was there, as were many of the writers he had met during the war. Capa finally promised to consider her invitation, recalling his interest in perhaps going into film in the Thirties when he had struggled to make a living as a freelance photographer. Besides, if he stopped covering wars, he would need a new challenge.

In early September, Bergman returned to Beverly Hills via New

York. She would, she told Capa before leaving, be returning to a gilded cage where she would have to pretend she was eighteen.* He vowed to see her again, perhaps in Hollywood. But he would have to see how being a photographer in peacetime worked out before deciding to try his luck there.

On 7 September, Capa was back in Berlin on assignment for *Life* to cover the first Rosh Hashanah (Jewish New Year) services held in the city's synagogues since 1938. One of his pictures shows a young private, Werner Nathan, with a prayer shawl over his US Army uniform, reading from a sacred scroll. Among the other 500 worshippers were Russian soldiers who prayed with a few dozen surviving Jews.†

'We are still in the dark,' said an assistant rabbi whose mentor had been killed by the Nazis. 'We are between two doors. We have opened and passed through only one. I ask God where we shall go from here . . .' When the service ended, Capa watched as an American soldier covered up the sacred Torah scrolls, hidden throughout the war for protection.[17]

While Capa photographed Europe waking from the Nazi nightmare, Bergman prepared for her next film project, wondering whether her lover would follow her to America. In late 1945, still pining after him, she met Ben Hecht, the screenwriter, and Alfred Hitchcock for a

* Her family life resumed its dull normality at 1220 Benedict Canyon, a chiselled stone and redwood one-storey house off Sunset Boulevard, with its enormous vaulted living-dining room which Bergman called 'the barn'. Bergman and Petter Lindstrom exchanged small talk over cups of coffee each morning. Then he left for work in a local hospital and Ingrid killed time reading scripts, sometimes obsessively cleaning the house and filling precious scrapbooks. To keep up appearances, the Bergmans ventured to the odd premiere or a party where briefly they might be seen on the dance floor. Petter was an elegant dancer, but not the ideal partner: he sweated easily and often had to change shirts midway through the evening. Ingrid, he later claimed, was too self-conscious to be a good dancer: 'She always had to look to see if others were watching.' (Details on domestic life are drawn primarily from Spoto and Leamer. See the bibliography for other sources on Hollywood and Bergman's career.)

† Well over half of the German Jewish population – around 308,000 in 1939 – had died in the 'Final Solution'.

story conference.[18] The shooting of *Notorious*, her next film, was about to begin.* After a couple of meetings, Ingrid and Hitchcock met for drinks one evening in his office. As they sat alone, sipping strong cocktails, she told him about Capa: that she desperately hoped he would come to Hollywood and make a new career. She was madly in love with him. But it seemed that he had already forgotten about her. Hitchcock reminded her of a speech in *Spellbound*, the last film they had made together. 'It is very sad to love and lose somebody,' Hitchcock said as Ingrid started to cry. 'But in a while you will forget and you will take up the threads of your life where you left off not long ago. And you will work hard. There is lots of happiness in working hard – maybe the most.'[19]

*According to Larry Adler, Bergman later complained that Hitchcock made repeated advances, which she diplomatically rejected, but which made filming a tense, frustrating experience. 'She told me that making pictures with Hitchcock was a horror, because he kept coming into her dressing room to try to make a pass. She always refused. She was a pretty tough girl – she never gave in to the status of the man making the pass.'

17 The End of the Affair

'The biggest piece of shit I ever stepped in.'

Robert Capa on Hollywood[1]

By late 1945, Capa had decided to try out Hollywood, as Bergman had urged. But he took his time getting there. He arrived in New York in October, and while Bergman pined he played poker, boasted about their affair to friends, and then finally, a few days before Christmas, checked into a bungalow at the Garden of Allah in Hollywood.*

At first, Capa and Bergman saw little of each other. *Notorious* consumed her every waking hour. In the meantime, he caught up with old acquaintances. While photographing Hemingway and Gellhorn in Idaho, he had met Gary Cooper and the director Howard Hawks and his ultra-elegant wife, Slim. Then there was his old poker gang from London: Stevens, Reis and Saroyan, as well as the screenwriter Peter Viertel. Eventually, Bergman wangled permission for him to visit the *Notorious* set at RKO. Mindful of the outcry if their affair went public, Hitchcock introduced the lovers as if they had never met. Unlike Europe, there were prying eyes everywhere: the tabloids would then, as now, pay well for salacious stories about the stars, and the gossip columnist Hedda Hopper, who could destroy a career with a whisper, had spies all over town. Because the Garden of Allah was monitored closely by reporters, Capa and Bergman met instead at Irwin Shaw's

*Among Capa's fellow guests at the hotel, notorious for its assignations between screen idols, were the actor Charles Laughton and the screenwriter Robert Benchley.

beach-house at 18 Malibu Road, where Larry Adler sometimes went to write.

In late January 1946, Capa took a job in production with William Goetz's company, International Pictures. Bergman was delighted: now he had a reason to stick around. But within weeks he was bored with the film industry and jaded with a social scene that was, as it is today, rigidly stratified according to the success of one's last picture. 'Capa couldn't take orders from anybody,' says Larry Adler, who shared his apartment in Beverly Hills with him for several weeks in early 1946. 'Had Bob really enlisted in the Hollywood game, he would have been very much under somebody's command. A producer would tell him what to do. A director would tell him what to do. Bob wouldn't have liked that.'

Unable to sit at a desk for more than a few minutes, Capa was soon spending his mornings playing tennis with Adler, afternoons sunbathing by the pool at the Hawkses' home, and weekends losing heavily on the horses at Santa Anita racetrack. Many a day was also whiled away with journalists and photographers such as Slim Aarons, who drank in an English pub, the Cock and Bull, across the road from *Time-Life*'s offices on Sunset Boulevard.

'We just used to sit in the bar and fool around with girls,' recalls Aarons, who soon nicknamed Capa 'Bob Caponey'. 'I also ran into him one time at a party with Howard Hughes and all of those big guys. He'd hang out playing cards with the rich boys, the big players, these producers who had a lot of money. When he didn't gamble with his life, he gambled with cards. He had to have the risk. You see, once the war was over, his charge was gone, and he needed excitement. He must have lost heavily a few times because he was always trying to borrow money from me.'

As with his father, gambling was often now the focus of Capa's life. But he'd chosen the wrong town in which to play for high stakes. Betting against the likes of Howard Hawks, card-sharp Humphrey Bogart, and the directors John Huston and Anatole Litvak was as potentially dangerous as parachuting out of a plane over the Rhine. Huston in particular was a notorious high-roller, who liked nothing more than staking a city of chips on the turn of a single card. 'I got into one of the big games one time,' says Slim Aarons. 'Capa might even have been in the same game because he was in town at the time. I remember being very lucky to get out of it. I never gambled again.'

By March, during trysts in Malibu, Capa was complaining about Bergman's indentured life in Hollywood. She was simply a meal ticket to Petter, and nothing but box-office gold to Selznick. 'Don't listen to your husband, Joe Steele, or anyone else who treats you like a schoolgirl,' he scolded. All she did was 'work, work, work'. She sacrificed far too much for her damned career, and he saw no point in doing so if it didn't make her any happier. 'You're mad. You have become an industry, an institution. You must return to the status of human being. You don't take the things you should out of life because you've got no time for living.'

'I am fulfilling myself,' she countered. 'And I'm going to make more films in Hollywood, and go back to the theater to do more plays.'[2]

Capa told Joe Steele angrily one day that Bergman was afraid to become her own person. She was still a child, avoiding maturity by escaping into celluloid fantasies.* 'For a grown woman, she's so naïve it hurts. She's afraid to let go. Scared to bust out of that goddam built-in conformity. Safeness and security – that's what motivates her. She hasn't the vaguest notion of what the world's about. It's a stinking shame.'[3]

Unable to see Bergman freely, and disillusioned by the reality of the film business, Capa was soon complaining that he and Los Angeles were not meant to be together. The city was the antithesis of a European capital such as Paris. It was difficult and expensive to take cabs, and so he was forced to drive, which he hated. During his stay in Hollywood he had several minor car collisions and near misses – rarely did he get behind the wheel sober, and Slim Aarons recalls that staff at

*Revealingly, Ingrid identified very much with the protagonist in her favourite book, Marcia Davenport's *Of Lena Geyer* (New York: Grosset and Dunlap, 1936). Lena is a poor Bohemian girl who becomes a world-famous opera singer. 'This isn't a question of career or money or anything,' she says at one point. 'It's my life, it's art, the one thing I've given up everything on earth for.'

the *Life* office in Los Angeles were worried that sooner or later he would kill himself. He and other Lifers also waited for the day when the car, which he never parked correctly, would roll down the hill outside the office and kill a pedestrian.

By May 1946, Capa had had his fill of Tinseltown. When Bergman told him she was going to New York for a break after *Notorious* wrapped, he packed his bags. In Manhattan, they decided that if they were to continue to see each other, they should stop hiding from the press. One night, they took a visible centre table at the swank Sheridan's Square nightclub. The gamble paid off. Reporters in shadowy corners assumed that they must be friends. Why be seen so publicly if they had something to hide?

Bergman also did her best to shake off her handler, Joe Steele, asking staff at the Drake Hotel to put her calls through directly to her. Steele soon guessed why. When he confronted her, asking if she had a date with Capa, she angrily denied his charges. The next day she slipped her schedule under Steele's door. She planned to have a drink with Cary Grant, go to the bathroom, and change for dinner. Then she would have 'Dinner (not with Cary)' and lastly, 'Home?'[4]

Night after night, Bergman and Capa were seen around Manhattan: smooching in smoky corners of Greenwich Village jazz bars, in the back row at art-house cinemas and strolling up Fifth Avenue at dawn after a boozy night on the town. Capa even took her to meet his mother, who duly made a wonderfully embroidered dress for her son's ultimate trophy girlfriend. 'Addicted to the attention and energy of a star's life,' her biographer Laurence Leamer has written, Bergman 'lived ever more on the edge, gambling with her saintly image, gambling with what was left of her marriage, gambling with personal scandal.'[5]

Steele's fears that Capa and Bergman's affair would become public knowledge seemed to be confirmed when the gossip columnist Sheila Graham reported rumours that the Bergmans' marriage was in trouble. Mercifully, Petter did not bring up the Graham story in one of his regular calls to Steele. Hoping this close shave would sober Bergman, Steele discovered the opposite: she believed they were meant to be together, precisely because their affair had not been exposed.

Steele tried to reason with her. Capa had a reputation as a penniless lothario. He boasted too loudly to his poker-playing buddies that he was balling Hollywood's ultimate 'babe'. He would never be the next Mr Ingrid Bergman. But she would not listen.

Steele was right. When she asked Capa about marriage, he shrugged and said he was not the 'marrying kind'.* She later wrote that if Capa had said 'come away with me, let's take our chance, hit the world, drink deep of the good red wine of life', she would probably have left Petter. And if he had said 'come marry me and be my love, and we will all the pleasures prove', she would have been at his side. But he said neither. Instead, he told her: 'I cannot tie myself down. If they say "Korea tomorrow" and we're married and we have a child, I won't be able to go to Korea. And that's impossible.'

One night, after several cocktails, Capa told her that if she wanted more than the here and now, she should look elsewhere. That was all he could ever provide, and if it was not enough, she should get on with her life.[6] But she could not bear to lose him, even if he refused to play the role she wanted. Throughout 1946, they continued their affair whenever they could find a free evening or weekend, Capa now becoming part-time husband/Svengali and Bergman his willing pupil. She started to read newspapers, peruse wine lists more closely, and take an interest in haute cuisine and European cinema. Most Hollywood films were overwrought pulp, Capa told her. If she wanted to be a true artist, she should collaborate with a decent director, someone like Roberto Rossellini.

One afternoon in New York, she saw *Roma, Città Aperta – Open City* – Rossellini's masterpiece, incorporating the kind of gritty documentary that had featured in many serious European films since the Twenties. She was mesmerized, too moved even to speak as she left the cinema. 'I'd rather be remembered for one great artistic film like this,' she told Capa, 'than any of my money making hits. Why can't

*Like Grace Kelly's character in Hitchcock's *Rear Window*, Bergman urged Capa to trade photojournalism for work as a studio photographer. In the film, James Stewart's character angrily scoffed at the idea. Hitchcock based Stewart's character largely on his knowledge of Capa and other veterans like Slim Aarons.

Roberto Rossellini come to Hollywood and make a movie like that with someone like me?'[7] Capa warned her that she should be careful not to confuse the nature of the artist with his work. But his advice fell on deaf ears.

In August 1946, he followed her back to Hollywood for the filming of her next movie, *Arch of Triumph*, based on Erich Maria Remarque's powerful novel of espionage and betrayal set in late-Thirties Paris.* Bergman asked the director, Lewis Milestone, if Capa could take pictures of the film actually being shot. Milestone was delighted to have the famous war photographer on his set, and was just as obsessed with Bergman as Hitchcock had been. Each evening, when the arc lights blacked out, Capa joined Bergman and her co-star Charles Boyer for cocktails in his office. To Bergman's dismay, he often got drunk to the point of embarrassment. He could hold his booze with remarkable élan in a war, when it served as painkiller and fuel. But by 1946, there was no life-or-death situation to distract him from the bottle. He took his first shot from a hip-flask well before lunch.

She quickly tired of Capa's morning testiness before he had restored his equilibrium over a long liquid lunch at Romanoff's or some other celebrity-studded restaurant – 'Drink had become something of a machismo challenge as well as an anodyne'[8] – and as filming continued their affair cooled. Irwin Shaw's home in Malibu was no longer a convenient place to rendezvous, given her even more frantic work schedule, and she did not want to risk being seen at the Garden of Allah. Capa's life, she realized, had become a depressing tedium, interrupted by adrenaline highs and drunken gambling. Peace bored him. But playing the 'impulsive Don Juan' didn't appear to satisfy him either.[9]

After more than a decade of war, Capa had started to exhibit many of the symptoms of post-traumatic stress disorder: restlessness, heavy drinking, irritability, depression, survivor's guilt, lack of direction and barely concealed nihilism. He had admitted early on in their relation-

*Bergman had enjoyed herself so much in New York that she arrived on the set twenty pounds overweight. The film's producer, Davis Lewis, claimed he asked Lindstrom 'to put a lock on the refrigerator at home'. (Leamer, *As Time Goes By*.)

ship that his dreams were haunted by death. Now she knew he had been telling the truth. She had finally seen behind his eternally 'debonair'[10] mask: as much a psychic shield as it was a necessary prop for a man who needed to pretend to be someone else to escape the emotional damage wreaked by war.

'Remaining debonair means', Irwin Shaw later explained, 'that one must always be ready to go to the next bar or the next war, no matter how late the hour or how unattractive the war. It means that a man must always sit through every poker pot and every hand; must lose six months' salary and buy the next round of drinks, lend thoughtlessly and borrow ceremoniously [and] consort only with very pretty women, preferably those who are mentioned in the newspapers.'[11]

Arch of Triumph was a gloomy failure at the box office. But Bergman did have some powerful scenes and, as *Illustrated* magazine proudly declared during the filming, it was innovative: 'Capa shot these pictures as movie cameras were turning. They are believed to be the first time stills have been taken during action.'[12] As with *Notorious*, there were plenty of parallels between the narrative and reality. Capa was present, in fact, for a scene in which Boyer, playing Dr Ravic, a Romanian-Italian cabaret singer, refuses to marry Bergman. 'I waited,' she said. 'WAITED. You never came . . .'[13]

While shooting Bergman at her most ethereal – his portraits were lovingly composed – Capa found time to appear before the camera himself. He had often joked that he should have been an actor. When not on the *Arch of Triumph* set, Capa got dressed up as an Egyptian servant in *Temptation*, directed by Irving Pichel.[14] Before *Temptation* wrapped, however, he left Hollywood for the last time, following Bergman once again to New York where she began rehearsals for her first Broadway role, as Joan of Arc. They saw each other several times but both knew the affair was doomed. He would not settle down and marry – domestication was worse than death, it seemed – and she would not jeopardize her career to be with a man who would not make the appropriate, face-saving commitment.

'I know the Hungarian influence,' she wrote to a friend. 'I'll always be grateful for it . . . I feel it has changed much in me . . . But [he] knows we are closing the chapter. It is a bad thing when all other things around him are bad too. But then you can't choose your time. We are drinking our last bottles of champagne. I am tearing a very dear piece away from my life, but we are both learning and also making a clean operation so that both patients will live happily ever after.'[15]

By the time *Joan of Arc* premiered in Washington, Capa had returned to Paris. Several weeks later, he wrote that he missed her terribly. He had bought a typewriter and a house. One was small, the other a little larger – ten miles from Paris, deep in a forest. Friends at the Ritz had been asking after her. He asked her to write to him, and hoped she would be faithful. He wanted her to keep a bottle of champagne chilled for the next time they saw each other. Again, he warned her about committing to more films and further imprisoning herself in Hollywood, becoming less human with every premiere. In his eyes, success was worse than failure. He knew the real Ingrid, a maid from Tinseltown whose heart belonged to Sweden. He ended the letter by telling her how much he was in love with her.[16]

Bergman's opening night on Broadway was a huge success, but after several standing ovations she fled to a bathroom, where she sat and cried from nervous exhaustion, suddenly feeling very much alone. The next day, among the stacks of congratulatory telegrams in her dressing room was one from Petter, who'd returned to Los Angeles: 'You made me cry.'[17] Day after day, the reviewers raved. Among bulging sacks of fan mail, she found letters from a lovesick Capa. Work had stolen her from him. He had met very few women who could make him laugh so hard, who made him enjoy life in the moment. He begged her not to fade from his life, for he had very little in his life now that he valued. Europe seemed very quiet and lonely without her. When he walked the streets, he felt her absence everywhere.

Capa kept moving, but he no longer found much solace in his nomadic lifestyle. As Martha Gellhorn wrote: 'He always had money to travel, never money to settle.'[18] That autumn, he flew to Istanbul where he directed a lacklustre documentary about Cold War tensions in the region. One Sunday afternoon he sat on the terrace of his hotel room overlooking the Bosphorus, but he was oblivious to the view.

Bergman filled his thoughts. The last time they'd been together, he'd told her he wanted to know how it would be to be far away from her, alone with his thoughts. Now he knew exactly how it was – he had begun to talk to himself.

He also wrote to her that the world was full of false values. People could no longer afford to fail. But being back on assignment reminded him of how living in the moment was what mattered. He had been trying to work out what had happened to him since meeting her. There was no decent champagne in Turkey. He was behaving himself. But he wondered about her. Was she seeing anyone? He wanted her to listen to his voices and to set herself free.

After finishing the documentary, Capa returned to Paris. He then went skiing in Megeve and finally flew back to New York. But Bergman had returned to Hollywood, so they arranged to see each other in Sun Valley, Idaho, after the Easter weekend. She would be at the ski resort there for several days with her husband. Nevertheless, they would find a way to see each other. In Sun Valley, they made love for the last time. Bergman then returned to her lodge to resume her hardest role – the faithful, joyous *Hausfrau*.[19]

Before leaving Sun Valley, Capa remained at the roulette and poker tables at the casino until he had lost $2,000 – his entire savings. The next morning, Bergman found him sleepless and hung over. 'What difference does it make?' he told her. 'It's very good for me. Now I have to work harder.'[20]

Around the same time, he ran into Petter Lindstrom on Sun Valley's slopes. According to Petter, Capa offered him some skiing tips. He was offended – he was an expert skier, far more proficient than Capa. Then Capa told him he thought Ingrid needed a vacation: she'd seemed pale and tired the last time he'd seen her in New York. Petter suspected him at last, and when he confronted Ingrid she admitted the affair but swore that it was over. She would lose everything if he sued for adultery: the scandal would ruin her career, as well as allow him to gain custody of Pia.

According to several accounts, Bergman and Capa ended their affair in Sun Valley on friendly terms. Bergman had listened to Capa's voices, and had tried to follow his advice. But she wasn't willing to give up everything to be with the man she later claimed she had 'come to love so much'. She would, however, always be deeply grateful to him for showing her that there was life outside Hollywood, and for opening her eyes to the possibility of working in Europe again. By contrast, she later claimed that Petter's only words of encouragement in their twelve years together were 'not bad'.[21]

18 Back in the USSR

> 'There is a war within the boundaries of the USSR . . . a war not for life, but unto death. You did not notice it however, although it can be clearly seen.'
>
> YURIY SHEREKH,
> 'What Did You Not Want to See, Mr. Steinbeck?'[1]

Not long after his affair with Bergman fizzled out, Capa met John Steinbeck in the bar of the Hotel Bedford in New York. Steinbeck's first marriage was failing. His career was in a slump, and he had hit the bottle with a vengeance. Capa sat down at the bar and they started to commiserate with each other. Steinbeck couldn't help cracking a smile when Capa, whom Steinbeck's second wife Elaine would call 'one of the most charming men in the world',[2] told him he was also depressed: a big poker game he'd been trying to arrange for weeks had fallen through.

Late into the evening they told jokes and war stories, compared each other's recent poker form (when Capa was in New York they often played together on Friday nights), and cheered each other up over bright green Suissesse cocktails, the speciality of Willy the bartender. Finally, the discussion got round to how unhappy they were with the way foreign affairs were being reported, especially coverage of the Eastern Bloc following Churchill's famous 1946 speech in Fulton, Missouri before President Truman in which he had praised 'the heroic Russian people and my war comrade Marshal Stalin', but then warned of a 'Red Threat': 'From Stettin in the Baltic to Trieste in the Adriatic, an iron curtain has descended across the Continent.'

As the first icy winds of the Cold War were sweeping through Washington and Moscow, Steinbeck and Capa decided to attempt a report on the ordinary Russian people – to make, in Capa's prophetic words, 'an old-fashioned Don Quixote and Sancho Panza quest – to ride behind the "iron curtain" and pit our lances and pens against the windmills of today'.[3] To be titled *A Russian Journal*, it would be a book on the real Russia, not a dry, political analysis of the country. Friends told them they didn't have a hope in hell of being allowed to tour the USSR at such a sensitive time.

Undeterred, Steinbeck visited the Soviet Consulate in New York, and to his delight his idea was greeted with enthusiasm. The author of *The Grapes of Wrath* (1939) and *Of Mice and Men* (1937) was the most famous living writer of proletarian fiction on the planet, and a safe enough bet in the Soviets' eyes.* His plan to focus on ordinary people, basing most of the book on a tour organized by Stalinist apparatchiks, was an opportunity for the Soviets to present the Soviet Union as a harmonious, industrious, highly productive nation.

'But why do you have to take a cameraman?' asked the Consul General. 'We have lots of cameramen in the Soviet Union.'

'But you have no Capas,' replied Steinbeck. 'If the thing is to be done at all, it must be done as a whole, as a collaboration.'[4]

His insistence paid off. The Soviets agreed to admit Capa. He had tried to get a visa to the Soviet Union in the Thirties and been denied, but now, thanks to Steinbeck's celebrity, he had the opportunity to photograph a country fast being demonized in the Western press.

Knowing Capa's camera could provide the most damaging evidence that all was not well in Stalin's empire, the Soviets began to make

*Steinbeck had visited Moscow in the summer of 1937, at the height of Stalin's purges when around five million people were executed or sent to work camps. He had not said a word against Stalin's regime. As he told a Soviet spy during his visit to the USSR: 'I was totally aware of what was going on and came to no false conclusions.' (CSA) Now Stalin was busy expanding a brutal network of gulags which in the late 1940s housed an estimated six million new undesirables. In Moscow, and among reporters familiar with the Soviet Union, Stalin's brutal repression was an open secret.

careful plans to thwart him.* The Deputy Chairman of UOKS (The Ukrainian Society for Cultural Relations) wrote in a secret report to his staff, who would conduct Steinbeck and Capa around the Ukraine, 'Capa, the photographer accompanying [Steinbeck], also needs to be watched to prevent him from taking pictures of what he shouldn't.'[5]

Days before they were due to leave for the Soviet Union, Steinbeck fell from a balcony in his New York apartment and broke his kneecap. The trip had to be postponed for several weeks. While he recuperated, Capa used the time to finally set up the agency he'd mentioned to George Rodger in Italy in 1943 and to Pierre Gassmann in 1945, and first imagined in the Thirties.

Since 1945, Capa had been active in the American Society of Magazine Photographers. He had eloquently argued that freelancers needed to push hard for some measure of protection from exploitative corporations such as *Life*, which had not only spoilt his most important story but then tried to cover up its responsibility by blaming Capa himself. Photographers also needed to gain as much control as feasible over the context of their work: in every article bearing his pictures for *Life*, his work had been captioned to support Henry Luce's worldview.† Last and most crucial, it was imperative that photographers gain copyright on pictures that could have immense future value, such as his shots of D-Day.

Capa wanted to own his work in perpetuity as well as to fundamentally redress the power imbalance between magazines and photographers. 'Why be exploited by others?' he told Gisèle Freund. 'Let's exploit ourselves.'[6] After contacting George Rodger, Chim and several other photographers, as well as his old boss at Alliance, Maria Eisner,

* Cameras profoundly unnerved the Soviets, who believed that Westerners more often than not used them for 'spy mapping'. As Steinbeck noted in *A Russian Journal*, the camera was a 'feared instrument', and 'a person with a camera is suspected and watched wherever he goes'.

† To this day, Magnum insists that the captions on its photographers' pictures should not be amended. It is a matter of some controversy as to whether this happens in practice. Often, single images are captioned to fit space and a particular report, and, of course, images used in newspapers with strong political views often take on a different significance to that intended by the photographer.

who had escaped the Nazis and made her way to America during the war, he held a special lunch to outline plans for a photographic agency run by photographers themselves. It took place in mid-April 1947, with champagne on hand, on the second floor of the Museum of Modern Art in New York.[7]

Those present included the American *Life* photographer Bill Vandivert and his wife, Rita, the elegant Maria Eisner, and David 'Chim' Seymour. The gathering, Capa announced, marked the formal birth of his brainchild – a 'cooperative' to be named Magnum. According to Pierre Gassmann, the agency's name arose spontaneously from an earlier meeting in Paris at which a magnum of champagne was uncorked and somebody shouted out: 'Magnum!' Its founder members would also include George Rodger and Henri Cartier-Bresson, who subsequently agreed to the broad strategy discussed over several glasses of champagne at MOMA. Chim would cover Europe, Cartier-Bresson would rove around India and the Far East, Rodger would concentrate on his beloved Africa and the Middle East and Vandivert would operate in the US. Capa would go where he pleased.

Each founder member was to provide $400 in start-up fees. The agency would take 40 per cent of the fees from assignments set up for photographer-members, 30 per cent of the fees from assignments the photographers found themselves, and 50 per cent of resales. The Vandiverts would run the New York office at 8th Street in the Greenwich Village, with Rita receiving $8,000 a year as the bureau's manager. Maria Eisner would run the Paris office from her home at 125 Rue du Faubourg-St-Honoré, and receive $4,000.[8]

There had been plenty of other organizations aimed at furthering the work of socially aware photographers.* What raised eyebrows in

*Capa was involved with the New York based Photo League in the early Forties. A loosely organized group of photographers, the League was designed to further left-leaning reportage, but did not operate as a business, rather a network of like-minded radical photographers. Capa spoke at meetings in February 1940 and April 1942 about his work in China, Spain and war photography in general, but, sadly, transcripts do not survive. In December 1947 the Photo League was declared subversive and placed on the infamous United States Department of Justice 'blacklist'. It dissolved in summer 1951, yet another victim of anti-communist hysteria during the Cold War.

editorial offices in New York, Paris and London was Magnum's bold pledge to retain ownership of its members' copyright and negatives – nothing short of a revolution in the way photographers dealt with major magazines such as *Life*.[9] The French photographer Romeo Martinez knew Capa and his fellow founders. 'Capa's idea – specifically, that the journalist is nothing if he doesn't own his negatives – will prove to be the sanest idea in the history of photojournalism,' he wrote in 1997. 'The co-op is the best formula for retaining those rights, and for ensuring the freedom of action of each of its members.'[10]

From the start, Capa was concerned that the agency might be labelled as the work of a group of dilettantes. To stand a chance, Magnum would need to perform like any other agency, however great its claim to sophistication and élan. In other words, it would have to provide commercial content: mainstream picture essays. Of all the founder members, only Cartier-Bresson could afford to ignore such practical constraints, and Capa didn't want his surrealist aesthetic to come to define Magnum in the eyes of workaday editors with money. 'Watch out for labels,' Capa had already warned him.* 'They're reassuring but somebody's going to stick one on you that you'll never get rid of – "the little surrealist photographer." You'll be lost – you'll get precious and mannered. Take instead the label of "photojournalist" and keep the other thing for yourself, in your heart of hearts.'†[11]

Pierre Gassmann recalls the early days of Magnum with particular fondness, for they marked the beginning of his association with the agency as its exclusive printer. To this day, he remains an honorary board member of Magnum. He also stresses that without Chim's influence, Magnum would have remained a fantasy. It was only when

*Capa had no need to worry. Cartier-Bresson distinguished himself as a world-class journalist in the following decades. In a rare appearance in 2000 on an American talk show, he grimaced at suggestions that he is one of the twentieth century's great artists, and repeated his frequent description of Capa as an instinctual picture-taker, one of photography's great adventurers.

†Cartier-Bresson sent me a fax in 1999 explaining that he had no interesting anecdotes to add to the ones he'd already repeated many times. Graciously, however, he sent me the poem that appears at the front of this book.

Chim agreed to Capa's plan to set up Magnum that the other fellow founders fell into line. And it was Chim who assessed risks more soberly and kept Magnum on course in its early years while Capa busied himself as its charismatic front man, charming editors and developing post-war contacts wherever he saw a possible revenue source.[12]

The agency's first important client was John Morris, who had left *Life* to be a picture editor of the *Ladies' Home Journal*: two-thirds of the $15,294 Magnum earned in its first five months derived from his patronage. Morris also developed with Capa an idea for a comparative reportage on families around the world, 'People are People', and convinced *Ladies' Home Journal* to back it. The *Journal* agreed a budget of $15,000. Chim would photograph a family in France and Germany, Rodger would cover families in Africa, Egypt and Pakistan and Capa would take portraits in the Soviet Union during his trip with Steinbeck.

Capa and Steinbeck finally arrived in Moscow on 31 July 1947. It was a unique opportunity. Surely if any photographer could slip his lens under the Iron Curtain, it was him. To this end, he took an enormous amount of equipment: several different cameras, hundreds of cartons of film and so much lighting equipment that he had to pay $300 in overweight baggage charges.

At the airport in Moscow, Capa quickly made sure that he had his ten pieces of luggage. He then had it locked in a room while he and Steinbeck waited to be picked up, telling several airport officials that they should guard it with their lives. 'Normally lighthearted and gay,' Steinbeck noted, 'Capa becomes a tyrant and a worrier where his cameras are concerned.'[13]

The officials had to guard it for far longer than Capa had expected. The two journalists were not greeted at the airport, as had been arranged, by the *Herald Tribune*'s Moscow correspondent, Ed Gilmore. It turned out that he was out of town on assignment, so Capa and Steinbeck found themselves stranded with no money – and no taxis to hire even if they'd had the requisite roubles.

A sympathetic French courier eventually drove them into Moscow.

The Metropole and Savoy Hotels, the only hotels assigned for foreigners, were fully booked. Finally, they got hold of a key to Gilmore's apartment where, in frustration, they polished off his whisky supply over several hands of gin rummy. Their spirits rose when the next day the Russian information agency handling their trip found them a suite at the Savoy with a huge bath for Capa's ritual soak each morning, but in the bar, other correspondents warned them that leaving the Moscow area would lead to greater frustrations than merely trying to find a bed for the night.

On his last trip, ten years before, Steinbeck had visited a shambolic capital. It was now far cleaner, and studded with new buildings and monuments to Stalin, but the people were grey and sombre. Indeed, they were exhausted, bone-weary from war, forced collectivization and the rigours of Stalinism. The women went without make-up, a bourgeois luxury, and most people's clothing was cheap and tawdry. Many men still wore their old military uniforms, the only clothes they had.*

While they waited for permission to leave Moscow, Steinbeck quickly got to know a different Capa from the charming figure he'd encountered in various bars and press camps. 'It was here that I discovered an unpleasant quality in Capa's nature, and I think it only right to set it down in case some young woman should ever listen to any suggestion of matrimony from him. He is a bathroom hog, and a very curious one.'[14] Sadly, he noted with some irony, Capa's ritual

*Steinbeck did not mention in *A Russian Journal* that in November 1946 many Jewish intellectuals in Moscow had been put under suspicion by Stalin and banned from the Soviet Writers' Group, with whom Steinbeck himself enjoyed an evening of self-congratulation. Several of those Jews soon died in the gulags where many of the Soviet Union's best scientists were slaving away to produce the country's first atomic bomb.

Nor did Steinbeck mention in his report about the lives of ordinary Soviets that in August 1946, exactly a year before they arrived, Stalin had ordered Yuri Zhdanov to launch a massive ideological campaign against Western cultural influence. Was Steinbeck unaware of these developments? Perhaps – this was a man who supported Elia Kazan during the McCarthy witch-hunt and throughout his life made political gaffe after political gaffe. In the Soviet Union, while talking to one spy, Steinbeck insisted that America had no class divisions. When the spy pointed out that Soviets knew about American social division from books like *The Grapes of Wrath*, Steinbeck 'blushed' but held firm and continued to deny the existence of 'antagonistic classes'. (CSA)

soaks ended because the rough, worn tub made his bottom bleed.

After almost a week in Moscow, Capa still had not been allowed to take pictures openly in the streets, and he pleaded with a Soviet press official for permission to photograph. The official promised to speed up the process. Capa drowned his frustrations at a party that left him feeling even more depressed about the prospects for the trip. Among his fellow guests were several sad-eyed Russian wives of foreign diplomats and journalists. Stalin would not allow these women to leave the country to join their husbands, even though Clement Attlee, Britain's Prime Minister, had requested they be given exit visas. If the Soviets could be so intransigent about such a simple humanitarian plea, what chance was there of being allowed to photograph what he wanted?

Capa finally received his permits and ventured on to the streets to photograph the preparations for Moscow's eight hundredth anniversary. But in every area he visited, policemen stopped him from taking pictures and demanded to see his papers over and over again. After a couple of days of this treatment, he was determined to leave Moscow as soon as possible. He hoped that far from the paranoia of the capital he would be free to be a photojournalist again. He had always found a way to circumvent red tape and get revealing pictures. He was confident that he could do so again, but that meant getting out in the field where he might be able to throw off his handlers, at least for a few hours.* Little did he know that plans had already been made to thwart any such attempt. A secret report by a UOKS operative in Kiev sums up what the Soviets had in mind: 'The task that the UOKS set for itself was to primarily show the visitors how the national economy and

*A close examination of Soviet archives in the Ukraine and Moscow reveals that Capa and Steinbeck were watched from the moment they arrived in the Soviet Union. They could not have known how cleverly their stay was being orchestrated towards propagandist purposes.

In order to see the Soviet Union, Capa and Steinbeck would have to visit every city by plane. They were told that roads were not yet repaired after the war. Even if they wanted to go just a few hundred miles from one city to another, they would have to do so via Moscow. Of course, this would allow agents to monitor their activities even further.

cultural valuables of the Ukrainian SSR were destroyed during the war and the great efforts of our people in restoration and reconstruction of the country.'[15]

By the time they left for their first destination – the Ukraine – Steinbeck and Capa's relationship was showing signs of strain. Capa had a nasty habit of stealing books, an unforgivable misdemeanour in Steinbeck's view. He pilfered anything he could get his hands on that was in English: *The Notebooks of Maxim Gorki*, a copy of *Vanity Fair*, and even a tattered report of the United States Department of Agriculture for 1927. From Ed Gilmore's shelves he took a new Ellery Queen mystery, a rare luxury in Moscow in 1947. Steinbeck wryly noted that he also stole women and cigarettes, but these crimes were far easier to forgive.

They finally arrived in Stalingrad at the height of a heatwave and were driven through mile after mile of ruins to a new 'Intourist' hotel at its centre. Their room overlooked the very square where Field Marshal von Paulus, the commander of Hitler's Sixth Army, had finally surrendered to the Red Army after the most epic siege of the Second World War.

Even after witnessing Berlin in 1945, Capa was shocked by the extent of the devastation. Fifteen per cent of the Ukraine's civilian population of 45 million in 1939 had been killed during the war and Stalingrad had lost tens of thousands. Not a building in the centre of the city was undamaged. Because Stalingrad was the great Soviet triumph of the war, Capa was allowed to photograph what he saw on the streets.*

He was pleased when he found a real story in the people still living like rats in warrens of tunnels and the cellars of their old homes. But then, to his bitter disappointment, he was barred from taking pictures of the famous tank factory where the Germans and Red Army had endured some of the bitterest fighting during the winter of 1942–43.†

*The Soviet victory had turned the tide decisively in favour of the Allies in 1943.

† During their time in the Ukraine, Capa and Steinbeck heard several gruesome stories about the siege of Stalingrad. One night, they sat listening to soft music and watching the Volga flow slowly below them. Their hosts talked of the unimaginable cold that had gripped the Ukraine during the winter of 1942, of how men had warmed their hands in the blood of dead comrades before they were able to fire at the fascists.

He and Steinbeck were given an official tour, but he was told he had to leave his cameras on the tour bus – a humiliating moment for a photojournalist of his reputation.

He seethed. To Steinbeck, who was not barred from taking notes, he appeared to be in mourning as they toured the factory where tractors were being forged from destroyed German Panzers. Everywhere, Capa saw wonderful images, 'contrasts, and angles, and pictures that had meaning beyond their meaning'. 'Here, with two pictures,' he told Steinbeck bitterly, 'I could have shown more than many thousands of words could say.'[16]

Ironically, there was a Soviet film crew in Stalingrad at the time, recreating the siege of the city for a propaganda film. But because of 'one accident or another', as Steinbeck put it, Capa was not even able to get shots of the film being made – yet another loss of a story with real commercial value in the West. He did, however, manage to photograph some of the remaining German prisoners. Still in uniform, they went through the streets guarded by a soldier, wretched survivors from the hundred thousand who had surrendered in 1944. Very few ever returned to their Fatherland.* In the shell of a chapel, Capa came across a woman lying on the ground in front of a damaged altar. He saw another woman, 'wild-eyed, half-crazed',[17] crossing herself again and again.†

Not long after this, judging by the dull nature of his pictures, it seems Capa decided to make the best of what remained of the 'vodka tour'[18] by treating it as precisely that – a junket to the Ukraine where at least the girls were as pretty as in Paris. '[Capa] felt that not only was this trip a failure,' wrote Steinbeck, 'but that everything was a failure, that he was a failure, that I was a failure. He brooded very deeply.'[19]

* Steinbeck observed that people looked away from the prisoners when they passed in the street. He did not say why. According to a contemporary writer, Soviet citizens were afraid of the 'slightest connection' with an alien. 'A person who has any connections with aliens in the USSR, outside the official rules and norms, disappears.' (Yuriy Sherekh, 'What Did You Not Want to See, Mr. Steinbeck?')

† The KGB made sure this image did not see publication, for it showed the reality of post-war Soviet Union – a country failing to recover from the loss of more than twenty million of its people.

The Deputy Chairman of UOKS in the Ukraine, a devious arch-Stalinist called Comrade Poltoratsky, reported:

> I was with Capa when he took all of his pictures. He had an opportunity to take pictures depicting beggars, queues, German prisoners of war, and secret sites (i.e. the construction of the gas pipe-line). He did not take photos of this kind and approached picture-taking without reporter imprudence. Of the photos which cannot be considered favorably, I can point to only two: in the Museum of Ukrainian Art, he took a picture of an emaciated woman-visitor, and on our way to the kolkhoz [collective farm], he took a picture of a kolkhoz family wearing shabby clothes . . . However, a close scrutiny of relations between Steinbeck and Capa also forces us to stipulate that Capa is more loyally and friendly disposed to us. Steinbeck in an underhand way gave Capa instructions to look for vulnerable, in his opinion, aspects of our life.

The Soviets had good reason to scrutinize Capa and Steinbeck as the pair continued the 'vodka tour' around the Ukraine: virtually the entire western part of the Soviet Union was engulfed in civil warfare.* Yet there was not the smallest hint of the Ukrainian people's bitter struggle against communism in *A Russian Journal*, either in Capa's pictures or in Steinbeck's words.

In 1948, the Ukrainian activist and writer Yuriy Sherekh wrote a blistering attack on Steinbeck, 'What Did You Not Want to See, Mr. Steinbeck?'. The piece appeared in the *Ukrainian Quarterly* in 1948 and has been perhaps conveniently overlooked by all Steinbeck's biographers.

'Just as you did not notice the utter weariness and despair of the Soviet man, so you did not notice the national repression in the USSR,' Sherekh wrote. 'You did not see the struggle of the Ukrainian and the Georgian nations for their liberation. You did not find out that even

*After the expulsion of German forces from western Ukraine, armed detachments of partisans had carried on the fight against the Soviet regime. Stalin had ordered his secret service chief Beria to finish off these 'outlaws in the shortest possible time', but it was not until 1950 that the most vigorous fighting ended in the area. (Dmitri Volkogonov, *Stalin, Triumph and Tragedy* (New York: Grove Weidenfeld, 1991).)

the Soviet press in Ukraine is full of articles against "Ukrainian nationalism" . . . There is a war within the boundaries of the USSR, a secret and masked war, a war not for life, but unto death. You did not notice it however, although it can be clearly seen.'

While Stalin's security forces murdered Ukrainian partisans fighting for independence, Capa and Steinbeck visited a 'Partisan Exhibit' in the Ukraine, where they watched a propaganda film, *People's Avengers*. Their UOKS guide noted in his diary:

> Capa became interested several times in the people who filmed those or other episodes, and gave an approving smile when the visiting operator filmed partisans as they posed for the camera. It was evident that Capa was inclined to believe especially this series of episodes. After *People's Avengers* was finished, the film *She is Fighting for her Motherland* immediately began, and both Capa and Steinbeck showed complete dissatisfaction, got bored, and began fidgeting. Then Capa said without any ceremony, 'I hope she will fight for her motherland very fast, because I'm starved to death.' Steinbeck gave a smile.[20]

As the weeks passed, Steinbeck and Capa succumbed to their hosts' lavish entertainment. According to a secret report from Comrade Poltoratsky, one night in a restaurant 'the last pieces of ice in Steinbeck's façade melted away . . . He was very animated, talkative.'[21] When they visited a circus, their handlers chose to introduce a friendly Ukrainian writer, a 'Comrade Korniychuk'. 'Steinbeck is plainly going to be "straight forward" to a large extent in his relations with Comrade Korniychuk,' reported Poltoratsky.*

As Comrade Korniychuk, a Soviet plant, regaled Steinbeck with folksy tales of proletarian life in Stalin's brave new society, Capa tucked

* Sherekh explains, Poltoratsky had 'on his conscience many a death and exile of the "true Ukrainian writer" . . . for this very reason he [Poltoratsky] was made a "Ukrainian writer", in order to give him the opportunity to spy on literary circles, with special instructions. This man, hated by all, was secretly called not Poltoratsky but Poltovratsky (from the Russian word "vrat" – which means to lie, tell a falsehood).'

Ironically, 'Poltovratsky' reported back to his bosses that Capa believed 'it preferable that evil should reveal itself rather than be concealed'.

into banquets now laid out wherever they went.* Before leaving the Ukraine, he wrote in the UOKS' 'Comments by Our Guests' book: 'Images of the Great Ukrainian people will arouse, I hope, in our people the same enthusiasm which made my stay so bright and fruitful.'

Their next stop was Georgia. After ten days, Capa and Steinbeck were exhausted from over-eating and drinking. Out of vanity, Capa refused to loosen his belt after each meal, priding himself on his thirty-two-inch waist. Stuffed and sun-tanned, Capa and Steinbeck returned to a surprisingly chilly Moscow in late August in time for the city's eight hundredth anniversary.

Banners and flags hung everywhere, like a scene from Orwell's *Nineteen Eighty-Four.* In the cavernous Dynamo Stadium, Capa photographed thousands of athletes. In a city-centre park devoted to captured German armaments, called Trophy Park, he watched Soviet families gather around Nazi aeroplanes and tanks. On the night of the eight hundredth anniversary, Capa joined more than a million people thronging Red Square and the surrounding streets. 'To the men in the Kremlin it was considerably more than fun and fireworks,' *Life* reported, reflecting Cold Warrior Luce's increasing paranoia about the spread of communism. 'Stalin in his anniversary speech made it clear that, no matter what the rest of the world thinks about the Russian example, he considers Moscow to be the symbol of a crusade to remake the world in the communist image.'[22]

Meanwhile, Henry Holt had published Capa's memoir *Slightly Out of Focus* in the US. Capa visited the American Embassy and, as he later told WNBC Radio in New York, looked through 'the papers [and] found the *New York Times*, which had a fairly big review'. When he showed it to Steinbeck, Steinbeck told him that any 'intelligent' writer should not read his critics. 'So I got ashamed,' he later joked, 'and I went with [the review] into the bathroom.'[23]

The *Times*' critic echoed many other reviewers. Nice pictures. Shame about the contrived narrative. The *Philadelphia Inquirer* was the most

* Steinbeck's text would make no mention of the 1946 famine that had killed millions of rural Russians or of the severe rationing that existed throughout the Soviet Union. Most people in fact ate no better than before the 1917 Revolution.

generous: 'What Tolstoy does with words for Sevastopol, Hemingway for Caporetto, Crane for the Civil War, Capa achieves with his camera.'[24] In *Photo Notes*, John Vachon perceptively noted: 'The brisk, personal and extremely funny story which Capa relates is pretty far removed from the grim and not often funny story he has photographed.'[25] Vachon went on to criticize the layout and Holt's poor reproduction. Many shots were fill-ins for magazine features and several pictures were similar to scenes that other photographers had captured many times.*

Though only early September, the bite of winter was already in the air. Capa and Steinbeck's room lacked adequate heating and soon they were wearing their overcoats when not in bed. Three days before they were due to leave, they learned that Capa's negatives would have to be developed and then inspected.† Reluctantly, he handed them over. The Soviets, he was certain, would rush through such a large number of rolls, and the printing would be worse than mediocre. The whole project, his idea and already a disaster, was surely now irredeemable? He paced about 'clucking like a mother hen who has lost her babies'.[26]

On the day of departure, at Moscow airport, the Soviets told Capa he could have his films back and take them out of the country. He was handed a large box of films but told he was not to break the seals until his plane was in the air, bound for Kiev, a refuelling stop before he crossed the Iron Curtain. Once aboard the plane, a grim-faced Capa held the box in his hands. 'It's light,' he told Steinbeck. 'It's only half heavy enough.'

* Today, Capa's story reads like a witty outline for a B-movie: vivid, tersely written but only fleetingly poignant. But as oral history – much of it was dictated to a young Turkish typist – *Slightly Out of Focus* ranks with the most charming of Second World War narratives. And, indeed, the current vogue for personal memoir has resurrected the book, with the help of Cornell Capa, from obscurity. In 1999, the American series the Modern Library reprinted it, thereby elevating it to the status of 'modern classic'. In so doing, the Modern Library included many excellent photographs that were not included in the original, and several that predate Capa's narrative. With twice as many pictures as the original, all superbly reproduced, the book's visual impact is far greater than the edition that John Vachon rightly criticized as sloppily designed.

† Capa had taken around 4,000 pictures in less than forty days (a few hundred in colour): an unusually large number for such an economical photographer.

'Maybe they put rocks in it,' said Steinbeck. 'Maybe there aren't any films in there at all.'

Capa shook the box. 'Sounds like films.'

'It could be old newspapers.'

'You son of a bitch,' replied Capa.

In Kiev, Capa opened the box after a rigorous customs inspection. According to Steinbeck, the picture of the half-crazed woman in Stalingrad and those of several German soldiers – doomed like millions of others to die under Stalin – were missing 'but nothing that mattered . . . was withheld'.[27] Dejected but relieved to have his film back, Capa fell asleep as the plane took off for Prague.

In *A Russian Journal*, after describing the final nail-biting moments of their trip, Steinbeck concluded: 'We know this journal will not be satisfactory either to the ecclesiastical Left, nor the lumpen Right. Surely it is superficial and how could it be otherwise? We have no conclusions to draw, except that Russian people are like all other people in the world. Some bad ones there are surely, but by far the greater are very good.'[28] Steinbeck did not mention in which camp 'Comrade Polto*vrat*sky' and his UOKS spies belonged.

19 The New Look

'He was very attractive, because of his looks, his gypsy lifestyle, the glamour of his work, the fame of his photographs, and the danger of his life.'

BETTINA GRAZIANI, former Dior model

After leaving the Soviet Union, Capa spent a few days in Prague, then went to the Slovak village of Furolac in the Carpathian Mountains, where he photographed a family for Morris's 'People Are People' series.* From Prague, Capa travelled to Budapest. The old part of the city around Buda's Royal Palace had been razed and elsewhere he found vast devastation.† Shocked by the disfigurement of his childhood home, he stayed less than twenty-four hours, but according to biographer Richard Whelan found time to see his brother László's widow, Angela, and her thirteen-year-old daughter.‡ Though his stay was short, Capa confronted for the first time the enormity of the Holocaust.** Most of

*He had promised Morris a Russian family, but had not bothered to shoot the story during the 'vodka tour'. Although Morris was later disappointed that he'd not done so, he was mollified by the fact that at least he had one family from the Eastern Bloc.

†Little had changed since the photographer Lee Miller had visited in late 1945. One of Miller's pictures was captioned 'Field of Blood' and showed an old woman scavenging for wood in an apocalyptic landscape.

‡ According to Richard Whelan, they had suffered enormously during the war, and were still barely making ends meet. Capa spent an evening with them and saw the American consul the next day about getting them out of Hungary, before leaving for New York.

** The Hungarian Jews had been the last major group of European Jewry to be annihilated. Most had been sent to Auschwitz as late in the war as summer 1944: between May and July that year, the Germans packed 437,000 into 147 trains. It was the last great barbaric act of

the city's Jews had been murdered, including several of his mother's relatives. He would seldom if ever talk about this, according to friends, perhaps because it was too painful.

Judy Freiburg worked as a researcher for Magnum in the late Forties, socialized with Capa many times, and fell in love with his 'closest friend', David 'Chim' Seymour. Capa and Seymour 'had escaped Hitler and knew what they had escaped,' she recalls. 'Every day they thanked God they were alive.' While working at the American Embassy in London in 1945, she saw hundreds of pictures taken in the liberated concentration camps – so many she 'can still smell them'. She believes the Holocaust was a 'terrible trauma' for Seymour and both the Capa brothers. 'They got around it in different ways. Chim went and saw [what had happened to his people by revisiting his former home in the Warsaw ghetto], but Bob and his brother Cornell tended to avoid it. They didn't want to be reminded. If you had survived, you didn't want to have your nose rubbed in it.'

When Capa returned to the US in early October, he checked into the Bedford Hotel, where Steinbeck was busy knocking out *A Russian Journal.** A few days later, Capa learned that he'd been awarded the Medal of Freedom for 'exceptionally meritorious achievement which aided the US in the prosecution of the war against the enemy in Continental Europe'.[1]

On 20 October, Capa got out of bed unusually early, ate a breakfast cooked by Steinbeck and then arrived in time for a live interview with WNBC Radio in New York to promote *Slightly Out of Focus* and *A Russian Journal.*

the Final Solution and resulted in the 'single most concentrated killing orgy at Auschwitz' (Goldhagen, *Hitler's Willing Executioners*). Most died in the showers of Auschwitz, the rest on death marches and in other concentration camps. Very few, perhaps one in ten, survived to return to Budapest.

*In the days following his return, Steinbeck confided in his friend Nathaniel Benchley that he liked Capa and admired his work, but he didn't want to work with him again: to get his photographs, Capa had promised to send people gifts from America, cameras or anything else they might fancy, but he didn't keep his word. According to Steinbeck's wife Gwyn, 'This made John angry, and he felt he had to make up for Capa's broken promises and send them himself.'

'Well now, Bob, you're on,' said Capa's jovial interviewer. 'And, incidentally, you can't talk with a cigarette in your mouth . . . What is it like working with a camera on the other side of the Iron Curtain?'

'You see,' replied Capa, 'you say it already – Iron Curtain . . . To me iron curtain is a kind of pocket iron curtain. Everybody's carrying it in his own head. The other Iron Curtain, I don't know. It does exist a little bit, maybe, as borders are concerned. But I didn't have much trouble.' He went on to make several jokes about Steinbeck and other incidents during the trip and to describe his and Steinbeck's visit as an attempt to simply 'see how those people lived'.[2]

On publication, *A Russian Journal* met with mixed reviews, and some fierce criticism from Soviet experts. Seeing how 'people lived' in 1947 in the Soviet Union was in itself a political act of either condemnation or tacit approval of Stalin's regime. The *New York Times*' Orville Prescott echoed many others: '*A Russian Journal* is a lot better written than most, but it is more superficial than many.' The noted New York critic Sterling North astutely concluded: 'The question arises: how superficial can books about Russia become . . . It could have been otherwise if the collaborators' knowledge of Russia, their interest in Russia and their attitude toward Russia had been above the level of eating, drinking and observing pleasant surface impressions.'[3]

The Stalinist press in Moscow, dutifully scathing of any Western view of the Soviet Union, was even less impressed than its capitalist counterpart: critics derided Capa and Steinbeck as 'gangsters' and 'hyenas'.[4] Yet the Soviet apparatchiks should have been pleased. *A Russian Journal* conformed to Comrade Poltoratsky's prediction: 'Steinbeck will rate the Soviet people favourably and will emphasize its sympathy to the American people. He will describe to some extent the ruin and will positively evaluate the heroic working of the Soviet Ukrainian people.'[5]

Its publication marked the lowest point of Capa's career. Given the quantity that he took, his pictures were uninspiring and strangely flat. Even considering the restrictions imposed on him, on the evidence of

A Russian Journal he was losing his touch. It appeared that his talents did not suit the complicated and politically delicate task of photographing the Cold War. It was as if only real combat could invigorate him with equal shots of adrenaline and compassion.

If his collaboration with Steinbeck was for the most part disappointing, it was, however, the biggest money-spinner of his entire career, thanks to John Morris at *Ladies' Home Journal*. In mid-October 1947, Capa met him for lunch at the Algonquin Hotel, and told him that the visit to the Soviet Union project had indeed been a disaster; but convinced that he could salvage something from the trip, Morris spent several hours going through a huge stack of eight-by-ten-inch prints in Capa's room at the Bedford.

Morris was impressed with several images, but they were all in black and white. Did he have any colour? Capa handed over around a dozen rolls of 120 Ektachrome film. Eventually, Morris found several decent images but he needed a cover shot. He looked more closely. Finally, he found 'just one frame, that was strong and tight enough. It showed a peasant woman in her babushka [headscarf], kneeling at work in a field.'[6]

Morris took a mock-up cover and several other images to his employers, Beatrice and Bruce Gould. He then convinced them to pay an extraordinarily high fee of $20,000 for first magazine rights to the pictures he had chosen, which would appear on the cover and over sixteen further pages. Capa was amazed when he heard about the windfall from Morris himself over lunch at the celebrity eaterie Toots Shor's. If he had held a grudge about the D-Day fiasco, after this sale Morris was more than forgiven. Steinbeck was not so grateful. He felt that he'd been sold short in the deal, yet his $3,000 fee for writing a few captions was more than most working Americans made in a year.

Capa's trip had paid off handsomely, to the tune of well over $2,000 for each week he'd spent behind the Iron Curtain, but in the long run it cost him dearly. As the FBI saw the trip, it was yet further evidence of his sympathy with the devil – communism – and they added a report to a file they'd kept since an informant claimed Capa had been a communist in the 1930s.*

Capa provided the FBI with further ammunition in the weeks following his return from Europe. At a *Herald Tribune* conference on the evening of Wednesday 22 October 1947, he read a statement summarizing his and Steinbeck's observations about the Soviets: 'These people were destroyed and hurt much more than any that I have seen during my ten years of battlefields and they hate war more than any one I ever talked to.' Capa then said the Soviets were very interested in hearing about 'the persecution of liberals' in America and that he and Steinbeck had told their Soviet hosts that 'there are no political prisoners in the United States yet'.

'I am holding my fingers crossed,' he added. 'We do not know who started this vicious and insane game of stupid accusation and violent criticism. It is not very important who started it. The important thing is who is going to stop it.'[7]

Despite their dismal collaboration on *A Russian Journal*, Capa and Steinbeck were soon involved in a far more acrimonious venture: a television production company called World Video. The company came about as a result of conversations between Steinbeck and Harry S. White, a smooth-talking promoter and former radio executive. Steinbeck believed television would 'make books, movies, newspapers, and other forms of communication nearly obsolete in the future'.[8] Capa was convinced that World Video was the route to sudden riches. Seeing another chance to profit from his association with Steinbeck, he decided to invest heavily in the company, buying $2,000 worth of stock.

It was an extraordinary move, particularly for Steinbeck. Annie

*One of several articles mentioned in Capa's FBI file is dated 24 October, only days after Morris had struck his deal with the Goulds. The *Daily Worker* reported: 'The word most frequently heard during their recent tour of the Soviet Union was "peace", author John Steinbeck and photographer Robert Capa told the fourth session of *Herald Tribune* Forum Wednesday evening.'

Laurie, his film and television agent, had told him in no uncertain terms that World Video was a bad idea and not worth his time and money. His wife Gwyn was even more blunt. Writing for television would grind him up 'like hamburger'.[9] Yet by January 1948 the author of *The Grapes of Wrath* was dashing off copy for World Video's first production, 'Paris: Cavalcade of Fashion'.

The series was Capa's idea and it made perfect sense at the time. The late Forties witnessed an extraordinary rebirth of high fashion in Parisian ateliers, led by the design geniuses Jacques Fath and, above all, Christian Dior. In a period of severe austerity in Europe, Dior's extravagant designs, with matching prices, were viewed by many as scandalous. A single Dior skirt took over twenty-five yards of fabric. In Britain, female MPs decried such extravagance as 'the ridiculous whim of idle people' and 'a stupidly exaggerated waste of material and manpower'.[10]

In Paris, models wearing Dior were accosted by women shouting 'forty thousand francs for a dress and our children have no milk'.[11] However, the protest movement was most vociferous in America where tens of thousands of women, to de-mobbed GIs' delight, started cutting their long skirts shorter to demonstrate their patriotic dedication to saving fabric. But as Mussolini had so perceptively observed, 'any power whatsoever is destined to fail before the fashion'.[12] War-weary women around the world, especially the wealthy in Manhattan and London, were enthralled by Dior's flamboyant return to lavishly cut dresses and sexy corsets.

In early 1948, Capa sailed from New York to Europe to direct 'Cavalcade of Fashion' for World Video. He had been given an impossible production schedule – eight one-hour shows to be shot in six weeks – and, to make matters worse, his budgets were far too low to do the subject justice. However, working under enormous stress and in difficult conditions – the world's press had flocked to Paris to sensationalize Dior's newest creations – he did an excellent job putting together enough material to fill eight hours of television time. He even found time to take stills for *Illustrated*, which reported that Dior again proved to be the 'sensation of the season, this time by failing to lengthen his skirts'.[13] Dior's new skirts were actually quite short. It was what his models wore beneath them that raised eyebrows: wonderfully sexy silk stockings and suspender belts. For several years, silk supplies had been devoted to making parachutes instead of frivolous hosiery, and European women had prided themselves on drawing straight lines down their calves. Now Capa photographed lithe models spinning on the catwalk, their dresses lifting to reveal ornate suspender belts and real silk stockings, not the cheap rayon items that GIs had used to entice women liberated from Nazism.

Forced to work within excessively tight production budgets, Capa literally went to town with his expense account. He took old friends like Pamela Churchill out for lavish lunches, and he wined and dined several models whom the New Look had made famous, including Bettina Graziani, a bewitching Breton with a sombre beauty who modelled for Jacques Fath and Dior. He introduced her to his favourite restaurant in Paris: a tiny bistro called Chez Anna, run by the eponymous proprietor, who cooked exquisite rustic French dishes. He adored it not least because Anna owned a pet chicken that would often sit perched on his table as he polished off yet another bottle of champagne.

Born Simone Micheline Bodin, Bettina had been renamed by Fath – 'we already have one Simone; you look to me like a Bettina'[14] – and was one of the century's first supermodels, rivalled in the Forties only by the English beauty Barbara Goalen. Capa was quickly infatuated with her but failed in his repeated approaches because she had already met and fallen in love with screenwriter and novelist Peter Viertel, who had decamped from Hollywood to Paris. Capa squired several of Bettina's fellow *cabine* models, notably 'Alla', a stunning Oriental with Russian blood, but it was Bettina – the freckle-faced daughter of a railway worker – with whom he formed a lasting friendship.

Seated in her elegant Parisian apartment, Bettina examines several portraits of Capa and smiles and remembers his immense charm and mischievous vitality. 'Capa was such a forceful presence,' she says, looking at a portrait by Ruth Orkin of him at his most debonair. 'When you lead such a dangerous life, and you know you can lose it any minute, you tend to live life to the full and truly appreciate it. He loved life, his friends, drinking, good food, and especially beautiful women.'

Bettina remembers Capa being enormously sexual. He always had a 'wicked look in his eye'. She never quite knew whether he was joking or not, and he was all the more attractive because his bravura and bravery were real – tested – and women knew it. 'He was not arrogant, and that made him attractive too – he was aware of his weaknesses. He was absolutely free. But that created difficulties with women who wanted to change him. I always had the impression he was searching for something that he could never find, something he may have lost – the perfect woman perhaps.' Gourmand, sensualist extraordinaire with immense natural charm, the Capa Bettina remembers was a survivor 'who lived in tragic times' but transcended the evil and horrors he had experienced to bring levity and joy to others' lives.

Capa's backers in New York were not as appreciative of his charms. Today, his documentaries constitute the best visual record of an important renaissance in fashion, but in 1948 Steinbeck and his colleagues were disappointed by their quality. Steinbeck was also upset by Capa's expense claims, amounting to over $1,500, and after close examination, World Video refused to pay them. Capa was then castigated for wasting the company's money and forced to sell back his stake in the company. His venture into television had ended in bitter disappointment.[15]

Steinbeck and Capa would never work together again but their friendship did survive the bitter fall-out over World Video. Steinbeck later said that Capa had many friends but none who loved him more, and the two saw each other several times before Capa's death, both in Paris and New York. On one visit to New York, it was Capa who orchestrated one of the most remarkable encounters in Steinbeck's literary career. According to Steinbeck's wife, Gwyn, he spent weeks trying to arrange a meeting between Steinbeck and America's other literary colossus, Hemingway. When the pair got together at a party at a popular bar called Tim Costello's on New York's Third Avenue, Capa 'clucked over the two of them like a mother hen.' But Steinbeck left the party in a funk, upset by Hemingway's macho and cruel behaviour: drunk, Hemingway had snapped the writer John O'Hara's blackthorn walking stick, a gift from Steinbeck, claiming that it was a cheap imitation.[16]

20 A Road of Death

'The Road to Jerusalem Was A Road of Death'

Illustrated, 5 July 1948

In early May 1948, Capa learned from press reports that a Jewish homeland was likely to be declared in Palestine in a matter of weeks. Here at last was a story he felt compelled to cover. He arrived in Tel Aviv on the 8th and took a room at the seafront Armon Hotel. Among his fellow guests, he quickly discovered, were his old colleague Quentin Reynolds, working for *Collier's*; the *Herald Tribune*'s Kenneth W. Bilby, whom he had met during the Second World War; and Jack Winocour of *Illustrated*.[1]

On 14 May, Capa woke early to prepare for what was bound to be a long and historic day. At precisely 8 a.m. the British High Commissioner, Sir Alan Cunningham, stepped out of the imposing Government House in Jerusalem to review an honour guard of the Highland Light Infantry. He then climbed into his bulletproof Daimler as bagpipes played a Scottish funeral dirge. By 1 p.m. he had wound his way to Kadandia airport with a heavily armed guard, and troops had lowered the last Union Jack in the city. The British had shuffled out, leaving Palestine to plunge into certain war.

Later that afternoon, in the Tel Aviv Museum, David Ben-Gurion rapped his gavel and the packed hall rose and sang a sacred hymn, the 'Hatikvah': Capa's cue to get closer to Ben-Gurion, Israel's first Prime Minister, as he prepared to read the Israeli Declaration of Independence. 'With trust in Almighty God, we set our hand to this

Declaration, at this Session of the Provisional State Council, on the soil of the Homeland, in this city of Tel Aviv, on this Sabbath eve, the fifth of Iyar, 5708, the fourteenth day of May, 1948.'

After Capa had photographed the birth of a Jewish homeland, he reloaded his Leicas and recorded Israel's first cabinet session. Emerging into the late afternoon light of Tel Aviv, he then focused on the exuberant crowds thronging the streets, and in particular on a young girl, waving an Israeli flag. She too was celebrating the moment her people had awaited for two thousand years. That night, war broke out between Israel and several surrounding Arab states.

Israel's war for independence was Capa's most personal war. It is difficult to find an example of any photographer before or since who has covered a war so brilliantly and bravely. The 'last great cowboy', in the photographer Jean-Jacques Naudet's words, was soon back at the top of his game, working with remarkable speed to provide the most lyrical and dynamic coverage of his career. One moment he was crawling under sniper fire into a camouflaged Israeli outpost on the roof of an Arab house, the next he was chatting up a gorgeous Sabra soldier.* One night, according to a possibly apocryphal story, a searchlight raked a hillside where Capa was clearly seen making love to one of these young female fighters.[2]

In late May, Capa joined *Life*'s Frank Scherschel and the Hungarian-born photographer Paul Goldman, and headed to the Negev Desert where the Israelis were fending off an Egyptian attack on a strategically vital kibbutz. Goldman later told Jozefa Stuart that the trio arrived to find it almost surrounded. For a couple of hours they lay on the ground while almost 300 Arab shells flew overhead.

'Who the hell can lie still when a fight is going on?' asked Capa, who jumped up and ran towards the kibbutz.

'Bob, keep low!' shouted Scherschel. 'You'll get hit!'

'My address isn't on those — shells,' replied Capa and kept running.[3]

When the group reached the settlement they were shown to shelters

*One of these female fighters – Jewish natives of Palestine – was strangely reminiscent of Bergman. Capa photographed her looking wonderfully seductive in khaki shorts with an ammunition belt flung casually around shapely hips.

where Capa greeted everyone with his 'spicy Hungarian-accented Shalom'. According to Goldman, Capa cracked a few jokes, relieving the tension, and was soon surrounded by a group of admiring women eager to tell their stories.

'Once again the violence of war has caught up with Robert Capa,' announced *Illustrated* in an introduction to a special report on Israel which featured more than twenty of Capa's pictures, many taken during the fighting in the Negev. 'These pictures tell the story of the Jewish settlements – Kibbutzim – dotted between the Arab villages and under constant rifle and machine-gun fire from the ground and bombs from the air . . . Capa and his cameras have captured the atmosphere of the Holy Land War, the misery of death, the peril that comes from a sniper's bullet. Robert Capa has found another war.'[4]

By far the most dramatic story Capa covered was the relief of Jerusalem. If part of the city was to be claimed by the Israelis, it was vital that a road was opened to Tel Aviv before a ceasefire, agreed at the United Nations, took effect on 11 June 1948. The man in charge of the operation was a remarkable West Point graduate, David Michael Marcus. Over several weeks, this Brooklyn-born Jewish American had inspired the rag-tag Israeli army under his command to daunting feats of perseverance and resistance. Capa greatly admired his courage, tenacity and pragmatism. Both were Jewish veterans of the Second World War and passionate idealists beneath their surface cynicism.

At first, however, Marcus found him an irritation. According to David Eldans, the head of the Israeli Press Office Photo Department, they played a game of bluff for several days:[5] Marcus would tell Capa that certain areas were dangerous in the hope that he would be distracted from the true danger zones, but even though Israeli front-line units had strict orders to turn correspondents away from key battle zones, through guile, cognac and charm Capa always got a story.*

*Many factors were not reported during the war because they would have undermined the romantic myth of a David and Goliath battle in which the Jews won against insurmountable odds. The Israelis were in fact well supplied from the start. As Bilby dared to point out, the United Jewish Appeal in America raised millions in 'hard cash' to procure weapons in several countries such as Czechoslovakia, 'which apparently had an abundance of military stores picked up from Nazi Germany or stockpiled there by the departing Allied armies.'

Correspondents were to be cheerleaders for the Israeli cause if reporting from the Jewish side – censorship had been introduced on all outgoing press dispatches as soon as the British mandate expired. Kenneth Bilby wrote after the war that this censorship was 'heavy-handed and often deceitful'. 'Coverage was usually distinguished by intense partisanship. You fell into a category, Arab or Jewish, soon after arrival and it became immutable.'[6]

In early June, Capa covered Marcus's major achievement: the creation of the so-called 'Burma Road' to relieve Jerusalem. In a matter of days, Israelis working mostly at night and often under the noses of the enemy carved a route through mountains and desert ravines. On the evening of 8 June, Capa joined Jack Winocour to travel the 'Burma Road' to Jerusalem. Their jeep was part of a convoy that would, it was hoped, reach the city with desperately needed medical supplies and food. As darkness fell, Capa and Winocour tied their handkerchiefs across their faces to protect them from dust and sand, and put out their last cigarettes of the night – even the faintest glow from a stub could betray their position to Arab mortars and snipers.

They drove along twisting paths beneath a bright moon. Every few miles, they could make out handpainted signposts in the moonlight, showing the direction to Jerusalem in Hebrew characters. Only a clumsy cluster of boulders indicated a nearby precipice. Tank-traps dotted the landscape. In a small mountain village, Capa parted ways with Winocour, joining Marcus to travel the last, and most perilous, stretches of the 'Burma Road'. By now, Marcus and Capa were calling each other 'Hadid', Hebrew for friend. Capa slept most of the way to Jerusalem, even though several times he was almost bounced out of the jeep.[7]

On the morning of 10 June 1948, Capa and Marcus talked in Marcus's temporary headquarters, the Monastère Notre Dame de la Nouvelle Alliance, 2,450 feet above the Judaean desert. The agreed truce between Israel and its six opposing Arab armies had been set for 10 a.m. the next day. No one was certain that the Arabs would keep to it. Marcus was worried that as long as fighting continued, the 'Burma Road' would remain in danger. If the road was cut before the ceasefire, Jerusalem might well go under. Capa confidently joked that the Eden

Hotel in Jerusalem was already 'preparing its highest honor' for Marcus – 'an authentic hot bath'. 'It'll be a delicious experience,' he added.

'If I ever make it,' Marcus replied. 'You can stretch a rubber band just so far, you know – and luck operates the same way.'[8]

That night, Marcus could not sleep.* In just a few hours, the long fight to create a Jewish homeland would be over. Around 3.30 a.m., he decided to take some air, pulled a sheet from his cot for warmth and then ambled around his camp. As Marcus headed back to his cot, he heard a sentry call out: '*Mi sham?*' ('Who goes there?')

Marcus replied and stepped forward. The sentry could only hear indistinct words in the wind. Marcus's ghostly figure came closer. The sentry trembled, raised his gun, his finger on the trigger. Marcus took another step. The sentry panicked and pressed the trigger. Marcus died instantly – shot through the heart at 3.50 a.m. on 11 June 1948, six hours and ten minutes before the truce began.[9] At 2.30 a.m. on 12 June, a grief-stricken Capa woke Winocour. 'Mike is dead,' he said very quietly.[10]

A letter to Marcus's wife Emma in Brooklyn from a woman who had housed him reads: 'I want you to know that when his men learned that Mickey was killed, they wept. Those boys, most of whom are but children, do not cry easily and death is a common, accepted thing with them . . . but this time they were not ashamed to cry.' Capa's reaction to the loss of his friend was the same.[11]

On 13 June, Capa and Winocour arrived in Jerusalem. Pale children were returning to their schools. Oriental Jews in their long robes wandered 'like ghosts'[12] through the shell-shocked city.† After a memorial

*Marcus knew that the Israelis had held off the Arabs on every front, but only just. Most of Galilee was in Israeli hands, as well as the majority of Jerusalem.

†'The new Jews in khaki grit their teeth on the dusty wind and endure,' Winocour reported in *Illustrated*'s issue of 3 July 1948. 'They have borne something more dreadful than any aerial blitz for over three weeks. They have crouched beneath artillery fire at short range, so dense that it was impossible to walk abroad. Hundreds have died. Hundreds upon hundreds more have been injured. The hospitals are full of wounded.' Later that day, Capa and Winocour met several other correspondents. One of them said he'd never seen so many dead and dying children littered about the streets of a city. He had seen twelve schoolboys singing one moment and, the next, one of them screaming in pain. He had seen a little girl gazing, stunned, at the stump of her arm. Yet again, civilians had paid a terrible price for 'victory'.

service in Jerusalem, it was announced that Marcus's coffin would be taken back to Tel Aviv before shipment back to Brooklyn. Capa decided to follow Marcus back to the port. Before leaving, he told Winocour about his last moments with him. Winocour chose not to repeat the story in his reports for *Illustrated*. 'It's Capa's story,' he wrote, 'and he'll want to tell all of it some day in his own way. I'll be silent.'[13]

Capa never did tell his story in print. Nor did many other correspondents who knew, like Winocour, how Marcus, the most famous martyr of the Israeli war for independence, had met his end: gunned down senselessly by one of his own men. According to Bilby, this silence was the worst example of censorship during the entire war. The official Israeli line was that he died in action from an Arab bullet while leading a patrol. Capa chose not to break rank with the censors, hence his silence. But two years later, Bilby did. In his 1950 book, *New Star in the East*, he explained that he was still violating the Israelis' 'censorship ban'.

By 21 June, Capa was back in Tel Aviv preparing to return to Paris. He had witnessed Israel's army repulse six Arab nations. The United Nations truce still held and the first waves of mass immigration were arriving from the Red Cross camps of Germany. In America, President Truman had recognized the new state, thereby assuring it a measure of international legitimacy and opening the way to massive American financial and military support. But then, as Capa was packing his bags, actual civil war threatened to tear asunder the previous months' miraculous achievements.

On 22 June, the leaders of Irgun Zvai Leumi, a right-wing group, decided to land an illegal shipment of weapons aboard a ship called the *Altalena*. The stash of weapons was a gift from wealthy American Jews who had also funded many terrorist attacks on the British before the mandate had expired. To land the arms would have violated the 11 June ceasefire agreement with the Arabs, and Ben-Gurion's government announced that any attempt to do so would be repulsed. From a balcony on the top floor of the Armon, Capa watched aghast as Irgun troops waded ashore from the ship while startled Haganah soldiers, loyal to Ben-Gurion's government, prepared to repel them. With Bilby and several others, Capa then sprinted to the beach where he discovered that the Irgunists had already set up a machine-gun emplacement. Then a second group of Irgunists waded ashore.

'Kill your own people, will you?' one shouted, taunting the Haganah troops. 'A fine reception for the Americans we brought with us! They come to fight for you and you try to kill them!'

The two groups faced off. Then Ben-Gurion gave the order to open fire. Kenneth Bilby saw what happened next: 'Fire commenced on the beach front, where the few Irgunists ashore were either killed or captured . . . Jews began killing Jews at point-blank range in a confused pattern of anarchical warfare. All the troops were dressed identically, and no other outsider could tell who was shooting at whom.' He watched in disbelief as a 'Haganah man fired at an Irgunist not ten yards away, his bullet tearing off the top of the other's head. The Irgun man trotted strangely in concentric circles for a minute or two and then fell over dead.'[14]

Ben-Gurion had also ordered the destruction of the *Altalena*, a powerful symbol of insurrection. When the ship exploded in flames, her surviving crew jumped overboard. Soon the cargo of ammunition caught fire. Capa heard 'a deeper roar' mix with the 'staccato crack of gunfire',[15] and then moved closer to take pictures of Irgunists jumping off the blazing ship and swimming ashore. For several minutes, he watched Jews on surfboards paddle out to the flaming ship as American bullets hit other Jews being carried to the shelter of American ambulances provided by the Jewish Red Cross, emblazoned with the 'Red Shield' of David.[16]

Suddenly, Capa felt a terrible pain in his groin. After a decade in the front line, a bullet had finally found him. For a few interminable seconds, he thought his genitals had been shot away. Thankfully, however, the bullet had merely grazed him. Relieved, he hobbled back to his room in the Armon Hotel and booked a flight back to Paris.[17] According to Irwin Shaw, Capa later quipped: 'That would be the final insult – being killed by the Jews!'[18]

A few days after his return to Paris, Capa sat drinking with a former night-fighter pilot called Noel Howard in his favourite nightclub, Chez Carrère, on the Champs-Elysées. They had first met at a dinner party and instantly hit it off when they discovered they were both wearing cufflinks given them by the same woman – Noel's ex-wife.

'I came back so fast,' Capa told him, 'I still had my flies undone when I got to the Lancaster.' As Raymond, the barman, dutifully refilled their glasses every few minutes, he said that he had decided that he and the other members of Magnum would no longer cover wars. 'They went too far, or rather got too close in Palestine. I'm not going to carry on recording for posterity these guys who play this little game.'[19]

While Capa had been covering the fight for Israeli independence, the Cold War had reached a new intensity. All summer, the only story worth reporting in Europe, it seemed, had been the Berlin airlift. On 18 September, a new record was set when Allied planes flew more than 7,000 US tons of supplies into the city in defiance of a three-month Soviet blockade. A few weeks later, Capa set out with Theodore White, the chief correspondent of the Overseas News Agency, on a well-timed tour of three Eastern Bloc countries: Poland, Czechoslovakia and Hungary.[20] They quickly found, in the words of the British journalist Richard Mayne, a wasteland that 'smelled of dust, oil, gunpowder and greasy metal; of drains and vermin; of sweat and vomit, dirty socks and excrement; of decay and unburied dead.'[21]

In Western Europe, many civilians still struggled to feed and clothe themselves adequately. Severe austerity scarred an entire generation in Britain. In Eva Besnyö's adopted country, Holland, adults lived on the 'caloric requirements of a six-year-old child'. But in Poland the suffering was far worse. In Warsaw, Capa photographed a landscape that looked as desolate as Nagasaki. In the Warsaw Ghetto, where 400,000 Poles had died, a Catholic church was the sole surviving building – the Soviets had levelled the rest of the area. Malnutrition and disease were rampant. Yet, miraculously, the exhausted Poles were already working long hours in mines and newly constructed factories, and rebuilding much of their devastated country by hand.

As White and Capa drove through the bleak countryside of southern Poland, they made a detour to visit a 'last awful monument': Auschwitz. The Nazis' most infamous death camp had been cleaned up and was now a museum. The paths Capa wandered were neat. Their guide had a well-practised spiel. Not far from Auschwitz lay several barren acres where many guides, some of them former inmates, feared to tread. Towards the end of the war, the Nazis had decided the gas chambers couldn't dispose of the Jews fast enough. It was cheaper and far quicker to simply dump corpses in pits and then burn them. Three years later, Capa could spot where pits had been filled in by the lush colour of the grass growing from soil fertilized by corpses. The Nazis had been in such a panic to escape the Red Army in 1945 that they left a couple of the pits open. Capa found them swamped with water. 'The half-burned bodies are still there and the water still bubbles,' reported White, 'with slow fermentation. If you bend down close to the water's edge . . . you can hear it.'[22]

When Capa arrived in Budapest a few weeks later, he found it only slightly less grim than on his previous twenty-four-hour visit. 'The Hungary of yesterday remains but a myth,' reported *Illustrated* on 26 March 1949 in an article that featured a dozen of Capa's pictures, several showing a military parade of newly armed Soviet-backed Hungarian troops. 'If the name of Kossuth, her great fighter for freedom, is mentioned today people think only of the Budapest Danube bridge named after him. And the Danube is red again with the blood of political victims whom Hungarian oppressors from time immemorial have sent to death in that river.'* Atop St Gellert Hill, where he had once skied, Capa discovered a memorial honouring Soviet soldiers who had died in the two-month siege of Budapest. Bullet holes riddled surviving landmarks, as they do to this day.

**Illustrated* also reported: 'The trial and imprisonment of Cardinal Mindszenty and his friends have completed the vassalage of the country which once found solace in the West and was fearful of the East. No other Cominform state has suffered so harshly. Poland and Jugoslavia are struggling to retain their own national tinge; in Hungary Soviet troops, ostensibly there to guard the lines of communication with the Russian garrison in Austria, are the real masters.'

For six weeks, Capa photographed the ruined city and later wrote a witty but shallow report for a new American travel magazine called *Holiday*. He couldn't bear, perhaps, to tell his up-market readers that hundreds of years of Jewish culture had been obliterated, along with much of what he had once found enchanting about the city. But he did intimate that he had been extremely lucky to get out of the country before the war. The day before he left Budapest, he went to get his exit visa stamped. A man in his mid-thirties examined his passport, stamped it and then asked what school he'd attended. It turned out that the official had left just two years after Capa. 'If you had been born two years later,' he said, 'today with your talents you would be dead or at least a secretary to a minister. The way it is, you are just a confused Western liberal. This is historical materialism.'[23]

In January 1949, the Israeli war for independence ended with a formal armistice. Capa discovered that Irwin Shaw planned to cover the post-war situation for the *New Yorker* and persuaded him to collaborate on a book project, *Report on Israel.** They arrived in Tel Aviv in early May, in time for the first anniversary of Israel. One of their first subjects was President Chaim Weizmann, whom Capa photographed sitting beside a pool with his English grandson, David, at his Tel Aviv home. They also sat in on a session of the Knesset and visited the rusting wreck of the *Altalena*. Shaw wrote that children had now made 'a plaything out of [the] tragic monument, swam up to the grounded ship, and the more daring ones clambered barefoot over it and dived from its side.'[24]

'Israel is the crudest and hardest place one can inhabit today,' Capa reported in the 27 August issue of *Illustrated* magazine. 'But it is a place where one hears the young people sing at night, and even the old ones talk about the bright future now awaiting them.' The country had already changed dramatically since Capa's hasty departure in July 1948.

*The book was Capa's most successful collaboration with a writer, far superior to *A Russian Journal*. Shaw's lyrical analysis and Capa's deeply sympathetic portraits combined to produce reportage of the highest calibre.

In the intervening months, Israel had become home to hundreds of thousands of young socialists who were now busy building a new country from scratch. They reminded Capa of the idealists he had met in Barcelona in summer 1936, before fascism had killed their dreams of a new, democratic nation.

What these hard-working zealots lacked in humour, they made up for in optimism. Indeed, their hope, bolstered by victory over several Arab armies, was quickly infectious. Capa noted that they were part of a massive 'Ingathering of Exiles' from exotic desert tribes such as the Habanim, from among the skeletal survivors of Auschwitz and from ghettos and villages throughout a war-ravaged Europe.[25] In the port city of Haifa, he photographed them arriving in their thousands each day. 'A few minutes after their arrival the passengers, most of them homeless for years, and citizens of no country, are becoming fully fledged nationals of Israel,' Capa reported. 'Then they pass a doctor and are packed into waiting trucks.' Now these survivors had to fight a new enemy – the desert. To survive in Israel, they would soon be working long hours to create settlements, basic infrastructure and water sources.*

In *Report on Israel*, Shaw noted, to his credit, how much the Arab Palestinians had suffered from the formation of a Zionist homeland for the Holocaust's survivors. But he didn't mention the full extent of the Palestinian Diaspora that Israel created, and his book did not include a single picture of an Arab. In all fairness, it should be pointed out that Shaw and Capa were prevented from covering the Arab side because it would have been too dangerous, particularly for Capa as a now famous Jew, to venture into the Arab-controlled areas bordering Jerusalem and other cities. But Capa did try, and in order to get inside Arab-controlled Jerusalem he was even prepared to disguise himself as a Bedouin camel driver, despite warnings that he'd probably be killed if he was discovered, although he finally opted to get pictures of the Arab

*In most of Capa's pictures, joy radiates from faces, young and old. The men sweat from dawn until dusk in grimy khaki in extreme heat. Their women, with deep tans and glittering teeth, trudge through the desert in their white ankle socks, smiling at a cheeky comment from Capa.

section from an Arab photographer instead, much to Shaw's relief. However, one revealing picture did appear in the 27 August 1949 issue of *Illustrated.* Captioned 'The Wandering Arab', the full-page picture showed a 'new tragic figure', a middle-aged Arab in traditional clothing, standing five to ten yards from him. Barbed wire separated them.*

Shaw also recalled that for most of the time he spent with Capa in Jerusalem he walked in his friend's shadow. Capa was a hero to many Israelis thanks to his 1948 coverage, Shaw was just a beak-nosed American with a notebook who held the famous Hungarian's lights. On 4 May, he joined Capa in covering the emotional first anniversary celebration of statehood and noted how he was able to get Orthodox Jews, who would rarely be photographed, to pose for him. Shaw was also with him when he recorded another moving ceremony in Israel's early history: a procession carrying the ashes of 200,000 Jews from concentration camps. Again, Capa placed his Leica only a few feet from the faces of grief-stricken women with hands clasped in supplication at a burial site near the ancient tombs of kings in Jerusalem.[26]

After several days in Jerusalem, Capa headed back alone to the coast and then visited the St Luke refugee camp, half an hour's drive from Haifa. This former British military base, surrounded by barbed wire, now housed thousands of Holocaust survivors. 'The "people of the barbed wire",' he reported, 'who have passed through scores of concentration camps in the last decade, reach the land of their dreams, only to be back once more behind barbed wire.'[27]

Conditions were very poor, food was rationed and the scenes he witnessed were perhaps more moving than anything he had covered in his career because of his personal stake in the fate of European Jewry. 'The camp of St Luke', he wrote bitterly, 'differs little from the

*Kenneth Bilby, who also returned for the first anniversary of Israel, reported in greater detail on the new Arab Diaspora in Palestine. Bilby reported in *New Star in the East* that Arab villages deemed 'uninhabitable' had been razed as 'insurance against their owners' return'. Eight hundred thousand Arabs had fled their homes during a year of war, and the Jewish state had hung out an 'unwanted sign . . . The Arabs of Palestine languished in perpetual exile.'

Displaced Persons camps they knew in Germany . . . Used to this life, they soon settle down to camp routine . . . In this new camp of Babel noisy loudspeakers blare as incessantly as any in Auschwitz or Belsen . . .'[28]

For several days, he took haunting pictures of orphaned children born during the Holocaust still screaming for love among the rocks and sand of new camps. They remain the most harrowing among the thousands of pictures he took of displaced children in his career.

Before leaving Israel, he visited the settlement of Gedera, where he roamed around a camp set up by a Polish lawyer for blinded Jews, many of them Yemenites who suffered from trachoma. One of his images shows a young girl leading three blinded men towards a dining hall – perhaps the most symbolic of all his pictures taken in nascent Israel. 'I remember when Bob came back from Israel after photographing the refugee camps,' recalls his cousin Suzy Marquis. 'He had been deeply affected by what he'd seen there. He left his photographs in the Paris office for someone else to edit. He told me he just couldn't bear to look at them again.'

21 The Realm of the Senses

> 'Capa gathered people around him, encouraged them, taught them, sometimes feeding and clothing them. A special quality of skill grew in their work – yet Capa himself appeared to be a wild, good-time, laughing, drinking man.'
>
> GAEL ELTON MAYO, *The Mad Mosaic*

Capa scanned the room crowded with models, actresses and Upper East Side debutantes, as was to be expected at the fashionable Greenwich Village nightclub Café Society. One woman stood out in Capa's eyes: Jemmy Hammond. 'She was tall, a light brunette, with beautiful big eyes and a nice straight nose that I always envied,' recalls Jozefa Stuart, who was then her neighbour and confidante. 'She photographed wonderfully and had once gone to Hollywood to be a movie star, but she couldn't act.'[1]

Hammond was delightful company, a heavy drinker, witty and available, having divorced the record producer John Hammond.* She would become Capa's most serious girlfriend for what remained of his life. According to her son, John Hammond Jr., she was instantly smitten with him but sadly he was unable to see her again for several months because he had to return to Europe the following morning: he had urgent business to attend to back in Paris.

Magnum badly needed to recruit new members if it was going to compete with other agencies in covering stories around the world. And so, between 1949 and his death, Capa brought in several photo-

*Hammond was already a legend in the music business, and went on to discover Bob Dylan, Bruce Springsteen and many others.

graphers. Most have since become famous in their own right and several still remain members of Magnum: Eve Arnold, Elliot Erwitt, Burt Glinn, Inge Morath and Marc Riboud.

Capa's first recruit was Werner Bischof, a Swiss photographer who had impressed him with a harrowing series of pictures taken in 1946 showing the plight of Europe's refugee children. He joined Magnum partly because of Capa's and Chim's political views and their involvement in the Spanish Civil War. Although Capa was only three years his senior, Bischof at first regarded him at times as a father figure. Over the years, Capa encouraged him to follow his instincts towards more artistic work while at the same time making a living by working for mainstream magazines, much to his frustration. Eventually, he tired of Magnum's inability to provide him with the financial support which *Life* could offer, and criticized Capa for not developing as a photographer. But he remained loyal to the agency. Father and rebellious son were destined to die within days of each other.[2]

The Austrian-born Inge Morath arrived in Paris in July 1949, and took a taxi from the Gare de l'Est straight to the Magnum office, still located on the fourth floor of the apartment building at 125 Rue du Faubourg-St-Honoré. A sign on a lift declared: 'The elevator can be taken up but not down.' When she entered the office, she saw that it 'looked like an apartment with a kitchen, bathroom, and bedroom. Only the big front room had a vaguely official air. Here were a long high table for editing, a phone on a long line that could be carried around, a few filing cabinets, and a couch on which I often slept when I had no money – a great convenience except for the absence of bed linen and the very early arrival each morning of the concierge to clean up.'[3]

That night she had dinner with Capa in St-Germain-des-Prés, and then waltzed in narrow streets below skies exploding with fireworks. It was Bastille Day. Morath says Capa quickly took her under his wing, advising her to assist Cartier-Bresson and find herself some smart clothes. Cartier-Bresson was 'the fastest' photographer she has ever seen at work. She learned to make herself inconspicuous like him, wearing plain overcoats, and always trying to have in mind an image she wanted. He told her to look at images upside down to 'judge composition'.

One of her first jobs for Magnum took her to Spain. 'I was at this party in Madrid,' she recalls, 'and I met the designer Balenciaga. I think he liked me because I was doing this dicey stuff, and he gave me a couple of suits, with pockets everywhere for cameras and film. They were so elegant – I still have one! Anyway, I got back to Paris and told Capa, "Come on! Take me out to dinner." I wore one of my suits and he said "Whooooh! Look at you!" After that, Balenciaga made all my clothes for a long time.'

Capa wined and dined his recruits, nursed them through heartbreak, found them the ideal jobs, and made their work for Magnum appear to be the most glamorous of callings. By all accounts, he was an inspirational mentor, and all of his recruits still remember him with enormous affection. 'He was extraordinarily generous with his time,' says Morath, 'and with money when he had it. He had the most amazing instinct for people, and for how to get the best out of people that I've ever seen.'

Inge Morath had arrived in Paris with one of the most engaging and perhaps the most creative of Capa's first recruits: Ernst Haas, described by former Magnum researcher Inge Bondi as 'a slender, lightly stepping young man with a shock of hair that rose like cascades in a Chinese landscape'.[4] Haas also joined Magnum in July 1949, after being introduced to Capa by the editor of *Heute*, Warren Trabant, and then rejecting an offer from *Life* magazine. Capa had convinced him that only Magnum offered what he wanted most – artistic freedom. After joining Magnum, he went to lunch with Capa. 'He congratulated me on becoming a "shareholder",' he recalled. But what did 'shareholder' mean? 'It means,' explained Capa, 'that your money is in Magnum, that Magnum is a nonprofit company, and that you will never see your money again.'[5]

Haas was particularly perceptive about Capa, noting that Magnum's founder was searching in his own work to create a 'poetry of war – a tragic poetry'. He 'considered himself anti-art, religion, poetry, sentimental, but it was his hands [that] really gave away his character.

They were tender and feminine and the opposite of his whole appearance, voice, and so on . . . Capa wanted to state purely "I was there", and he wanted to do it without any composition so you would really feel the reality of a happening. And you don't really compose if you just land with a parachute. That is a feeling, and he created this kind of feeling.'[6]

Shortly after recruiting Haas to the agency, Capa took a much-needed break and headed south to a favourite summer destination, the Côte d'Azur, where many friends such as Irwin Shaw and Peter Viertel rented villas and beach-houses for a couple of months each year.[7] He had last visited France's summer playground for the rich in July 1948, after returning from Israel. When not gambling in local casinos, he had spent several days photographing Pablo Picasso with his one-year-old son Claude and Claude's mother, Françoise Gilot. One of his many portraits, showing Picasso holding a beach umbrella to shade the ravishing Gilot, is now the classic image of the couple.

That summer Capa spent several days with Henri Matisse in his home in Nice, whose walls were lined with huge murals that eventually decorated a local church. Matisse, seventy-nine, portly and white-bearded, spent most of his time in bed, his beloved cat at his side, struggling with arthritis. The illness had left his fingers crippled, and Capa photographed him using a bamboo stick with a carbon pencil attached to it – a less painful method of marking the outlines of his images.

That same summer, Capa stayed with Irwin Shaw and his wife Marion at their pine-shaded summer home in Antibes, the 'Villa Shady Rock', which looked out on to the Mediterranean, and was still painted in camouflage patterns from the war. One evening shortly after his arrival, Shaw took Capa to his favourite bar, popular with sailors who often played a bizarre game of chest-hair pulling. 'The players merely reached inside their shirts, grabbed as much hair as possible, and yanked,' Shaw wrote. 'Then they carefully laid the hairs out on a paper napkin to be counted by a referee chosen for his honesty.' The loser bought the next round.[8]

One day, Gijon Mili, a *Life* photographer, turned up on the Shaws' doorstep to join the party. He and Capa soon joined forces, hunting women by day and hitting the casino at night. 'You'd lend [Capa] the 200 dollars he needed to replace the 200 you'd lent him the night before,'[9] Shaw recalled, 'and which he promptly lost at the casino in Cannes . . . He was not a proper guest or a proper friend or anything – he was Capa and splendid and doomed . . .' More often than not, Capa would return to Villa Shady Rock penniless but with a local girl or prostitute as a consolation prize. According to Shaw's biographer Michael Shnayerson, 'More than one morning Shaw had to raid Marion's closet for clothes that the photographer's dates could wear to avoid shocking the neighborhood as they left.'[10]

According to James Salter, a writer who was a friend of Shaw in his final years, Capa also burned holes in the furniture, spending endless hours sitting 'lazily with cigarette ashes drifting on to his clothes',[11] and Marion Shaw's patience was soon stretched beyond breaking point. She concluded that Capa had spun out of control without war to give him some purpose and finally insisted that he had to leave. Shaw was the one who told him to go – 'an act for which he never forgave himself'.[12] He later drew on Capa's stay for his novel *Evening in Byzantium*, in which the protagonist remembers 'a houseguest who went a long way toward wrecking' a summer on the Côte d'Azur.

In early September 1949, Capa was on a plane headed back to New York. One autumnal morning, he reappeared on Jemmy Hammond's Greenwich Village doorstep. Having concluded that he had gone for good, she was overjoyed to see him. 'I once told Capa I thought Jamie was a real beauty,' recalls Jozefa Stuart. 'Capa said: "That isn't what attracted me, what attracted me was when I went to see her again after several months she was so happy to see me." He really needed to be wanted.'

Capa and Hammond were soon deeply involved. But she was not free to follow him back to Paris. She had two young sons by her marriage to John Hammond, and under the terms of their divorce she could not take them away from America. According to John Hammond Jr., for the next five years, until Capa's death, she waited for him to return from his latest adventure, spent a few weeks with him in Paris each summer and occasionally joined him for skiing in the Alps.

As the years passed, she urged him to make a commitment, but he would not. 'She once told me, "if only he'd stop running around, gambling all the time," ' recalls Jozefa Stuart, ' "I'd go and live in Little Rock, if that's what it took to have a normal life." '

Above all, Capa did not want a normal life – his father had set the example of how to avoid mundane routine at all costs. It was as if slowing down or settling in one place represented a slow death. And so he opted to play the footloose bon viveur instead – the professional boulevardier that his father had always aspired to be, and which he had actually now become. Capa's oldest friend, Eva Besnyö, remembers going to Paris in the early Fifties. Capa invited her to meet him, not over a quiet dinner as she hoped, but at a cocktail party. The Capa she'd known for twenty-five years had become depressingly 'superficial'. 'At the end, our friendship was not there,' she says. 'I felt like I'd lost him.'

When she enquired whether she might find work through Magnum, Capa told the woman who had got him started in photography that she was not suited to the agency – she was 'not journalistic'. Her aesthetic was too abstract. He may also have not wanted her around to remind him and others of his former self: André Friedmann, the young hustler she'd known in Hungary and Berlin.

Other photographers such as Fenno Jacobs, Herbert List, Homer Page and Gisèle Freund were brought in as stringers but not full members. Gisèle Freund later maintained that Capa told her she was a full member and she duly handed over several hundred dollars. After she left Magnum, she claimed that he denied she had ever given him any money. 'At the end of an incredibly brilliant career,' she has written without bitterness, 'he had nothing but a few well-cut suits, though his work as a whole was of immeasurable value.'[13]

In 1951, Maria Eisner dared to become pregnant and Capa quickly took her place as president of Magnum. But he soon discovered that being its front man was infinitely preferable to the tedium of running its day-to-day business, and within months he had started to cast around for someone to replace him. One of those he approached was Warren Trabant, who was now working in Paris for NATO. 'I'd already told him that I didn't want to run a photographers' club,'

Trabant recalls. 'A professional picture agency, now that would have been different.' He had also told Capa he didn't want to 'change diapers'. Now he joked that he didn't want to run a 'nursery'.

By Christmas 1951, it looked as if Magnum in New York might finally clear a profit, as much as $700. Capa decided to hold a party in a private bar at the Algonquin Hotel and, according to John Morris, 'declared it open to friends of Magnum'. When it started to snow heavily, the heavy drinkers 'decided to hunker down for the night'.[14] The bill came to far more than $700, and while the largesse may have endeared Magnum to several editors, it annoyed many Magnum staffers.

Managing an organization such as Magnum was not Capa's forte. He liked to play the businessman, especially at expensed lunches, but actually organizing and administering Magnum quickly became an onerous bore. He was too restless, too fundamentally anarchic, to focus on minutiae such as balance sheets and to worry very much about their bottom line.

'[Capa] knew he was incapable of settling down to a normal life with one woman, a regular job, and an apartment in Paris or New York instead of the pleasant impermanence of living in a hotel,' his friend Peter Viertel has written. 'He was such an incurable bohemian that he didn't even like going to someone's house for dinner, preferring restaurants and cafés and standing at a bar late at night chatting to strangers.'[15]

Chaos suited Capa, not the discipline and order necessary to keep a medium-sized business such as Magnum afloat. Perhaps his greatest aptitude as a manager was finding and inspiring people to work for next to nothing. Magnum at times resembled a modelling agency on first impression due to the presence of the invariably pretty researchers whom Capa hired to scurry around attending to the founders' needs and egos. The talented English writer Gael Elton Mayo was the most beautiful of them all: she found Capa 'sturdy and dark, with a warm, animal attraction' and would melt whenever he came close and whispered: 'You are my sort of creature.'* 'The memories are glamorous,'

*In a photograph provided by her daughter, Capa can be seen gently kissing Mayo's forehead. She looks utterly infatuated.

she wrote later. 'Capa and I with Chim in the White Tower in Soho; Capa with his cigarette stub, looking into space to see a future story while Chim took care of the menu . . . [Capa's] creased, laughing eyes; the eternal cigarette stub; the way he went anywhere, but never owned a dinner jacket.'[16] Another of her indelible memories was of Capa playing pinball in the cafe below Magnum, wincing through clouds of blue smoke as he fired silver balls at bright lights for hour after hour.

Warren Trabant says Capa rarely talked business for more than a few minutes in the cafe, which became the true Magnum office, preferring to chat, glass of red wine in hand, about a racehorse, a new restaurant Chim had found, or a long-planned game of poker. To others, it often seemed that gambling had finally replaced photography as his main occupation.

Had an independent auditor scanned Magnum's books in the early Fifties, he would have found financial irregularities that would today constitute embezzlement.[17] Capa dipped into his partners' and recruits' earnings to pay for women, expensive clothes, restaurants and, above all, his gambling. It wasn't as if he was going to be sacked from the agency he'd started. Those he'd recruited owed their careers to him, so there was no prospect of serious protest about his regular use of their earnings.

But his attitude was not deliberate fraud. The Magnum stalwart Elliot Erwitt, who has been perhaps the agency's most consistent earner over fifty years, remembers visiting Magnum's Paris office in the early Fifties – or rather the cafe below its office. 'Capa had won a double at Longchamps. He came into the cafe with literally an armful of money which he sorted and then started distributing to all the people he owed in the café and the office upstairs. By the time he'd finished, it had all gone.'

During her time as president, Maria Eisner was constantly afraid that one of the founders would come back from a foreign assignment and demand to be paid all their back earnings.[18] This actually happened when Cartier-Bresson returned after three years in India. He was owed several thousand dollars and told Capa he needed the money badly. 'Why?' asked Capa. 'Your wife has got a fur coat, she doesn't need a second one. You don't like cars, what are you going to do with the money?'

Cartier-Bresson wanted to buy a house, at a bargain price, and use the money to restore it.

'I've taken your money because we were practically bankrupt,' replied Capa.

'Oh, you could have warned me.'

'Don't jiggle like a frog. Come on, Preminger is making a film, you go and shoot pictures of that film.'

'Money was not the problem between us,' Cartier-Bresson later claimed. 'We had to live, he was gambling, providing work. It was always like this.'[19]

According to Suzy Marquis, who kept the key to Magnum's petty-cash box, Cartier-Bresson was not quite so blasé. She remembers fierce shouting matches between Capa and his aristocratic comrade. 'Cartier-Bresson thought Capa was from another world,' she recalls. 'He loved Bob but he didn't understand him at all, or what Bob was actually saying most of the time – his mixture of broken English, bits of German and a little Hungarian. When things got really heated, Bob would pound on the table. Chim was always trying to smooth things out. After a while, there would be a ceasefire. Eventually, Henri accepted that Bob would never change. So, as long as Henri could go out and take photographs of what he wanted to cover in his own way, he was fairly happy.'

George Rodger's widow, Jinx, remembers Capa's gambling as a constant concern among Magnum's co-founders. Her husband would argue with him over money, just as Cartier-Bresson did. 'Capa gambled the money away,' she says. 'He didn't seem to care, but we did. Finally, Chim and Cartier-Bresson decided they couldn't rely on Capa's gambling to run Magnum. They would have to do something else.'

Capa remained not only a compulsive gambler but also a seeker of anonymous sex with prostitutes right to the end. If he'd won on a horse, there were the model-hookers smoking Lucky Strikes in bars around the Champs-Elysées, his favoured hunting ground. If he preferred a visit to a brothel to a quickie back at the Lancaster, there was La Maison des Nations, where the rooms were appropriately decorated for a man of such international tastes: the Oriental room came with a tatami and a wood-block print of Mount Fuji. The girls were, of course, ravishingly exotic and young. And if Capa was down on his luck, there were the twenty thousand or more cherry-lipped, over-perfumed but budget-priced *putains* who hovered in the shadows around the Place de la Bastille and other *coins de plaisir* throughout Paris.

Capa's compulsions may have had a simple explanation. He was bored. 'You have to remember that Bob was a man of action,' says Suzy Marquis. 'He wanted to be a witness to his times. He always had to move, act, be in the right place at the right time . . . All his life, he had kept moving, mostly as a way to survive.' Born and raised in conflict, the longer he played pinball in a smoky bar in Paris, dealing with petty squabbles over money in Magnum and arguments over bylines, the more he may have missed the challenge of war photography. One contemporary of his who covered the Second World War admits: 'I have never had an orgasm to compare with the highs I got after a day in combat, adrenaline rushing for hour after hour. It was a hell of an experience – the most intense you can ever have is being in the front lines, under fire, in a war.'

Capa told friends he loathed war and was 'happy to be an unemployed war photographer',[20] yet war had made him a legend, and if he was going to maintain it, he would have to return to the battlefield. But he also knew how short the odds of returning from the next war zone were. He had already covered four wars, and the near miss in Tel Aviv had left him badly shaken, very much aware of his mortality. It was perhaps for this reason that he did not cover the Korean War in the early Fifties, thereby sacrificing his status as the pre-eminent war photographer of his generation.*

Several of Capa's contemporaries believe he did not feel strongly enough about the Korean War to gamble with his life once again. 'In

*The war was covered superbly by several photographers, but perhaps most dramatically by the American ex-marine David Douglas Duncan, a proud champion of the average GI, whose stoicism he glorified in the pages of *Life*. Although Capa did not go to Korea, his first recruit, Werner Bischof, photographed the war for Magnum, concentrating on the victims of American bombing. But as Miller notes in *Magnum*, Capa described these pictures as 'too soft' to sell to *Life*, more than ever a cheerleader for American aggression in the Far East.

a war you must hate somebody or love somebody,' he had once told Martha Gellhorn, 'you must have a position or you cannot stand what goes on.'[21] But there may also have been a less prosaic reason: bank-rolled by Magnum, he had no desperate need for money. Watching an imperial power kill peasants was not yet worth the risk.

22 How Can I Be Old?

> 'Bob had a special way of showing his amusement: his eyes half closed, his mouth split from ear to ear, and clasping a cigarette, he chuckled, very softly, with little gasps. You waited for him to burst into laughter, but he never did. From this purring one discerned an immense interior joy.'
>
> NOËL HOWARD, *Hollywood sur Nil*

While other photographers were stealing his glory in Korea, Capa saved Magnum from going under by courting several important clients: *Picture Post* in London, the public relations office of the Marshall Plan and, most lucrative of all, Ted Patrick's *Holiday* magazine. The fruits of his relationship with Patrick and his picture editor, Frank Zachary, sustained Magnum for much of the early Fifties.

Zachary fondly remembers Capa's work and friendship. The worldly photographer and bon vivant, with entrée into the most glamorous circles, was the 'ideal contributor' to his magazine. 'Bob had a great sense of humour and it came across in his pictures,' he recalls. 'He didn't lie in his pictures – he told the truth as he saw it. Irony was a great part of his visual philosophy. You couldn't be a Hungarian Jew back then and not have a sense of irony.'*

*For one story on Paris, which eventually appeared in April 1953, Zachary hired Cartier-Bresson to take colour photographs. He only later discovered that Cartier-Bresson hated to work in colour, and had asked Capa to take the pictures instead. When the issue appeared, with Capa's pictures besides Cartier-Bresson's byline, many photographers 'dashed out to pick up all the copies they could get to see the first and only colour shots of Cartier-Bresson. They got fooled like everybody else.'

Capa spent the winter of 1950 preparing a long feature on skiing in the Alps for *Holiday*.* On his first visit to Klosters, which he much preferred to more snooty resorts such as Davos, Capa stayed in a hotel called the Chesa-Grischuna. The hotel's owner, Hans Guler – a handsome former skiing champion – offered a 'wood-paneled [room] with chromium shower, three meals, heating and atmosphere included, for about six dollars a day.'[1]

In the hotel's cellar bar, where a pianist played Chopin and Strauss, Capa met Judith Thorne, a stunning young American Ivy League student from Vassar College. She had glossy dark hair and mischievous eyes, a great sense of humour and an athletic body that turned heads – especially when she wore figure-hugging ski-pants – and she was alone in Switzerland on a six-week skiing trip. He ran into her again in the bar of the exclusive Grand Hôtel du Mont-Cervin in Zermat, in the lee of the famous Matterhorn. They skied together, with Thorne modelling for him, and began an affair that continued sporadically for three years.[2]

As he jetted around the world with a healthy expense account, Capa appeared content, and Eve Arnold remembers him animating many a gathering with an irresistible zest and charisma.† 'Capa was a chameleon, endlessly changing. There was nothing set, fixed, about him. He would spend huge amounts of time and energy and thought with you. I found that rather special.' She agrees that Capa was too sensitive not to be affected deeply by the 'tragedies that had happened to him'. 'But he never showed it in my company,' she stresses. 'He was too involved in living to show that to many people.' She can still picture Capa 'walking down the Champs-Elysées with a coat draped

*By 1954, Capa had received assignments to write about and photograph Norway, Holland, Jerusalem, Indianapolis, Paris, Munich, Biarritz and Rome.

†She says Capa and his fellow Magnum founders were her 'photographic university', and she spent hours going through files studying their pictures. She also recalls one night when she attended a party where she met the *New Yorker* writer Janet Flanner, who knew Capa. When Flanner discovered that the petite, fiery Arnold was with Magnum, she asked about Capa. 'She said: "What do you think of Capa's pictures?" I said: "Well, I don't think they are very well designed." And she looked at me with pity and said: "My dear, history doesn't design well either."'

across his shoulder like a cape and a cigarette dangling from his mouth. How he ever kept the cigarette in there, I don't know, because it seemed to touch his chin. Behind him would be one of the world's top models, also with a coat draped around her. He had wonderful girlfriends.'

Capa's days in Paris often began with a long soak in the tub at the Lancaster Hotel. During his bath he would read cheap detective novels – Simenon was a favourite – and then scour the daily papers to check up on stories before studying the racing form for that day at Longchamps. 'Capa would lie there in the tub with his newspaper and hand out jobs he'd found,' recalls Inge Morath. 'Then he'd go and arrange his bets. "You see, guys," he'd tell us, "I have to stay in the Lancaster because that's how I get my connections. You don't need connections. You just stay in some cheap hotel." And you knew he was right. God, he was so much fun.'

Capa's companions to Longchamps included John Huston, Howard Hawks, Irwin Shaw, Gene Kelly and the Aga Khan's fabulously wealthy son, Aly Khan. Capa and Huston both liked to bet heavily on Huston's American friend, the jockey Billy Pearson. On one occasion when Pearson was riding in France, Capa and Huston marshalled their friends together to go to Longchamps. French jockeys had fouled him outrageously in an earlier race and, according to Huston, the massed support was part of a plan to surround him in the winner's enclosure and protect him from the xenophobic French crowd. After he had whipped and elbowed his way past the winning post, Capa and Huston's army of supporters sure enough provided a protective cordon. He was duly disqualified, but he was content to have exacted revenge on the French jockeys.[3]

If Capa didn't go to Longchamps, he would often have lunch at some celebrity-studded restaurant. Like Irwin Shaw, after a bottle of good burgundy he liked to retire for afternoon sex. Sometimes he took lovers to a magnificent former Rothschild residence owned by the American businessman Arthur Stanton, who had met Capa in Paris after the liberation in 1944. Stanton had told him he could use the apartment when he wasn't in Paris, and Capa took him at his word.

Burt Glinn remembers staying in the apartment, which came complete with a Moroccan butler called Israel.

'Chim told me a story which was so typical of Capa. Stanton hadn't visited Paris in years because he'd been so busy. But one day he called Israel and announced that he should prepare the master bedroom because he was going to be arriving with his wife. There was an uncomfortable silence and then Israel told Stanton that Mr Capa was in the master bedroom with a companion. Stanton loved Bob and told Israel he should prepare a second bedroom instead. But Israel had to explain that the second room was taken too – by one of Mr Capa's friends. By now, Stanton was losing his patience. He told Israel to go and fetch Capa. Israel said he didn't think Mr Capa would appreciate being disturbed. There was a long silence while someone went to fetch Capa. Finally, Capa picked up the phone. "Arthur, don't worry," he said. "We have a wonderful room for you at the Lancaster Hotel." '

The women Capa bedded at Stanton's place and at the Lancaster varied enormously, but all were beautiful. Pamela Churchill was still a favourite and recalled Capa chasing her laughing down the hundreds of steps leading to the Sacré Cœur in Montmartre one afternoon. He was one of the many poor men she slept with, she later told her biographer; he had 'champagne tastes – he bought his shirts and ties at Sulka – but a beer budget.'[4]

A former *Washington Post* editor, Ben Bradlee, ran into Capa many times in Paris while working for *Newsweek* in the early Fifties. 'He instinctually liked you or he didn't. It was as uncomplicated as that with Capa,' he recalls. 'All women adored Capa. They mothered him. Then he fucked their brains out. His *laissez-passer* was that he was this little lost child.'[5]

Hedy Lamarr, the raunchy star of the 1949 movie *Samson and Delilah*, was one of the few women who may have conquered Capa rather than vice versa. 'I like oversexed people. The few I knew were always talented and sensitive.'[6] She and Capa were often seen on the town, but Lamarr was perhaps too fond of ordering her men around in bed for their relationship to progress past whirls of the roulette wheel followed by a roll in her silk sheets. In following years, according to surviving friends, Capa had one-night stands or brief affairs with many other Hollywood beauties. 'He never lied to [these] women,' insists Suzy Marquis. 'He didn't promise anything he couldn't give, and the women knew what kind of life he led. He didn't want security . . . The idea of living the rest of his life with just one woman – he couldn't think about that.'

In need of a post-coital pick-me-up, Capa would then head for late afternoon drinks at the Hôtel Crillon, popular with journalists and the best place in Paris for tips about possible foreign assignments or which editor to approach next. If time allowed before fixing that night's date, he'd fit in a quick gin-rummy game in the photographers' locker room, sometimes with Slim Aarons and Gjon Mili, at the *Time* office off the Place de la Concorde.

A favourite spot for arranging that night's date was the bar of the Hotel California opposite the *New York Herald Tribune* office. 'Chim told me he was there one Saturday afternoon with Bob and Irwin Shaw,' says Burt Glinn. 'Chim was very quiet while Capa and Shaw went through a long list of courtesan types – really glamorous women. They called everyone but no one was available at such short notice. Eventually, Chim announced that he had to leave. He had a dinner date. It must have been a bit galling for Bob when Chim told him who his date was – Ingrid Bergman. She and Chim got on very well, in fact because of Bob. That was how she knew him.'

Dinner, with or without a date, would be at one of Paris's best restaurants, often recommended by Chim, a devoted gourmand. 'Then there [was] Alexandre's, on the Avenue George V,' fellow sybarite Irwin Shaw reminisced, 'where every midnight American friends would congregate . . . Bob Capa drawling out his Hungarian-accented English, a cigarette drooping from his mouth, saying "I am not happy". John Huston, in town to make *Moulin Rouge* . . . Billy Wilder, caustically witty, in town for the shooting of *Love in the Afternoon* . . . Art Buchwald, the next day's column just finished, looking for a poker game.'[7]

Late-night poker games sometimes followed, often with Shaw, and Huston if he was in town, and then Capa would stagger outside into the grey streets at dawn. 'Jemmy told me that towards the end Capa was no longer really interested in sex,' says Jozefa Stuart. 'He preferred gambling.'

Capa's relationship with Hammond now followed the pattern of his love affairs with Bergman and Pinky: he would not commit to marriage, and instead drifted in and out of her life. Stuart says that when Hammond did visit Paris to be with Capa, she so relied on him to entertain her, thereby cramping his style, that he was somewhat relieved when she returned to New York. But when she was gone, typically, he began to miss her.

Unwilling to tie himself down, Capa nevertheless made a point of spending every Christmas with Hammond and her two sons. 'Whenever Capa came to visit,' recalls John Hammond Jr., 'my mother would come alive. I'd wish them goodnight before I went to bed, and they always seemed very comfortable with each other. It was hard not to feel the warmth of them being together. Capa was a kind of a father figure to me and my brother . . . I used to paint and draw and do sculptures when I was a boy, and he would be very encouraging and complimentary. My mother very much wanted to marry him.'

While in New York, Capa would also hustle editors such as *Holiday*'s Ted Patrick and pay a brief visit to Cornell and his new wife Edie, as well as to his mother Julia. Cornell had changed his surname to Capa in 1944 upon becoming an American citizen, and now worked for *Life*, thanks in part to his brother. It was rare that Capa spent more than an evening or two with his family on his visits, though, probably finding his mother, whom his friends nicknamed 'Mother Goose',[8] as overbearing as ever.

Throughout the early Fifties, Capa would return to Europe for the ski season each January. His favourite resort was still Klosters, which was also popular with Irwin Shaw, Charlie Chaplin's son Sydney, and Peter Viertel, who would often drink late into the night with him in the cellar bar of the Chesa Greschuna. The bar had not changed since Capa's first visit: it still had carved wooden ceilings, smelled of furniture polish, and stayed open until the last customer fell off his stool.

Viertel liked Klosters so much he eventually spent many winters there with his wife, the actress Deborah Kerr. 'The first time I met Capa,' recalls Viertel, who worked in military intelligence in the war, 'he said to me: "Yeah, I know you, you're the spy!" We all had a bond in those days, going back to the war . . . What drew me to him among many things was that he was so phenomenally brave. In war, it is a highly esteemed quality, though it fades when the shooting's over. And he was very funny. In Klosters, he was loved by the waitresses, the chambermaids, everyone.'

Viertel and others recall that Capa was an average skier. He was often accompanied on the slopes by a witty local farmer called Peter Hitch, who doubled as a ski instructor in the winter. According to Viertel, Capa once asked him which he preferred, being a ski instructor or a farmer. 'Peter said, "I go up into the mountains in the summertime with the cows, and in the winter I go up there with English ladies. It's pretty much the same thing." Capa told the story later in *Holiday* magazine and it caused an outcry among British readers.'

Ben Bradlee sometimes joined Capa and his drinking pals in the Chesa Greschuna's bar. 'One night Noel Howard appeared with this heartbreakingly beautiful child,' he remembers. 'She couldn't have been more than sixteen. Capa was enchanted with her. We all were. When Howard left with her, either Peter Viertel or Irwin Shaw said, "I'll bet you she'll be back tomorrow." And she was – summoned by Capa. It didn't even make you jealous. It was funny to watch.'

While Bradlee joined Shaw and others each morning on the slopes of the local mountain, the Gotshnagrat, Capa often remained in bed. 'I don't remember him doing much skiing,' says Bradlee. 'He was busy bonking while the rest of us were out on the slopes.' One of his many conquests at Klosters was Colette Harrison, Rex Harrison's first wife. 'A thin, pretty blonde, she appeared to be as lightly involved with Capa,' Viertel has written, 'as many of his Paris girlfriends had been.' According to Viertel's girlfriend at the time, Bettina Graziani, Vivien Leigh also fell for his charms one evening. As she remembers the occasion, 'She was alone and fragile. We were all having a drink in the bar. She came down and Capa started to drink with her and then they danced – Russian dances. He was incredible, so much fun. I don't think it lasted long with her. I don't know if he had a life with any woman that lasted very long.'

According to several other contemporaries, as middle age threatened, Capa confronted a profound identity crisis. What would he do with the rest of his life if he stopped playing the light-hearted gypsy with a Leica dangling from his neck? Was it too late to reinvent himself as a successful businessman outside photography? He was a fount of new ideas, the creative drive behind almost all of Magnum's team projects, but ideas did not in themselves guarantee a secure financial future. When Noel Howard told him he could easily be a rich man, he replied: 'The difficult thing in life is not having ideas, but getting people who can make them happen believe that they came up with them.'[9] One thing was certain: being a freelance journalist was no way for a man with such jaded tastes to enjoy life's great delights. 'If you want to make money, give up your job as a reporter,' he told Gisèle Freund and others at Magnum many times. 'It will earn you a good living, but you'll never get rich. There are too many expenses.'[10]

He was also beginning to tire of constantly having to maintain the Capa legend, acting the impulsive Don Juan, and wearing his eternally 'debonair mask'. 'Capa was very much trapped by it,' confirms Inge Morath. 'If he wanted an early night, he couldn't go to bed. He was Capa and Capa always stays up until three and plays poker. And yet he was tired of it all. As with anyone who is always telling jokes, eventually things stopped being funny. He had a sadness, which may have been just part of his Slavic, Jewish background. But I think it came from all the wars.'

Irwin Shaw, who had moved to Paris in summer 1951, saw the man who had seen too much:

> Only in the morning, as he staggers out of bed, does Capa show that the tragedy and sorrow through which he has passed have left their marks on him. His face is gray, his eyes are dull and haunted by the dark dreams of the night; here, at last, is the man whose camera has

> peered at so much death and so much evil, here is a man despairing and in pain, regretful, not stylish, undebonair. Then Capa drinks down a strong, bubbling draught, shakes himself, experimentally tries on his afternoon smile, discovers that it works, knows once more that he has the strength to climb the glittering hill of the day, dresses, sets out, nonchalant, carefully light-hearted, to the bar of '21', or the Scribe, or the Dorchester, all places where this homeless man can be at home, where he can find his friends and amuse them and where his friends can help him forget the bitter, lonely, friendless hours of the night behind him and the night ahead.[11]

By 1952, Capa's appetite for the 'glittering' life, as well as his commitment to Magnum, had started to wane. In a February report to Magnum's stockholders, Capa quipped: 'After five years Magnum is solvent and I am bankrupt.'[12] A few months later, he was allocated $10,000 a year to cover his travelling and entertaining expenses alone, but declined the offer of a salary to continue running the agency,[13] telling his brother Cornell, 'Do you think I would want to be employed by those bastards?'[14]

It was not until January 1953 that he found someone willing to head the financially strapped agency: John Morris, whom he coaxed into leaving *Ladies' Home Journal* to become the 'international executive editor' of Magnum, in charge of the London and Paris offices, for a salary of $12,000.[15] 'It was not a business,' Morris recalled. 'It was a story, a romance.'[16] Capa announced the appointment at a gathering of Magnum staff in New York later that month. 'Well, boys, from now on take your problems to him!' he cried, pointing at his new executive editor.[17]

Around the time he was handing over responsibility for running Magnum, he received a letter from the US Embassy in Paris asking him to consult them about his passport. On 7 October 1952, he had applied to renew his passport, which was due to expire on 5 October 1954. He handed it over and to his shock was told that it would not be returned. When he demanded to know why, he was told that he was suspected of being a communist.[18] 'All [Capa's] connections and friendships were of little help to him at that moment,' Peter Viertel has written. 'He had never been a member of the Communist Party – he had been a journalist whose sympathies had been anti-fascist and nothing more.'[19]

Capa told Noel Howard and Viertel that he'd immediately cabled a lawyer in New York, Morris Ernst. A co-counsel of the American Civil Liberties Union, he had helped *Life* photographer Margaret Bourke-White overcome the same problem successfully, and Capa hoped he would be able to solve the crisis as quickly as possible because without a passport he could not work, and he needed the foreign assignments with *Holiday* magazine to claw his way out of debt and also to help Magnum's dire cash-flow.

From a close examination of Capa's FBI file, it would appear that his past had finally caught up with him.

The first detailed report on Capa in his FBI file is a summary requested by J. Edgar Hoover's office dated 28 March 1948. 'It has been reported,' the summary states, 'that the subject became a member of the FFR Communist Party during the Spanish Civil War when he sold his photographs to the Communist front weekly, *Regards*.' The summary provided Hoover's G-men with several other examples of Capa's subversive activities:

> The 1938 edition of the magazine, *Friends of Abraham Lincoln Brigade* contains a group of photographs taken by the subject . . . On June 2, 1942 an informant reported that the subject was either a member or honorary member of the radical anti-Fascist 'Photographic League of New York' at 31 East 21st Street, New York City . . . On December 18, 1947, the *Magyar Jovo*, a Communist Hungarian language newspaper, said that the subject was present at a meeting held at the Park Central Hotel in New York City on December 14, 1947 by the '48 Committee.' This committee was organized to form a pilgrimage to Hungary in order to participate in the Centennial celebrations to be held in 1948 on the occasion of the 100th anniversary of the Hungarian War for Independence in 1848 . . . The subject, together with John Steinbeck, made a tour of Russia during the summer of 1947 . . . Upon his return numerous articles appeared in various papers recording what the subject and Steinbeck observed in Russia . . . *The Daily Worker* for October 24, 1947, said

> that the subject in speaking before the 4th session of the *Herald Tribune* Forum on the Wednesday previous had stated that the Russian people did not want war and that a 'halt of the vicious and insane game' of recriminations between Russia and the United States would meet with the immediate approval of the Russians.*

Morris Ernst advised Capa to make a full statement to the passport authorities detailing his earlier political activities, and the resulting affidavit was a long and fascinating document in which he named names. He stated that 'at no time during my entire life have I ever been a member of the Communist Party'.[20] In Hungary he had 'studied socialism, but found [himself] in immediate disagreement with the aims and methods of the Communist Party'. In Nazi Germany he had become 'ever more opposed to the Communist Party, which, in [his] opinion, seemed to be furthering Hitler's rise to power'. He then explained why he had changed his name: there was 'already an established photographer named Friedman working in France'.

He maintained that his work for *Ce Soir*, the 'Communist controlled newspaper', did not mean he had been a communist, neglecting to mention that only communist sympathizers became staff photographers, then stated that the 'editor of *Ce Soir*, Louis Aragon, was a Communist'. To underscore his respectability, he went on to mention famous friends and employers such as Hemingway and Ed Thompson, the managing editor of *Life* magazine. In a brief passage about his time in China, he revealed that the documentary he'd made there had been yet another propaganda effort – 'directly sponsored and supervised by Mme. Chiang Kai Chek [sic]'. He also named his old colleague and friend Joris Ivens as 'probably a communist'.

Capa's FBI file includes another declassified document that suggests that he considered working for the US State Department. According to one document, 'a confidential source of known reliability' reported on 14 April 1953 that he had not worked for propaganda arms of the US

*Much of this material was provided by an informant code-named 'T-1'. By 1953, there had been several others. The FBI even looked through police files in New York for dirt but came up empty-handed.

State Department. The source also stated that 'the Information Division . . . had at one time considered using Capa on a contract basis, and in line with normal procedures clearing contract personnel, Capa was given an application form to execute . . . Capa refused to fill out an application form.'

Several heavily censored letters between the CIA and Hoover's office reveal that throughout 1953 he was closely watched and made the subject of much discussion. His file ends in 1955, a year after his death, with several blanked-out letters referring to information which is still too sensitive for the CIA to allow to be made public.

On 6 May, Miss Agnes Schneider, Chief of the Passport Section at the American Embassy in Paris, validated his passport until October 1954, 'for all countries with the exception of the Iron Curtain countries.' It is worth asking how he got his passport back so quickly (within two months of its seizure) when other suspected subversives had to fight for years and in one case all the way to the Supreme Court.

There may be a very simple answer: Peter Viertel says he contacted Henry Hyde, a former boss in the Office of Strategic Services, the wartime intelligence service, and asked him to put in a word with Mrs Shipley, at that time the famously reactionary head of the passport division. 'Hyde was very Republican, and had been my boss during the war. He had a good relationship with Shipley, and eventually managed to get Capa's passport back without even asking for a fee.'

But others have questioned whether Hyde exerted such influence. Is it possible that Capa considered a deal to try to regain his passport? Did this even entail providing information to the CIA? We may never know unless the CIA decides to reveal exactly what dealings it had with him. Larry Collins, a journalist friend of Capa's who had close connections to the CIA during his time as a *Newsweek* correspondent, believes 'Capa would have made the perfect asset'. Warren Trabant, who had worked during the war in counter-intelligence, jokes that Capa 'was perhaps on the verge of becoming the ultimate male Mata Hari.'

*

Capa's *annus horribilis* went from bad to worse. In May 1953, he slipped a disc after carrying too much heavy camera equipment. John Morris recalled a day when the pain got so bad that he lay on the floor of the Magnum office and 'simply wept',[21] and in June he went to London to see a Harley Street specialist. He started to take large doses of codeine, and tried traction, but still the pain continued.[22]

That summer, Capa travelled back to the south of France with Jemmy Hammond and stayed in John Huston's summer villa. Peter Viertel remembers Huston's wife Ricki walking barefoot on the small of Capa's back while he lay moaning on the floor. 'It was distressing to see the once debonair Capa partially crippled by an injury that was in no way connected with the many wars he had been in . . . We often discussed his future, but he said he was tired of going to wars, tired of looking at horror through the finder of his Leica . . . tired of living in crummy hotels in godforsaken corners of the globe . . . His personal life was equally unsettled. He was devoted to Jemmy Hammond, but he knew full well that he would never make any woman a good husband.'[23]

Capa told Viertel he still felt a 'great affection' for the American skier Judy Thorne, but when he was with Jemmy he thought of Judy, and when he was with Judy he thought of Jemmy. He didn't like to be reminded that having a girl in every port didn't work so well in peacetime. 'It's all different now,' he told Viertel. 'Now it's worse to have two girlfriends than one.' Viertel already knew of Gerda's tragic death, from Hemingway. '[Capa] had never gotten over the loss of her and that perhaps kept him from committing himself completely in any other relationship.'[24]

In July, Capa went to Italy for *Picture Post* to report on the making of the John Huston film *Beat the Devil*, scripted by Truman Capote and starring Humphrey Bogart. Huston had chosen a magical place for his shoot. The town of Ravello was high in the mountains behind Sorrento, and famous for a grand villa that overlooked the sea. Greta Garbo and Stokowski had stayed there during a much-publicized romantic holiday. Much of the film was shot at the villa, surrounded by mountains and terraced with grape vines and fruit trees. On many nights, Capa played poker with members of the cast and crew. The table was dominated by Bogart and Huston: 'Bob Capa, who was there to take promotion shots, and Truman were our main victims. Their services on the picture came pretty cheap because we regularly won back whatever salaries were paid them.'*

Capa couldn't afford to lose a single dollar to Huston. By autumn 1953, he was in the worst financial trouble of his career. In order to pay his medical expenses and legal bills for Morris Ernst, he was forced to borrow several thousand dollars from Magnum, adding to the agency's already severe cash-flow problems.

At the last Magnum shareholders' meeting he attended, in September 1953, Capa spoke eloquently about how the moving image would one day usurp the still in importance. Jinx Rodger remembers him suggesting that Magnum members should start carrying movie cameras.† He was fifty years ahead of his time. Today the veteran photojournalist Dirck Halstead, winner of the Robert Capa Medal in 1974, recommends Capa's dual approach as the only way to revivify serious photojournalism.

The French photographer Marc Riboud, whom Capa had recruited earlier that year, remembers visiting Capa in his room, dubbed 'The Racing Room', in London's Pastoria Hotel that autumn. '[Capa] had told me to go to London to learn English and meet the girls there. I went but didn't meet any girls. I was too shy. But I met Capa twice in London. One time, I talked to him for maybe fifteen minutes while he

*One night during a game, Huston left the table to make himself a martini. As he records in *An Open Book*, he strolled out on to a terrace, marvelling at his surroundings. Below was a 'bay with the sodium lights on the fishing boats . . . making constellations to rival those above.' He slipped and fell, glass in hand. Fortunately, a tree broke his fall and he dropped to the ground forty feet below the terrace. He was unhurt. He called up for help and was soon brought back to the villa where he nonchalantly mixed himself another martini and returned to his place at the poker table.

†'I remember Bob saying several times that we had to start looking to the future. Television was going to change everything. We all felt that Bob would not have gone on being a photographer. He was a restless soul who had to keep doing something new and take on fresh challenges.'

soaked in the bathtub in his hotel room. He told me photography was finished. Television would take over.'

On 22 October, depressed, still in pain, practically bankrupt, Capa celebrated his fortieth birthday. 'I can't be forty, how can anybody be forty?' he told Inge Morath. 'I don't know how I am going to do it.' He again visited his family in New York that Christmas and then returned to Klosters in the New Year.

One afternoon on the slopes, Capa almost fell to his death. The ski instructor Flury Clavadetscher saved Capa just in time: 'We were going down a very steep slope above a rock face. He was wearing French skis and boots, and he fell and I jumped on him, grabbed his leg and stopped him. We had a party that night in the Chesa Greschuna to celebrate him not falling over the edge. He probably would have died, because it was about a hundred-foot sheer drop.' Clavadetscher remembers Capa as a heavy Scotch drinker and as having immense charm, but there was now a melancholy about him, especially in the mornings as he tried to find his skiing gear and talked to Clavadetscher about Jemmy Hammond and other women. He loved Jemmy but still refused to tie himself down.

In early February 1954, while still at Klosters, Capa received an offer he couldn't refuse. A Japanese publishing conglomerate, Mainichi Press, invited him to spend several weeks photographing Japan. The company would pay all his expenses and a fat fee, and provide him with new Japanese-manufactured cameras to use while touring. Irwin Shaw was also in Klosters that winter. 'I had made [Capa] promise not to get involved in any more wars. When I asked him to bring back a camera for me, he glanced at me peculiarly, which should have warned me that he was not going to spend his time in the Orient photographing the peaceful rehabilitation of the Japanese civilian population.' Shaw accompanied him to the railway station when he left for Paris: '[Capa] was serenaded by the town band as he climbed aboard the train with a bottle of champagne and someone else's wife.'[25]

Inge Morath remembers one evening in late spring 1954, when a group of Magnum recruits went down to the cafe under the Paris office to say goodbye to Capa before he left for Japan. They had seen each other off to many places for many years, but this time was different. 'It was so weird, because we'd never had a feeling of any kind of doom about Capa. But that evening we all did. We felt terrible. We had our last pinball game together. It was kind of sad because we felt he didn't want to go.' Capa again spent most of his time hammering away on the pinball machine, muttering about what he'd do in his old age.

Later, outside in the rain-splashed streets, Capa and his young recruits embraced each other. '*Bonne chance, mon vieux,*' Inge Morath told the man who had been a 'brother and father' to them all. Capa then headed back to the Lancaster where Suzy Marquis found him in one of the maids' rooms – the Lancaster's manager had kindly set it aside for him, now he could no longer afford the standard rates. For several years, she had helped Capa pack his bags before a trip. 'We would talk as I packed,' she says. 'I always knew how he felt about going to different places. At the end, Bob didn't want to go to war any more. He had been terribly affected psychologically by what he had seen – he never talked about it with others, but he did with me.'

Suzy discovered that he had already packed his bags. He had already told her: 'If I have to go to war again, I'll shoot myself because I've seen far too much.' Now she suddenly felt that she wouldn't see him again, and somehow he knew it too. 'Bob wasn't the writing type. But I later got a short hand-written letter from him. It ended with his last words to me – "live intelligently, Love Bob." '

23 Forward Lies the Delta

'He had this marvelous capacity to get on
with generals and peasants.'

JINX RODGER

The Mainichi Press put on a rousing tour for Capa in Japan. To his delight, he was fêted wherever he went. Large groups gathered to hear him talk about his work, and long lines formed outside an exhibit of his photographs in Tokyo. 'There were hundreds and hundreds of Japanese photographers running after Capa,' says Jinx Rodger. 'He was their hero.' In a cable to Magnum's Paris office, he explained how he had been given five new cameras, fifteen lenses and thirty bunches of flowers in only a few days.

Throughout the six-week trip, Capa chose children as his primary subjects. He also recorded a May Day celebration in Tokyo and scenes inside several Buddhist temples. Focusing on joyous children and places of worship, he was soon enjoying photography for the first time in years. He told a Japanese contact, Hiroshi Kawazoe, that Japan was a 'photographer's paradise'.[1]

While Capa regained some of his former enthusiasm for photography, events were conspiring elsewhere to cut his stay in Japan short. That April, *Life*'s Howard Sochurek, who was covering the French war in nearby Indo-China, returned to San Francisco on compassionate leave. *Life* needed a replacement badly. According to Sochurek: 'Ed Thompson [*Life*'s managing editor] said, ' "You're coming back through Tokyo. See Capa there. He may cover Indochina while you're gone." ' Capa was exhibiting his pictures at one of the department stores.'[2]

Life knew what Capa always responded positively to and also cabled him directly with an offer: $2,000 for a month with a $25,000 Lloyd's of London insurance policy thrown in for good measure. Thompson then telephoned Capa in Tokyo.* 'Look, you don't have to do this and I know you won't if you don't want to,' Thompson told him, 'but if you want to take a whack at this for a month or so, how about taking Howard's place in Indo-China?'

Thompson later insisted that he didn't 'try to talk' him into taking the dangerous assignment. Capa apparently told him he already had an idea for a story called 'Bitter Rice', which would juxtapose 'in the form of an essay, pictures of peasants in the Delta against the military activity'.[3]

A cable Capa then got from John Morris at Magnum emphasized how much *Life* wanted him: 'PRICE SUBJECT TO CONSIDERABLE UPRAISING IF BECOMES HAZARDOUS.'†

On 29 April, Howard Sochurek met Capa in Tokyo before returning to America. 'We had dinner together in the old Imperial Hotel that Frank Lloyd Wright built,' Sochurek recalled.[4] 'It had five foot six inch ceilings, or so it seemed, but they had a grill downstairs that served terrific steaks. We talked from seven at night until one in the morning about what I had covered, and how the war was going, and how dangerous it was. He kept saying, "This is one war I've never covered, and I've never wanted to cover." He was under great pressure from his brother not to go. I know he needed the money. He said a little bit about that. In those days, the money was quite good.'‡ Capa

* Henry Luce had ordered Thompson to provide upbeat coverage of the war to compensate for Douglas's report, which had provoked the French Foreign Ministry into talking of 'defamation and slander'.

† Morris has said that he called Capa to try to dissuade him. It was a bad connection. 'Bob, you don't have to do this,' he shouted, 'it's not our war.'

'Don't worry,' Capa shouted back, 'it's only a few weeks.'

Capa subsequently sent Morris a letter, apologizing for having shouted at him, and explaining that he wasn't taking the job because he felt duty-bound, but because he was genuinely excited by the prospect of taking on a real assignment again. In Japan, he had recharged and regained some of his enthusiasm for shooting, he added.

‡ Why Capa took his final assignment remains an emotive question to this day. Was he

accepted *Life*'s offer on 30 April 1954 and then flew to Bangkok.[5]

Capa's time in Japan had coincided with the epic siege of Dien Bien Phu. Hoping to draw Ho Chi Minh's guerrillas into a classic battle, the French had decided to build up a garrison there. But as they did so, Vietminh guerrillas and troops from the People's Army of Vietnam surrounded the town under cover of darkness. With immense ingenuity and determination, the Vietminh also managed to move entire gun batteries across precipitous gorges and mountains to within range of the garrison.

When the Vietminh attacked the French on 13 March, they had immediately proved how vulnerable and flawed the French defences were. Within days, they had surrounded the garrison. Closed off from the outside world, under constant fire and flooded by monsoon rains, conditions inside Dien Bien Phu rapidly became inhuman. Men went insane. Hundreds and then thousands of casualties piled up inside the garrison's hospital as days stretched into weeks. On 7 May, Dien Bien Phu fell to the communists. At least 2,200 members of the French forces had died during the siege. Thousands more were taken prisoner.

Capa was still in Bangkok awaiting a visa to fly to Hanoi when the news of Dien Bien Phu's fall came across the wire. Two days later, on 9 May, he arrived in Hanoi, in French Indo-China. The fall of Dien Bien Phu, which had caused headlines around the globe, meant Capa would inevitably see action. The release of French prisoners by the Vietminh and the French strategy in the wake of this crushing defeat

keen to burnish his legend as the greatest war photographer of his time? Indeed, was he envious of Duncan, whose coverage of Korea was fast making him photojournalism's new battlefield star? Duncan denies there was any competition between him and Capa. 'I never felt in competition with anybody in war photography,' he insists. 'You're lucky to get your ass in and out again. It's as simple as that. It's the easiest photography in the world to shoot somebody who's been shot up. It doesn't take a genius. That's easy. The only thing you need to do is know your photography. Get in and if you're lucky get out. And get as close as you can get.'

'I have always thought,' Irwin Shaw later wrote, 'it was to disprove semi-official allegations that he was a Communist sympathizer that Capa accepted the job.' Peter Viertel discounts this theory, suggesting it stemmed from Shaw's later obsession about McCarthyism in America. 'Capa really needed the dough,' he says.

were now big news. *Life* would need suitably dramatic images.

Expecting to find nightclubs deserted and the city in mourning, Capa toured crowded restaurants where premier vintages were being uncorked with decadent abandon. Bamboo bars were propped up by French officers clinging to their petite whores who clucked mock-hatred for Ho Chi Minh as they eyed the competition's silken bedroom couture.[6]

The *Paris-Match* photographer Michel Descamps drank cognac several times with Capa in Hanoi.

> He was a very good friend of mine. We had met many times in Paris, often in the marvellous bar at the American Legion near the *Paris-Match* offices. In Vietnam, we spent a lot of time in the press club in Hanoi, if you know what I mean. I respected him because he made a lot of human pictures, and he worked very fast. We got talking about *Paris-Match* one time. Very often, the editors would look at the name of the photographer and only then at the photograph. Capa said: 'Michel, come to me when you're back in Paris and we'll stamp my name on the back of your photos and then you'll be the best!'

After three days in Hanoi, Capa accompanied Descamps and the *Life* reporter Don Wilson to Luang Prabang, in northern Laos, to cover the evacuation of wounded French from Dien Bien Phu. A week after its fall, according to *Life*, only '183 of 753'[7] wounded men had left the stricken town, leading the Vietminh to declare: 'See, we are ready to evacuate you but the French are not interested in getting you out.' An unseen newsreel shows Capa taking a picture of a wounded French soldier. He looks fit, relaxed, focused, and extremely quick on his feet as he darts closer to a stretcher to get within a few feet of the man's face. One of his photographs shows a weary sore-footed soldier resting after a helicopter has lifted him to safety. In other images, sodden men carry their comrades through a tent encampment mired in foot-deep mud.[8]

In Luang Prabang itself, Capa found an idyllic setting around the Royal Palace on the banks of the Mekong River. 'The city, nestled in rich green mountains covered with frangipani trees, is the unlikeliest location for modern war,' reported Don Wilson. 'Between the soldiers digging trenches rise the golden spires of Phousi Pagoda. The signs of trouble don't bother the pretty barefooted girls softly pedaling bicycles along shaded streets . . . But ask Governor Tiao Rattava Panya, who wears a green rubber fedora, and he'll tell you the Viets could still come before the rains.'[9]

On 17 May, Capa and Descamps returned to Hanoi, where Capa heard that several French commanders believed that all was not yet lost, and one in particular insisted that the war against the Vietminh could still be won. General René Cogny, a tall and sophisticated leader, insisted fiercely that what was needed was a war of rapid movement, tactics designed to beat Ho Chi Minh at his own game. The French should fight as marauders, in small groups. Capa agreed with his tactics, if not with the political impulse behind them.

It was during a visit to Cogny's headquarters on 21 May that Descamps, on a whim, whipped out his camera and snapped the last picture of Capa alive.

> I just pulled out the camera, took one shot, that was it. Bob was walking along with a doctor, a professor of medicine called Huard. Not long afterwards, he asked me to take a camera back to France. He said: 'Michel, you're going back to France in a military aircraft so you don't have any customs. You go straight through. May I give you my camera, and you give it me back in Paris?' So I said, 'OK, Bob,' and I took it. But I made a mistake. I gave the camera to Cartier-Bresson at Magnum. It would have been much better if I had kept it for me, as a souvenir. Later, I told myself, 'Michel, you're crazy to give back this camera.'

According to Descamps, Cogny and Capa got on well: 'Capa was very well known and Cogny liked the press very much.' Cogny's daughter, Marie-Claude, remembers her father talking about Capa with affection until his death in an air crash in 1967: 'My father and Capa had the same views on how the war should have been waged.' Cogny was humorous and genuinely brave, a soldier's soldier, and Capa quickly recognized him as such. 'He and Capa had both come from modest beginnings. By the time they met, they'd both travelled very far. Perhaps they both recognized that.'

On 24 May 1954, beneath a cloudless sky, Capa flew with Cogny to the troubled southern zone of the Red River delta. He then watched the general present a military honour to the elite 2nd Amphibious Group, 1st Foreign Legion Cavalry Regiment. It was a public relations exercise, of course, intended to demonstrate that the French had not lost heart, and Capa knew his pictures would suit *Life*'s political stance: they'd project the French in a positive light.

'There's nothing wrong with us when we fight,'[10] Cogny told the men, in earshot of Capa and other correspondents, hiding his bitter sadness after the fall of Dien Bien Phu. He had begged to be allowed to relieve the garrison, but he'd been refused. To have relieved the garrison would have contravened the mandates of a Geneva peace conference. Powerless to save his comrades, he had remained in contact until the last moment, agonizing as the voices crackling over the radio had grown more desperate and fearful before finally going silent.

That morning of the 24th, Capa watched as Cogny tied a traditional 'fanon', an Arabian horse's tail, to the unit's regimental colours, then called his officers to him. 'Dien Bien Phu was a blow,' he said, 'but that's all over now. We must turn the page. We must look forward – and forward lies the Battle of the Delta.'[11]

Over lunch, Lieutenant Colonel Jean Lacapelle, one of Cogny's senior officers, invited Capa to accompany him on a mission to evacuate and raze two small forts, Doaithan and Thantine, along a road leading from the village of Namdinh to Thaibinh, twenty miles to the east. Lacapelle assured him he'd get plenty of good pictures. Capa accepted the offer.

In Namdinh that night, 'in a seedy and bug-ridden hotel' calling itself the Modern Hotel, Capa agreed to join forces with *Time-Life*'s John Mecklin and Jim Lucas, who was working for Scripps-Howard and was one of the century's very best American war correspondents. Lucas later covered Vietnam aged fifty before dying of alcoholism.

Mecklin, Lucas and Capa sat up until 3 a.m., fuelled by Capa's cognac. Capa was angry about the slack attitude of many correspondents and contemptuous of their work: they were too afraid to get close enough to show what was really happening in French Indo-China. 'This is maybe the last good war,' he said as he swilled cognac and soda around a glass. 'The trouble with all you guys who complain so much about French public relations is that you don't appreciate this is a reporter's war. Nobody knows anything and nobody tells you anything, and that means a good reporter is free to go out and get a beat every day.'

Capa did not mention his own compromised position. He was, after all, covering the war for a magazine whose publisher was vehemently opposed to communist expansion in the Far East. Indeed, he was very much on the wrong side, for the first time in his career. Luce would want pictures of French victory, not of imperialism's victims. It was a far cry from the days when Capa had staged scenes in Spain, believing so passionately in the cause that he became the Republic's most able propagandist armed with a Leica.

At 7 a.m. on Tuesday 25 May, one of La Capelle's men collected Capa, Mecklin and Lucas. Capa had prepared a flask of cognac and a thermos of iced tea. 'This is going to be a beautiful story,' Capa said. 'I will be on my good behaviour today. I will not insult my colleagues, and I will not once mention the excellence of my work.'

They crossed the Red River and then the column began toward Doaithan. At 8.40 a.m., shots rang out. The correspondents instinctively dived for cover. Several French tanks further back in the convoy opened fire. Capa jumped down from his jeep and began to photograph seemingly oblivious peasants as they continued to pick rice in surrounding fields.

While the convoy waited to move on, Capa waded out into a paddy to get closer to several women, determined to complete the 'Bitter Rice' project he'd discussed with *Life*'s Ed Thompson. Finally, the column started up again. But a few minutes later, an explosion halted it once more. Word came down the line that a truck had driven over a mine. Four were dead, six wounded. Then Vietminh mortars opened up. The more chaotic and dangerous the situation became, the more Capa appeared to be energized. Lucas saw him brave mortar fire to load a wounded Vietnamese soldier into a jeep that he then drove back to an outpost for medical aid.

In lulls between shelling, Capa photographed a dead Vietminh soldier stripped of his rifle, shoes and rice ration – the corpse lay sprawled on top of a dyke. He took another picture of a soldier carrying a mine detector, and of other soldiers in a rice paddy, searching for a mortar position. He moved with agility and a keen sense of the risks involved in taking each new picture that only a forty-year-old veteran of five wars could possess. 'He was cautious about crossing exposed areas,' observed Mecklin, 'but if he saw a good picture which could only be made with risk he took the risk.'

A French colonel invited Mecklin, Lucas and Capa to have lunch with him at Dong Q'ui Thon. Capa declined the invitation. He wanted to carry on shooting his 'Bitter Rice' story, even though *Life* might not run images that captured the injustice of the war. To avoid the midday sun, he napped under a truck, where Mecklin and Lucas found him dozing just after 2 p.m. on returning from lunch. They asked how much film he had left.

'That's what I'm doing here,' he smiled, 'saving film.'

The trio got back into their jeep and manoeuvred around other vehicles in the column. At 2.25, they arrived at a fort surrounded by barbed wire. Demolition experts were planting explosives.

'The story's almost done,' said Capa, 'but I need the fort blowing up.'

A few hundred yards further on the column was again halted by a Vietminh ambush. The journalists approached Lacapelle.

'What's new?' asked Capa.

'Vietminh everywhere,' he replied.

Capa leapt on to the hood of the jeep to get a better shot of mortars opening up yet again. A truck full of soldiers behind the journalists honked angrily several times for them to get moving. Capa took his time getting his shot. 'That was a good picture,' he said, finally climbing back into the jeep, allowing the column to advance again. Three miles from the next fort at Thanh Ne, as the sun blazed above them, the most intense fighting of the day began. French artillery, tanks and mortars opened up to their rear. Small-arms fire responded from trees around a village about a mile away. Within seconds, all that could be heard was 'the sporadic ping of slugs passing overhead, the harrowing curr-rump of mines and enemy mortars.'

Capa looked bored. 'I'm going up the road a little bit,' he told Lucas and Mecklin. 'Look for me when you get started again.' They thought it far too dangerous but he shrugged off their concerns. 'For a long, indecisive minute,' recalled Lucas, 'Capa crouched behind the protective bulk of our jeep, ready to leap back or spring ahead – as if testing the temper of Viet Minh fire. He decided he'd risk it.'

They watched as Capa walked ahead and then left the road and began to cross a sheltered area between the road and a dyke. He photographed a platoon advancing through tall grass, fanned out against the humid horizon. Mecklin checked his watch. Five minutes later, there was the sound of a heavy explosion. A French lieutenant nearby tried to crack a joke, asking him: 'Does the atomic bomb look like that?'

'Dammit,' swore Lucas. 'There goes the picture Capa wanted.'

Suddenly, a young Vietnamese soldier arrived and spoke to the lieutenant, who said, in French and without a trace of emotion, 'The photographer is dead.'

'Pardon?' asked Mecklin.

'*Le photographe est mort.*'

Mecklin turned to Lucas. He wasn't sure whether the lieutenant was trying to be funny again. 'I think this guy's trying to tell me Capa's dead,' said a disbelieving Mecklin. The lieutenant nodded and then spelled out 'd-e-a-t-h' in a heavy French accent. Another soldier ran up and spoke to him. 'Maybe not dead but wounded by mortar, very serious,' he added.

Mecklin and Lucas ran towards Capa, scrambling on all fours across the road and into a small field. Capa lay on his back, soaked in blood. His left leg had been blown to pieces. The stump lay a foot from a hole gouged in the ground by a landmine. He had a serious chest wound. With his left hand, he clutched his Contax camera. *

* Capa's last photograph, frame 11 of his film, showed men walking along a dyke.

'Capa. Capa! Capa!' called Mecklin.

Capa's lips quivered and then they moved no more. It was 3.10 p.m. Mecklin screamed for a medic. A few minutes later, a husky Frenchman carrying a stretcher arrived, took one look at Capa, shrugged and turned to walk away. He was done for, a hopeless case. Plenty of other men could be saved. But then he turned back towards Mecklin and Lucas. '*Camarade?*' Mecklin nodded. The medic shrugged again and unfolded his stretcher.

They placed Capa's mangled body in the stretcher and then hurried towards a less exposed area across the road. As they reached relative safety, they heard a huge blast on the road. Another landmine had exploded, throwing three screaming Vietnamese soldiers into a nearby ditch. The seconds passed slowly. Then Colonel Lacapelle arrived on the scene, flagged down an ambulance and Capa's body was taken to Dong Q'ui Thon, three miles away, where a Vietnamese doctor pronounced '*le photographe*' dead.[12]

Outside the medical station, Mecklin and Lucas encountered the operational commander in the area, Lieutenant Colonel Jacques Navarre. Mecklin told him Capa was dead. '*C'est l'Indochine*,' he replied, then turned away and walked past the truck in whose shade Capa had dozed earlier that afternoon.

'Is this the first American correspondent killed in Indochina?' asked the Vietnamese doctor.

Mecklin nodded.

'It is a harsh way for America to learn.'*

* It was another two decades, after the loss of 60,000 young men, before America learned how futile it can be to engage a fiercely ideological enemy in a guerrilla war in inhospitable terrain halfway around the globe. Indeed, Capa was the first correspondent to die in what would become the Vietnam War, known to the Vietnamese as 'the American War'. Tragically, more than a hundred other journalists died before the Americans learned the lesson of Dien Bien Phu – the Vietminh should never be underestimated.

By a particularly poignant twist of fate, Larry Burrows, a skinny eighteen-year-old when he spent fifty-two hours straight developing Capa and other *Life* staff photographers' D-Day pictures, also died in Indo-China while on assignment for *Life* magazine. He lost his life working for Henry Luce in 1968, becoming the first British war photographer to die in Indo-China, and winning the Robert Capa Medal in the process.

*

The sun cut through the hazy afternoon, bleaching the dust, forcing their hands across the sad, burnt faces of the young Frenchmen as they carried Robert Capa's casket aboard a C-47 for shipment to Hanoi. In Saigon, General Navarre had already sent condolences to the US Embassy. Capa would be buried in Hanoi until arrangements could be made for transport to New York. When the plane landed in the capital, a Senegalese honour guard waited on the runway.

At the memorial service in Hanoi, the sun blazed down again, on the last days of the French occupation of Indo-China and General René Cogny, dressed in full uniform. Cogny stood frozen in grief, his hand stiffly saluting his dead friend. When the long minute of silence ended, he turned towards Capa's press colleagues: hardened battle veterans, many struggling to hold back tears. 'Capa fell as a soldier among soldiers,' he said. He then pinned a medal on the American flag draped over Capa's casket. It was one of France's highest honours: the Croix de Guerre with Palm, Order of the Army. Several wreaths were then placed on Capa's temporary grave. One was from the French army's press information service. Another was inscribed: '*A notre ami.*' It came from La Bonne Casserole, a local restaurant where, according to Mecklin, Capa had 'terrified the waiters, charmed the hostess and taught the bartender to mix American martinis'.

EPILOGUE The Legend

> 'Capa: He was a good friend and a great and very brave photographer. It is bad luck for everybody that the percentages caught up with him. It is especially bad for Capa. He was so much alive that it is a hard long day to think of him as dead.'
>
> ERNEST HEMINGWAY, Madrid, 27 May 1954

While Capa's death on assignment was perhaps inevitable – he knew better than anyone how luck would one day desert him – it nevertheless left his friends, family and Magnum colleagues deeply shocked. John Steinbeck is said to have wandered around Paris in a daze for fourteen hours, so devastated was he by the news. John Hammond Jr. remembers being with his mother Jemmy when she received a telephone call. 'There was no consoling her – she never got over his death. He was the great love of her life, and she changed after he'd gone. She became withdrawn, less social, and began to drink a lot more. Perhaps they are together now.'*

Magnum staffers such as Inge Bondi, who worked in the New York office, recall May 1954 with particular poignancy. 'We just couldn't believe it. It was a terrible, terrible time.' The tragedy was compounded by another death in the Magnum family: Capa's protégé, Werner Bischof, had died on 16 May in a car accident in Peru, falling 1,500 feet when his car slid off a road. It took nine days for the news to reach New York – at the same time as Capa's death was being announced. It was Bondi who broke the news of Werner Bischof's death to John Morris: 'John, I have terrible news. Werner is dead. Dead!'[1]

*Jemmy Hammond died in 1993. John Hammond Jr. says she never stopped loving Capa.

Morris was stunned by Werner's death, having befriended him and his wife, Rosellina, who was pregnant with the photographer's second child. 'Overwhelmed by happy and sad memories', Morris returned to New York from Chicago. That evening, a researcher from *Life* called him at home. 'You've heard the awful news?' she asked.

'Yes,' replied Morris, assuming the researcher was referring to Bischof.

'Do you mind if I ask you some questions about Robert Capa?'

'Capa?'[2]

The added news of Capa's death was just too much for one day. Somehow, he prepared obituaries for both Magnum photographers, taking particular care that Bischof's accomplishments would not go unnoticed – Capa was famous, but Bischof's greatness was not yet widely acknowledged. The following morning, he met a distraught Julia and Cornell. As he recalls, Julia was undecided on what funeral arrangements should be made for the son she had adored so much. It was, however, decided that there should not be a burial at Arlington National Cemetery. 'Bob, the greatest war photographer of the bloodiest century, hated war and scorned its monuments and memorials,' Morris has written. 'Père-Lachaise Cemetery, in Capa's beloved Paris, was considered seriously for a few hours, but there were too many women in Bob's life since Gerda Taro, who was interred there.'

Nor did Julia want her son to be sent to a funeral home, as usually happened in the case of non-practising Jews in New York. He was too special for such an anonymous ending. John Morris had become a Quaker in recent years and suggested a simple ceremony at a meeting-house in Purchase, near Armonk, an hour's drive north of New York. To the surprise of Jews such as Judy Freiburg, Julia agreed to the proposal. The Quakers' informal, non-denominational ceremony, Morris hoped, would be a fitting send-off.

On the Sunday after Capa's death, the meeting-house in Purchase was packed. The photographer Edward Steichen stood and announced: 'We salute you, Robert Capa and Werner Bischof.'[3] Tributes from around the globe were read, including a message from Ingrid Bergman. Two weeks later, Capa was buried in a Quaker cemetery in

Amawalk, thirty miles north of Purchase. Only members of his family and closest friends were invited. To Inge Bondi's surprise, a young photographer began to take pictures as the coffin was lowered into the grave. She asked Morris if he couldn't tell the photographer to stop. He approached eighteen-year-old Dirck Halstead, and began to admonish him, but then stopped. 'After all,' he told Bondi, 'whom are we burying?'[4]

'I had heard that Capa had been killed the previous week,' Halstead recalls. 'I was thunderstruck, because it was Capa, and I had idolized him, and because I heard he was going to be buried in my coverage area for my local newspaper . . . I was wandering around the cemetery and then suddenly the procession arrived and this casket appeared. I was amazed – he was in a packing case. It wasn't really a casket. It had "Robert Capa, photographe" written on it. I wasn't used back then to seeing bodies in packing cases.'

Halstead's pictures of Capa's burial did not jump-start his career but his meeting with Morris did lead to a first foreign assignment with *Life*. His subsequent career has seen him win most of photojournalism's most prestigious awards. In 1974, he won what most war photographers consider the ultimate accolade, the Robert Capa Medal, for his coverage of Vietnam. *Life* and the Overseas Press Club established the award to honour 'superlative photography requiring exceptional courage and enterprise abroad'.[5] Its first recipient in 1955 was Howard Sochurek, whom Capa had filled in for on his final, fatal assignment. Asked in 1993 how he felt when he learned that Capa had died, Sochurek replied: 'I felt I was responsible. That was my beat he was covering . . . If Capa had lived another three days, he would have been back in Tokyo.'[6]

'What immediately attracted me to Capa,' says Halstead, 'was the legend, the fact that he created himself, this great character. To me, it was like Clark Kent turning into Superman.' Capa was the first photographer to make photojournalism appear glamorous and sexy.

His example has inspired many great photojournalists such as Donald McCullin, Jim Natchwey and Magnum's Luc Delahaye, as well as Halstead: all have won the Robert Capa Medal. As Steinbeck wrote in a eulogy to Capa: 'The effect of Capa will be found in the men who worked with him. They will carry a little part of Capa all their lives and perhaps hand him on to their young men.'[7]

The other founders of Magnum – George Rodger, Henri Cartier-Bresson and Capa's close friend, David 'Chim' Seymour – vowed to sustain Magnum after the loss of Capa, its figurehead, and Bischof, one of its most promising recruits. Tragically, Seymour was killed in 1956 by Egyptian machine-gun fire while covering the Suez crisis. Despite the loss of two of its founders in as many years, Magnum somehow struggled on. To many people's surprise, Capa's brainchild survives to this day, although its prestige is not what it was during the heyday of photojournalism in the 1940s and 1950s before television usurped the still image as the primary medium for relaying visual information to the world.

After his brother's death, Cornell Capa left his staff job at *Life* and dedicated himself to the survival of Magnum. In the late Fifties, he set about burnishing his brother's reputation, as well as that of subsequent photojournalists who have devoted their lives to what he has dubbed 'concerned photography'. With tenacity and guile, he established the International Center of Photography in New York in the 1970s. Today, it is the most influential institution of its kind. His mother Julia died in 1961, and is buried beside Robert Capa in Amawalk. To her dying day, she continued to idolize her favourite son.

Capa's greatest legacy is not an institution, nor a medal, nor the inspirational example he set. It is, as with any photographer, his photographs. 'During his short time on earth he lived and loved a great deal,' Cornell wrote in April 1999 of his brother. 'What he left behind is the story of his unique voyage and a visual testimony affirming his own faith in humankind's capacity to endure and occasionally to overcome.'[8]

Notes

Full details of primary and secondary sources are given in the extensive bibliography. I have not included sources where it is obvious from the text that the person being quoted was interviewed by the author. A full list of interviewees appears in the acknowledgements. Where the source is given in the text – most often the date of magazine issues – I have not repeated the attribution in the notes.

Three Thousand Miles From Omaha

I spent several days in Bedford, talking to survivors of Company A. Professor Bill McIntosh provided invaluable insight into what D-Day had meant to Bedford. Several days in Normandy, particularly in Caen, a visit to the superb Memorial museum in Bayeux, and to the Normandy beaches provided further insight. See other sources in the bibliography and the D-Day section – chapter 13.

1 John Steinbeck, *Popular Photography*, September 1954.
2 Robert Capa, *Slightly Out of Focus*.
3 Interview with the author.

1 Conversation in Budapest

The writer Jozefa Stuart conducted extensive research in the late Fifties for a biography of Capa which she chose not to complete. All accounts of Capa's childhood necessarily rely heavily on her work, and indeed Richard Whelan's authorized 1985 work acknowledges the debt all biographers owe

Stuart, who obtained the only interview with Julia before her death in 1961.

To obtain my version of Capa's childhood, I also relied on the work of Stuart and my own interviews with her. The following were very helpful: the photographer Liesl Steiner, a close friend of Julia's at the end of her life; the veteran Hungarian photojournalist Éva Keleti, who was immensely knowledgeable and helpful before and after my visit to Budapest in September 2000; Karoly Kincses, another Hungarian expert on photography; interviews with Cornell Capa, specifically one of John Loengard's excellent collection of interviews with *Life* veterans; and last but not least, the remarkable Eva Besnyö – Capa's sole surviving childhood friend and confidante.

I am also indebted to Katya Steiner, who provided an invaluable tour of Capa's childhood haunts, homes, schools and other important spots. Please see detailed bibliography for books on Budapest and Hungary, which provided the historical context. John A. Lukacs, *Budapest 1900: A Historical Portrait of a City and its Culture*, pp. 92–6, was particularly illuminating.

The first section is based largely on Capa's article for *Holiday* magazine, November 1949, and *Illustrated*, 26 March 1949.

1 John Hersey, 'The Man Who Invented Himself'.
2 Ibid.
3 György Markos, 'My Friend Capa'.
4 Ibid.
5 For details on Capa's early childhood and birth see Richard Whelan, *Robert Capa*, and Jozefa Stuart's manuscript and interview transcripts held at ICP, New York.
6 Whelan, *Robert Capa*, and Jozefa Stuart, ibid.
7 Adam de Hegedus, *Hungarian Background.*
8 Julia Friedmann, interview with Jozefa Stuart.
9 Whelan, *Robert Capa.*
10 FBI file, affidavit, sworn by Capa, October 3 1952, witnessed by Jerome Weiss, Notary Public of the State of New York, No. 24–4207225, p. 2.
11 *Capa and Capa: catalogue for exhibition of pictures at International Center of Photography.*
12 Ibid.
13 *Capa and Capa: catalogue for exhibition of pictures at International Center of Photography.*

2 Barbarians at the Gate

1 For the Frau Bohen incident, and the desperation of poverty in Berlin: Suzy Marquis, interview with author, April 2000, Paris.
2 FBI file, 1953 affidavit, p. 2.
3 For Dephot, Felix Man and Guttmann, see Gisèle Freund, *Photography and Society*.
4 Jay Deutsch, director of the Leica Gallery in New York, was particularly helpful in providing historical information about the Leica.
5 Lechenperg incident, see Richard Whelan, *Robert Capa*.
6 '*Aufnahmen: Friedmann – Dephot*', *Der Welt Spiegel*, 11 December 1932, p. 3.
7 Eva Besnyö, *Eva Besnyö*.
8 Eva Besnyö, interview with author.
9 For the Veres travel agency, the details of his return to Hungary, and his departure for Paris, see Whelan, *Robert Capa*, and Jozefa Stuart, Robert Capa biography, incomplete manuscript, ICP, New York.

3 The Man Who Invented Himself

For this chapter I have relied on interviews with surviving contemporaries of Capa: Jozefa Stuart, Ruth Cerf, Pierre Gassmann, and Suzy Marquis. I also drew on John Hersey's *47 Magazine* article, 'The Man Who Invented Himself', and Irme Schaber's exhaustively researched biography of Gerda Taro (*Gerta Taro: Fotoreporterin im spanischen Bürgerkrieg: eine Biografie*) for much of this chapter, as well as Capa's first magazine pieces. Schaber had access to the Capa estate archives held at ICP, and obtained some of her information from the many long interviews conducted by Jozefa Stuart.

1 John Hersey, 'The Man Who Invented Himself'.
2 Hervé Le Goff, *Pierre Gassmann*.
3 From a poem by Henri Cartier-Bresson, sent to the author with permission to quote in full.
4 Henri Cartier-Bresson, *The Decisive Moment*.
5 Pierre Gassmann interview with author.

6 Whelan, *Robert Capa.*
7 Information on Gerda and first meeting: Pierre Gassmann interview, April 2000; Ruth Cerf interview, April 2001; Irme Schaber interview, October 2000; Schaber's book, *Gerta Taro.*
8 Schaber, *Gerta Taro.*
9 Whelan, *Robert Capa.*
10 Ibid.
11 *Berliner Illustrierte Zeitung*, 20 June 1935.
12 Ibid.
13 *World Illustrated*, 14 April 1936.
14 Schaber, *Gerta Taro.*
15 Ibid.
16 Whelan, *Robert Capa.*
17 Cornell Capa, interview with John Loengard, in *Life Photographers: What They Saw.*
18 Whelan, *Robert Capa.*
19 Hersey, 'Man Who Invented Himself'.
20 Radio interview, WNBC (N.Y.), 20 October 1947.
21 Information on Kertész, *Vu*, and Vogel based on interviews with Professor Hans Puttnies, Gisèle Freund's *Photography and Society*, and *André Kertész, His Life and Work*, essay pp. 83–197, by Dominique Baqué.
22 Hersey, 'Man Who Invented Himself'.
23 Ibid.
24 *Vu* magazine, 8 July 1936.
25 Ibid.
26 For the Alliance agency and Capa's work for it, and his relationship with Eisner, see also Gunther, *Alliance photo.*

4 The Passionate War

1 Ernest Hemingway, Preface to Gustav Regler, *Great Crusade.*
2 Martha Gellhorn, 'Till Death Do Us Part', *Two by Two.*
3 Schaber, *Gerta Taro.*
4 Gustav Regler, *The Owl of Minerva.*
5 Schaber, *Gerta Taro.*

6 Richard Whelan, *Robert Capa.*
7 Ibid.
8 Franz Borkenau, *The Spanish Cockpit.*

5 'The Falling Soldier'

1 'Heart of Spain – Robert Capa's photographs of the Spanish Civil War', *Aperture*, New York, 1999.
2 Ibid.
3 Jimmy Fox, e-mail to author, April 2000.
4 *New York World-Telegram*, 2 September 1937.
5 Hansel Mieth, letter to Richard Whelan, 19 March 1982, quoted with permission from Georgia Brown and the Center for Creative Photography.
6 Gisèle Freund, *Photography and Society.*
7 Phillip Knightley, *The First Casualty.*
8 Ibid.
9 *Vu* magazine, 23 September 1936.
10 Georges Soria, Robert Capa, David Seymour-Chim, *Les grandes photos de la guerre d'Espagne.*
11 Ibid.
12 Mario Brotons Jorda, *Retazos de una epoca de inquietudes.*
13 Rita Grosvenor and Arnold Kemp, 'Spain's Falling Soldier Really Did Die That Day', *Observer*, 1 September 1996.
14 Caroline Brothers, *War and Photography.*

6 'La Paquena Rubena'

1 Jay Allen, Preface, Robert Capa and Gerda Taro, *Death in the Making: Photographs by Robert Capa and Gerda Taro.*
2 Schaber, *Gerta Taro.*
3 Regler, *The Owl of Minerva.*
4 *World Illustrated*, 2 January 1937.
5 Bernard Knox, 'Remembering Madrid', *New York Review of Books*, 6 November 1980.

6 Peter Weyden, *The Passionate War.*
7 Capa, *Slightly Out of Focus.*
8 Letter to the editor, *47 Magazine*, October 1947.
9 Jimmy Shute, quoted in Raymond Fielding, *The March of Time, 1935–1951.*
10 Ibid.
11 Ibid.
12 Alfred Kantorowicz, *Spanisches Tagebuch.*
13 Ibid.
14 Ibid.
15 Dr Norman Allan, untitled and unpublished biography of his father Ted Allan, containing extensively quoted memoirs of Allan. Permission to quote, courtesy of Dr Allan.
16 Ibid.
17 Details on Cockburn drawn from Peter Weyden, *The Passionate War.*
18 Norman Allan, unpublished biography.
19 Ibid.
20 Weyden, *The Passionate War.* The Non-Intervention Committee was set up to prevent foreign involvement in the Civil War. Delegates from twenty-seven nations formed the committee, which was widely derided as completely ineffectual and which the Nazi foreign minister, Joachim von Ribbentrop, jokingly referred to as the 'Intervention Committee'.
21 Schaber, *Gerta Taro.*
22 Ibid.
23 Norman Allan, unpublished biography.
24 Heinrich Jaenecke, *Es lebe der Tod, Die Tragödie des spanischen Burgerkrieges.*
25 Norman Allan, unpublished biography.
26 Interview with author.
27 Details of Gerda's death, her funeral and Capa's reaction come from several sources – Eva Besnyö's, Pierre Gassmann's and Ruth Cerf's interviews with the author; Peter Weyden's excellent *The Passionate War*; Irme Schaber's biography; and above all Dr Norman Allan's book about his father.
28 *Life*, 16 August 1937.
29 Hansel Mieth, undated letter to Irme Schaber.

30 György Markos, 'My Friend Capa'.
31 Le Goff, *Pierre Gassmann.*
32 *Ce Soir,* 8 January 1938.
33 Details of the siege of Teruel and quotes are drawn from Herbert L. Matthews, *The Education of a Correspondent.*

7 'The 400 Million'

1 Joris Ivens, *The Camera and I.*
2 Christopher Isherwood, *Journey to a War.*
3 *Picture Post,* 3 December 1938.
4 The source for this and much of the team's movements is Ivens' *The Camera and I.*
5 Ibid. All Ivens' descriptions of the trip are quoted from this volume.
6 Agnes Smedley, *Battle Hymn of China.*
7 Quoted in Barbara W. Tuchman, *Stilwell and the American Experience in China, 1911–45.*
8 György Markos, 'My Friend Capa'.
9 For the details of the letter to Peter Koester, see Whelan, *Robert Capa.*

8 The Final Defeat

1 Juan Negrín, quoted, Weyden, *The Passionate War.*
2 Ibid.
3 Details of the farewell parade, ibid.
4 Vincent Sheean, *Not Peace But a Sword.*
5 Herbert L. Matthews, *The Education of a Correspondent.*
6 Details of the Ebro crossing drawn from Matthews' and Sheean's accounts.
7 *Picture Post,* 3 December 1938.
8 *Picture Post,* 4 February 1939.
9 Ibid.
10 Ibid.
11 Details of the flight from Barcelona are based on *Picture Post,* and Weyden's, Matthews' and Sheean's accounts.

12 Weyden, *The Passionate War.*
13 Robert Capa, *Images of War.*
14 Ibid.
15 Letter from Wilson Hicks, in care of Mrs Olivia Chambers of the Paris office of *March of Time*, 31 January 1939.
16 *Picture Post*, 15 April 1939.
17 Ibid.

9 Splendid Isolation

1 Edward K. Thompson, *A Love Affair with Life & Smithsonian.*
2 Ibid.
3 Irwin Shaw, *Views of Paris; Notes on a Parisian.*
4 Thompson, *A Love Affair.*
5 Hansel Mieth, *The Singing Hills of Jackass Flat* (unpublished manuscript, quoted courtesy of Georgia Brown and Center for Creative Photography).
6 Account of Capa's marriage, ibid.
7 Hansel Mieth, undated letter to Irme Schaber, quoted with permission from Georgia Brown and the Center of Contemporary Photography.
8 Richard Whelan, *Robert Capa.*
9 Thompson, *A Love Affair.*
10 For details of McCombs's relationship with Capa, see Whelan, *Robert Capa.*
11 *Life*, 10 June 1940.
12 *Life*, 22 July 1940.
13 Robert Payne, *The Life and Death of Trotsky.*
14 *Life*, 6 January 1941.
15 *Life*, 20 January 1941.
16 Gordon Parks, *A Choice of Weapons.*
17 Capa's personnel file, held in the *Life* magazine archives, reviewed for the author by Bill Hooper.

10 Muddling Through

1 Capa, *Slightly Out of Focus.*
2 *Illustrated,* 13 June 1942.
3 Ibid.
4 *Collier's,* 7 November 1942.
5 Ibid.
6 *Collier's,* 24 October 1942.
7 Christopher Ogden, *Life of the Party: the Biography of Pamela Digby Churchill Hayward Harriman.*
8 Gellhorn, *Till Death Do Us Part.*
9 Radio interview, WNBC (New York), 20 October 1947.
10 *Illustrated,* 5 December 1942.
11 Radio interview, WNBC, 20 October 1947.
12 Whelan, *Robert Capa.*
13 Jozefa Stuart, interview with author.

11 The Desert

1 Quoted in James Tobin, *Ernie Pyle's War.*
2 Ernie Pyle, quoted in Phillip Knightley, *The First Casualty.*
3 Capa, *Slightly Out of Focus.*
4 Ibid.
5 *Collier's,* 19 June 1943.
6 Ibid.
7 Capa, *Slightly Out of Focus.*
8 Jackson Benson, *The True Adventures of John Steinbeck, Writer.*
9 Hemingway, Mary Welsh, *How It Was.*
10 Ibid.
11 Capa, *Slightly Out of Focus.*
12 See the *Life* personnel file, *Life* archives, courtesy of Bill Hooper.
13 For details on Capa's attempt to provide an exclusive, see *Slightly Out of Focus.*
14 Ibid.
15 Hersey, 'The Man Who Invented Himself'.
16 Letter to the editor, *47 Magazine,* October 1947.

17 Matthews, *The Education of a Correspondent.*
18 Capa, *Slightly Out of Focus.*
19 He officially went on contract on 15 July 1943.
20 John Steinbeck, *Louisville Courier-Journal*, 21 April 1957.
21 Jackson Benson, *The True Adventures of John Steinbeck, Writer.*
22 Capa, *Slightly Out of Focus.*

12 It's a Tough War

1 Will Lang, 'Story of Fort Schuster', *Life*, 25 October 1943.
2 *Life*, 8 November 1943.
3 *Illustrated*, 13 May 1944.
4 Capa, *Slightly Out of Focus.*
5 John Huston, *An Open Book.*
6 *Life*, 1 November 1943.
7 Ibid.
8 Ibid.
9 *Life*, 22 November 1943.
10 All quotes from Rodger's diary reproduced with the permission of Jinx Rodger.
11 George Rodger, quoted, *The Magnum Story*, BBC2, October 1989.
12 Ibid.
13 *Life*, 14 February 1944.
14 Capa, *Slightly Out of Focus.*
15 *Life*, 31 January 1944.
16 Vicki Goldberg, *The Power of Photography.*
17 Capa, *Slightly Out of Focus.*
18 Ibid.
19 *Illustrated*, 1 April 1944.
20 Bill Mauldin, *The Brass Ring.*
21 Capa, *Slightly Out of Focus.*

13 The Longest Day

1 Omar Bradley and Clay Blair, *A General's Life: An Autobiography.*

2 Ernie Pyle, *Scripps-Howard* column, 10 June 1944.
3 Richard Whelan, *Robert Capa.*
4 Irwin Shaw, Robert Capa profile (an amended version of Shaw's introduction to *Views Of Paris*), *US Vogue*, April 1982.
5 Lawrence Lee and Barry Gifford, *Saroyan.*
6 William Saroyan, 'Letter to the editor', *47 Magazine.*
7 Irwin Shaw, *US Vogue.*
8 Leicester Hemingway, *My Brother, Ernest Hemingway.*
9 Records of the Public Relations Division, SHAEF, Record Group 331, National Archives, Washington DC.
10 Leicester Hemingway, *My Brother, Ernest Hemingway.*
11 William Saroyan, *47 Magazine.*
12 Leicester Hemingway, *My Brother, Ernest Hemingway.*
13 Ryan, *The Longest Day.*
14 Capa, *Slightly Out of Focus.*
15 Stephen E. Ambrose, *D-Day: The Climactic Battle of World War II.*
16 The account of D-Day is based on Capa's memoir, the Wertenbaker interview with Capa, the histories given in the bibliography as well as oral histories at the Eisenhower Center.
17 Oscar Rich, interview transcript, Eisenhower Center, New Orleans.
18 Charles Wertenbaker, *Invasion!.*
19 Ryan, *The Longest Day.*
20 Wertenbaker, *Invasion!.*
21 Capa, *Slightly Out of Focus.*
22 Wertenbaker, *Invasion!.*
23 Ibid.
24 Capa, *Slightly Out of Focus.*
25 Charles Jarreau interview transcript, Eisenhower Center, New Orleans.
26 Wertenbaker, *Invasion!.*
27 Ibid.
28 Interview with author and *Get The Picture.*
29 Charles Jarreau interview.
30 Wertenbaker, *Invasion!.*
31 Capa, *Slightly Out of Focus.*
32 John Morris, *International Herald Tribune*, 3 June 1994.
33 The account of developing the pictures and meeting *Life* deadline is

also based on an interview with Morris and his extraordinarily detailed memoir, *Get The Picture.*

34 Wertenbaker, *Invasion!.*

35 Quoted, Introduction, Steinbeck, *A Russian Journal*, 1999 edition.

36 Marie-Monique Robin, *The Photos of the Century: 100 Historic Moments.*

14 The Bocage

1 *Life*, 3 July 1944.

2 Capa, *Slightly Out of Focus.*

3 *Life*, 10 July 1944.

4 Wertenbaker, *Invasion!.*

5 Stephen Ambrose, *Citizen Soldiers.*

6 Wertenbaker, *Invasion!.*

7 Hastings, *Overlord.*

8 The account of the entry into Cherbourg is based on Pyle's column 'Street Fighting' in *Brave Men*, from which all the quotations are taken, and Wertenbaker's detailed account in *Invasion!.*

9 Capa, *Slightly Out of Focus.*

10 Tobin, *Ernie Pyle's War.*

11 Ibid.

12 Ibid.

13 Wertenbaker, *Invasion!.*

14 Ibid.

15 Richard Whelan, *Robert Capa.*

16 Irwin Shaw, Robert Capa profile, *Vogue.*

17 Capa, *Slightly Out of Focus.*

18 Alfred G. Aronowitz and Peter Hamill, *Ernest Hemingway, The Life and Death of A Man.*

19 Capa, *Slightly Out of Focus.*

20 Aronowitz and Hamill, *Ernest Hemingway.*

21 Ibid.

22 Wertenbaker, *Invasion!.*

23 Ibid.

24 Wertenbaker, *Time*, 4 September 1944.

25 Ibid.

15 Victory

1 Wertenbaker, *Invasion!*
2 Capa, *Slightly Out of Focus.*
3 *Life*, 13 November 1944.
4 Capa, *Slightly Out of Focus.*
5 Bill Graffis, letter to editor, *47 Magazine.*
6 For the conversation see Richard Whelan's interview with Gellhorn in Whelan, *Robert Capa.*
7 Capa, *Slightly Out of Focus.*
8 Ibid.
9 Ibid.
10 Ibid.
11 Andy Rooney, *My War.*
12 Capa, *Slightly Out of Focus.*
13 Le Goff, *Pierre Gassmann.*
14 Hersey, 'The Man Who Invented Himself'.
15 Ibid.
16 Ibid.
17 Ibid.
18 Ed Murrow, CBS report, 22 April 1945.
19 Radio interview, WNBC (N.Y.), 20 October 1947.
20 *Life*, 14 May 1945.
21 John Steinbeck, *Once There Was a War.*
22 Tobin, *Ernie Pyle's War.*

16 'Here's Looking At You, Kid'

1 Laurence Leamer, *As Time Goes By: The Life of Ingrid Bergman.*
2 Bergman and Burgess, *My Story.*
3 Leamer, *As Time Goes By.*
4 Bergman and Burgess, *My Story.*
5 Leamer, *As Time Goes By.*
6 Ibid.
7 Donald Spoto, *Notorious: The Life of Ingrid Bergman.*
8 Joseph Henry Steele, *Ingrid Bergman: An Intimate Portrait.*

9 Spoto, *Notorious.*
10 Bergman and Burgess, *My Story.*
11 Spoto, *Notorious.*
12 Bergman and Burgess, *My Story.*
13 Ibid.
14 Ibid.
15 Ibid.
16 Russell Miller, *Magnum: Fifty Years at the Front Line of History.*
17 *Life*, 8 October 1945.
18 For details on the meeting with Hitchcock, see Spoto's *Notorious* and his equally insightful *The Dark Side of Genius: The Life of Alfred Hitchcock.*
19 Spoto, *Notorious.*

17 The End of the Affair

1 Whelan, *Robert Capa.*
2 Bergman and Burgess, *My Story.*
3 Steele, *Ingrid Bergman.*
4 Leamer, *As Time Goes By.*
5 Ibid.
6 Spoto, *Notorious.*
7 Leamer, *As Time Goes By.*
8 Ibid.
9 Ibid.
10 Irwin Shaw, 'Letter to the editor', *47 Magazine.*
11 Ibid.
12 *Illustrated*, 6 September 1947.
13 Ibid.
14 For details on Capa's minor role of Hamza and his involvement with Hollywood, see Alain Bergala's introduction to *Magnum Cinema.*
15 Bergman and Burgess, *My Story.* Quoted with permission of Delacorte Press.
16 Ibid.
17 Leamer, *As Time Goes By.*
18 Gellhorn, *Till Death Do Us Part.*

19 For the details of the last meeting, see Leamer's, Spoto's and Bergman's accounts. Leamer's book includes extensive interviews with Petter Lindstrom, who sadly died before I could arrange an interview.

20 Bergman and Burgess, *My Story*.

21 Ibid.

18 Back in the USSR

1 Yuriy Sherekh, 'What Did You Not Want to See, Mr. Steinbeck?', *Ukrainian Quarterly*, 4, 1948. Sherekh was the pen name of Yuriy Shevelov, who later became Professor of Slavic Philology and Linguistics at Columbia University in New York.

I am indebted to Professor Wolodymyr Stojko, editor of the *Ukrainian Quarterly*, for the enormous detail and new information which he helped bring to light about Steinbeck and Capa's stay in the USSR. Susan Shillinglaw, a leading Steinbeck scholar, also pointed me in the direction of several new sources.

All the secret Soviet files quoted in this chapter derive from the Ukraine's Central State Archive in Kiev. The specific documents, translated for Professor Stojko in the Ukraine, are labelled Fond 1; Opys, 23; Sprava 4365 (resolution 4363 pp. 16–23 and 54–50). For the purpose of brevity, they are attributed as CSA.

For a superb overview of what was actually happening under Stalin's regime at this time, see Edvard Radzinsky's *Stalin*. The best account of inside dealings at the Kremlin is Dmitri Volkogonov's definitive *Stalin, Triumph and Tragedy*.

2 Jay Parini, *John Steinbeck*. For a superb account of Steinbeck's many escapades see Jackson Benson, *The True Adventures of John Steinbeck, Writer*.

3 Steinbeck, *A Russian Journal*.

4 Ibid.

5 CSA.

6 Gisèle Freund, *The World in My Camera*.

7 For the best account on the formation of Magnum and Capa's motivation, see Russell Miller's *Magnum: Fifty Years at the Front Line*

of History. John Morris's *Get The Picture* is also extremely detailed, and benefits from the author's personal involvement with all the founders.

8 Miller, *Magnum*.
9 Ibid.
10 Jean Lacoutre, *Robert Capa*.
11 Miller, *Magnum*.
12 Le Goff, *Pierre Gassmann*.
13 Steinbeck, *A Russian Journal*.
14 Ibid.
15 CSA.
16 Steinbeck, *A Russian Journal*.
17 Ibid.
18 Interview with Professor Wolodymyr Stojko, October 2000.
19 Steinbeck, *A Russian Journal*.
20 CSA.
21 Ibid.
22 *Life*, 6 October 1947.
23 Radio interview, WNBC (N.Y.), 20 October 1947.
24 Quoted, Introduction to *Slightly Out of Focus*, Modern Library, New York, 1999.
25 John Vachon, *Photo Notes*, March 1948.
26 Steinbeck, *A Russian Journal*.
27 Ibid.

19 The New Look

1 Miller, *Magnum*.
2 Radio interview, WNBC (N.Y.), 20 October 1947.
3 Introduction, *Russian Journal*, 1999 edition.
4 Reviews quoted in ibid.
5 CSA.
6 John Morris, *Get The Picture*.
7 *Daily Worker*, 22 October 1947.
8 Jackson J. Benson, *The True Adventures of John Steinbeck, Writer*. For the details of the financial investment and later problems with Capa,

see Steinbeck's business correspondence relating to World Video, Columbia University, and Richard Whelan, *Robert Capa*.

9 Ibid.

10 Nigel Cawthorne, *The Dior Revolution*.

11 Ibid.

12 Ibid.

13 *Illustrated*, 3 April 1948.

14 Michael Gross, *Model*.

15 For these financial dealings, see nine letters between 1947 and 1948, held at the Anne Watkins Collection, Columbia University.

16 Benson, *The True Adventures of John Steinbeck*.

20 A Road of Death

1 Details of Capa's stay are drawn from interviews conducted by Jozefa Stuart; Kenneth Bilby, *New Star in the East*; and several articles by Jack Winocour and Quentin Reynolds.

2 Whelan, *Robert Capa*.

3 Goldman interview with Jozefa Stuart.

4 *Illustrated*, 19 June 1948.

5 Whelan, *Robert Capa*.

6 Bilby, *New Star in the East*.

7 For the journey across Burma Road, see Winocour's elegiac piece for *Illustrated*, 3 July 1948.

8 Ted Berkham, *Cast a Giant Shadow, The Story of Mickey Marcus*.

9 Ibid.

10 *Illustrated*, 3 July 1948.

11 Berkham, *Cast a Giant Shadow*.

12 *Illustrated*, 3 July 1948.

13 Ibid.

14 Bilby, *New Star in the East*.

15 Ibid.

16 For details of the landing, see *Illustrated*, 17 July 1948, *Life*, 12 July 1948.

17 See Noël Howard's *Hollywood sur Nil* and Miller's *Magnum*.

18 *US Vogue*, April 1982.

19 Ibid.
20 For details of the visit to Eastern Europe, see *Illustrated*, 26 March 1949; *Holiday*, June 1949; *Illustrated*, 20 August 1949, *Holiday*, November 1949.
21 Mary Blume, *After the War was Over.*
22 *Holiday*, June 1949.
23 *Holiday*, November 1949.
24 Irwin Shaw, *Report on Israel.*
25 All details and quotes derive from *Illustrated*, 27 August 1949.
26 For Shaw's recollections see *US Vogue*, April 1982.
27 *Illustrated*, 27 August 1949.
28 Ibid.

21 The Realm of the Senses

1 Details of Capa's first meeting with Hammond are based on Jozefa Stuart interview and John Hammond Jr. interview, October 2000.
2 Burri and Bischof, *Werner Bischof.*
3 Inge Morath, 'Meeting Magnum' in *Paris Magnum – Photographs 1935–1981.*
4 Inge Bondi, quoted, Miller, *Magnum.*
5 Ibid.
6 Inge Bondi, *Ernst Haas: Colour Photography.*
7 See Michael Shnayerson's *Irwin Shaw*, and *Illustrated*, 4 March 1950.
8 Irwin Shaw, 'How to Live Abroad', *Holiday*, July 1951.
9 Irwin Shaw, *Vogue.*
10 Shnayerson, *Shaw.*
11 James Salter, *Burning the Days.*
12 Ibid.
13 Freund, *The World in My Camera.*
14 Morris, *Get The Picture.*
15 Viertel, *Dangerous Friends.*
16 Gael Elton Mayo, *The Mad Mosaic.*
17 The financial dealings at Magnum and other issues in this chapter pertaining to the agency are based on Miller's *Magnum*, and interviews by the author with Suzy Marquis, Warren Trabant, Inge

Morath, Jinx Rodger, Judy Freiburg, Jimmy Fox, Pierre Gassmann, Elliot Erwitt and John Morris.
18 Miller, *Magnum.*
19 Ibid.
20 Morris, *Get The Picture.*
21 Quoted, ibid.

22 How Can I Be Old?

1 *Holiday*, January 1951.
2 Details about Thorne and skiing, ibid.
3 Details of Capa's days in Paris are based on Noël Howard's memoirs; John Huston's *An Open Book*; Christopher Ogden's *Pamela Harriman*; Irwin Shaw's *Vogue* profile and 'Notes on a Parisian'; Peter Viertel's *Dangerous Friends*; and the author's interviews with Suzy Marquis, Burt Glinn, Inge Morath, Elliot Erwitt, Pierre Gassmann, Bettina Graziani, Ben Bradlee, Michel Descamps, Inge Bondi, John Morris, Peter Viertel, Eve Arnold and Warren Trabant.
4 Christopher Ogden, *Pamela Harriman.*
5 Ibid.
6 Hedy Lamarr, *Ecstasy and Me.*
7 Irwin Shaw, *Paris! Paris!*
8 Morris, *Get The Picture.*
9 Howard, *Hollywood sur Nil.*
10 Freund, *The World in My Camera.*
11 Irwin Shaw, 'Letter to the editor', *47 Magazine.*
12 Miller, *Magnum.*
13 For details of Capa's pay, see Miller's *Magnum* and Morris's *Get The Picture.*
14 Miller, *Magnum.*
15 For details of Morris's appointment and terms, see Miller's *Magnum* and Morris's *Get The Picture.*
16 Ibid.
17 Morris, *Get The Picture.*
18 For details of the passport crisis, see Morris's *Get The Picture*, and Capa's FBI file, released under the Freedom of Information Act.

The file is referred to as FOIA 923304 under FBI procedure for release to the author. For the sake of abbreviation, references are referred to as 'FBI file' and where relevant the dates are given in the text.

19 Viertel, *Dangerous Friends.*

20 FBI file, affidavit, sworn by Capa, 3 October 1952, witnessed by Jerome Weiss, Notary Republic of the State of New York, No. 24–4207225.

21 Morris, *Get The Picture.*

22 Details on Capa's *annus horribilis*, depression and bad back are drawn from interviews with John Morris, Jinx Rodger, Inge Morath, Ben Bradlee, Flury Clavadetscher, Ruth Guler, Larry Collins, Bettina Graziani, Suzy Marquis, Peter Viertel, and Jozefa Stuart.

23 Viertel, *Dangerous Friends.*

24 Ibid.

25 Irwin Shaw, *US Vogue.*

23 Forward Lies the Delta

1 Whelan, *Robert Capa.*

2 Interview with John Loengard, *Life Photographers.*

3 Thompson, *A Love Affair with Life & Smithsonian.*

4 Interview with John Loengard, *Life Photographers.*

5 For further details of how Capa came to take his last assignment, see Morris, *Get The Picture*, and Miller, *Magnum.*

6 Details of Capa's time in Hanoi are drawn from an interview with Michel Descamps, *Life* magazine articles, obituaries, Miller's *Magnum* and Morris' detailed account in *Get The Picture*, and the author's interviews with Inge Bondi, John Morris and Suzy Marquis.

7 *Life*, 31 May 1954.

8 Details on the newsreel are drawn from the Patrick Jeudy interview. He has several fascinating clips of Capa in action. All newsreel mention in this book is courtesy of him.

9 *Life*, 31 May 1954.

10 *Life*, 7 June 1954.

11 Ibid.

12 The account of Capa's death is based largely on two sources, John Mecklin and Jim Lucas. Mecklin's 'Forward Lies the Delta', *Time*, 7 June 1954, is a detailed account of the days leading up to the end. 'He Said: "This Is Going to Be a Beautiful Story"', *Life*, June 7 1954, recreates with great drama and detail Capa's last day. The author acknowledges permission from *Time-Life* to quote at length. The other eyewitness was Jim Lucas. His article 'Bob Capa Planned to Leave Indo-China by Sea' appeared in the *Washington Daily News* first, on 27 May 1954. The author has relied on both accounts, and a close examination of Capa's last pictures, to reconstruct Capa's last assignment.

Epilogue – The Legend

1 Morris, *Get The Picture.*
2 Ibid.
3 Ibid.
4 Ibid.
5 Catalogue for Inhumanity and Humanity, Robert Capa Gold Medal Winners Exhibition, Tokyo Fuji Art Museum, Tokyo, 2000. Robert Capa Medal shown to author by Anthony Suau, Paris, April 2000. Suau won the award in 1995.
6 Interview with John Loengard, *Life Photographers.*
7 John Steinbeck, *Popular Photography.*
8 Cornell Capa, Foreword to *Slightly Out of Focus,* Modern Library, New York, 1999.

Bibliography

Adler, Larry, *It Ain't Necessarily So* (Grove Press, 1984).
Aldridge, John W., *After the Lost Generation* (Arbor House, 1985).
Allan, Ted, *This Time a Better Earth* (Morrow, 1939).
Ambrose, Stephen E., *Americans at War* (Berkley, 1997).
– *Citizen Soldiers* (Simon and Schuster, 1997).
– *D-Day: The Climactic Battle of World War II* (Simon and Schuster, 1994).
– *Eisenhower and Berlin, 1945* (Norton, 1967).
Aragon, Louis, *Adieu Capa*, in *Les Lettres Françaises*, May 27–June 3, 1954.
Arnold, Eve, *The Unretouched Woman* (Alfred A. Knopf, 1976).
Aronowitz, Alfred G. and Peter Hamill, *Ernest Hemingway, The Life and Death of A Man* (Lancer Books, 1961).

Baker, Carlos, *Ernest Hemingway: A Life Story* (Charles Scribner's Sons, 1969).
Baltermants, Dmitri, *Dmitri Baltermants* (Photo Poche, 1997).
Barea, Arturo, *The Forging of a Rebel* (Reynal & Hitchcock, 1946).
Bataille, Georges, *La Part Maudite* (Editions de Minuit, 1967).
Beaton, Cecil, and Gail Buckland, *The Magic Image* (Little, Brown, 1975).
Belden, Jack, 'The Fall of Troina', *Time*, 23 August 1943.
Benson, Jackson J., *The True Adventures of John Steinbeck, Writer* (Viking, 1984).
Bergala, Alain, *Magnum Cinema* (Phaidon, 1995).
Bergman, Ingrid, and Alan Burgess, *My Story* (Delacorte, 1980).
Berkham, Ted, *Cast a Giant Shadow, The Story of Mickey Marcus* (Doubleday, 1962)
Bernard, Bruce, *George Rodger: Humanity and Inhumanity* (Phaidon, 1994).

Besnyö, Eva, *Eva Besnyö* (Focus Publishing, 2000).
– *N'eue Halve Eeuw Werk* (Feministische Uitgeverij Sara, 1982).
Bilby, Kenneth, *New Star in the East* (Doubleday, 1950).
Blume, Mary, *After the War was Over* (Thames and Hudson, 1985).
Boatz, Willfried, *Photography, A Concise History* (Laurence King, 1995).
Bondi, Inge, *Ernst Haas: Colour Photography* (Harry N. Abrams, 1989).
Boorstin, Daniel J., *The Image* (Vintage, 1992).
Boot, Chris, *Great Photographers of World War II* (Magna Books, 1993).
Borkenau, Franz, *The Spanish Cockpit* (Faber and Faber, 1937).
Bourke-White, Margaret, *Dear Fatherland, Rest Quietly* (Simon & Schuster, 1946).
– *Portrait of Myself* (Simon & Schuster, 1963).
Boyle, David, *World War 2 in Photographs* (Rebo, 1998).
Bradley, Gen. Omar N., and Clay Blair, *A General's Life: An Autobiography* (Simon and Schuster, 1983).
Brotons Jorda, Mario, *Retazos de una epoca de inquietudes* (self-published, 1995).
Braham, Randolph L., *The Politics of Genocide: The Holocaust in Hungary* (Columbia University Press, 1981).
Brinnin, John Malcolm, *Sextet* (Delacorte, 1981).
Brothers, Caroline, *War and Photography* (Routledge, 1997).
Buchwald, Art, *Seems Like Yesterday* (G. P. Putnam's Sons, 1980).
Burri, René, and Marco Bischof, *Werner Bischof 1916–1954: His Life and Work* (Thames & Hudson, 1990).
Burri, Rossellina Bischof, and René Burri, eds, *Werner Bischof, 1916–1954* (Grossman, 1974).

Calvocoressi, Peter, Guy Wint, and John Pritchard, *Total War* (Pantheon, 1989).
Camera (Lucerne), March 1961.
Capa, Cornell, *The Concerned Photographer* (Grossman, 1968).
– *Cornell Capa* (Little, Brown, 1992).
– 'Truth: The First Casualty of War', *Sunday Times Magazine*, 28 September 1975.
– ed., *Israel – The Reality* (World Publishing, 1969).
Capa, Robert, 'Coal Mine Characters', *US Camera*, June 1943
– *Heart of Spain* (Aperture, 1999).

– *Holiday* magazine, November 1949, January 1951, January 1952, January 1953.
– *Illustrated* magazine, 6 September 1947.
– *Images of War, Photographs by Robert Capa, with text from his own writings* (Grossman, 1964).
– *Photographs* (Aperture, 1996).
– *Robert Capa* (Pacific Press Service, 1980).
– *Robert Capa* (Pacific Press Service, 1984).
– *Robert Capa* (ed. Anna Farova: Grossman, 1969).
– *Robert Capa* (ed. Cornell Capa and Bhupendra Karia: Grossman, 1974).
– *Robert Capa* (ed. Romeo Martinez: Mondadori, 1979).
– *Robert Capa* (Pantheon, Random House, 1989).
– *Slightly Out of Focus* (Henry Holt, 1947).
– and Gerda Taro, *Death in the Making: Photographs by Robert Capa and Gerda Tavo* (Covici, Friede, 1938).
Capa and Capa: catalogue for exhibition of pictures at International Center of Photography, 1990.
'Capa's Camera', *Time*, 28 February 1938.
Carlson, Evans Fordyce, *Twin Stars of China* (Dodd, Mead, 1940).
Cartier-Bresson, Henri, *The Decisive Moment* (Simon & Schuster with Editions Verve de Paris, 1952).
– *Masters of Photography* (Aperture, 1987).
– *The Mind's Eye*, (Aperture, 1998).
Cawthorne, Nigel, *The Dior Revolution* (Reed International Books, 1996).
Cerassi, John, *The Premature Antifascists* (Praeger, 1986).
Churchill, Winston, *The Second World War* (Houghton Mifflin, 1948–1953).
Cockburn, Claud, *In Time of Trouble* (Rupert Hart-Davis, 1957).
Coke, Van Deren, *Avant-Garde Photography in Germany, 1919–1939* (Museum of Modern Art [San Francisco], 1980).
Colodny, Robert, *The Struggle for Madrid* (Paine-Whitman, 1958).
Corum, James, S., *The Luftwaffe* (University Press of Kansas, 1997.
Cox, Geoffrey, *Defence of Madrid* (Victor Gollancz, 1937).
Crozier, Brian, *Franco* (Little, Brown, 1967).

Davenport, Marcia, *Of Lena Geyer* (Grosset and Dunlap, 1936).
Davis, Franklin M., Jr., and the editors of Time-Life Books, *Across the Rhine* (Time-Life Books, 1980).
Devillers, Philippe, and Jean Lacouture, *End of a War: Indochina, 1954* (Praeger, 1969).
Dorfman, John, 'Looking for the Face Behind the Camera', *The Ethnic NewsWatch Forward*, vol. CII.
Dos Passos, John, *1919* (Harcourt, Brace, 1932).

Eisenhower, Dwight D., *Crusade in Europe* (Doubleday, 1948).
Elgey, Georgette, *Front Populaire, Photos by Robert Capa and David Seymour* (Chene-Magnum, 1976).
Ellis, John, *The Sharp End: The Fighting Man in World War II* (Charles Scribner's Sons, 1980).
Elson, Robert T., *Time Inc.: The Intimate History of a Publishing Enterprise, 1923–1941* (Atheneum, 1968).
Esquire, April 1974.
Ewing, Joseph H., *29 Let's Go* (Washington Infantry Journal Press, 1948).

Fielding, Raymond, *The March of Time, 1935-1951* (Oxford University Press, 1978).
Flanner, Janet, *Janet Flanner's World: Uncollected Writings 1932–1975* (Harcourt Brace Jovanovich, 1979).
– *Paris Journal 1944–1965* (ed. William Shawn, Atheneum, 1965).
– *Paris Was Yesterday 1925–1939* (ed. Irving Drutman, Viking Press, 1972).
Fondiller, Harvey V., 'Magnum: Image and Reality', *35mm Photography*, Winter 1976.
Forbes-Robertson, Diana, *The Battle of Waterloo Road* (Random House, 1941).
Fotografia Italiana, June 1972.
Fraser, Ronald, *Blood of Spain: An Oral History of the Spanish Civil War* (Pantheon, 1979).
Freund, Gisèle, *Photography and Society* (David R. Godine, 1980).
– *The World in My Camera* (Dial, 1974).
Fritzsche, Peter, *Germans into Nazis* (Harvard University Press, 1998).
Fussell, Paul, *Wartime* (Oxford University Press, 1989).

Gabler, Neal, *Winchell: Gossip, Power and the Culture of Celebrity* (Alfred A. Knopf, 1994).
Gavin, Gen. James M., Letter to the editor, *47: The Magazine of the Year*, October 1947.
– *On to Berlin* (Viking, 1978).
Gay, Peter, *Weimar Culture: The Outsider as Insider* (Harper & Row, 1968).
Gellhorn, Martha, *The Face of War* (Atlantic Monthly Press, 1988).
– *A Stricken Field* (Charles Scribner's Sons, 1940).
– *Travels with Myself and Another* (Dodd, Mead, 1978).
– *Two by Two* (Simon and Schuster, 1958).
Gidal, Tim N., *Modern Photojournalism: Origin and Evolution, 1910–1933* (Macmillan, 1973).
Giles, James R., *Irwin Shaw* (Twayne, 1983).
Gilot, Françoise, and Carlton Lake, *Life with Picasso* (McGraw-Hill, 1964).
Goldberg, Vicki, *Margaret Bourke-White* (Harper & Row, 1986).
– *The Power of Photography* (Abbeville Press, 1991).
Goldhagen, Daniel Jonah, *Hitler's Willing Executioners, Ordinary Germans and the Holocaust* (Random House, 1997).
Goldsmith, Arthur, 'Moment of Truth', *Camera Arts*, March/April 1981.
Goodwin, Doris Kearns, *No Ordinary Time* (Simon & Schuster, 1994).
Graffis, Bill, Letter to the editor, *47: The Magazine of the Year*, October 1947.
Gross, Michael, *Model* (William Morrow, 1995).
Gunther, Thomas Michael, and Marie de Thézy, *Alliance photo, agence photographique 1934–1940: Bibliothèque historique de la ville de Paris, Hôtel de Lamoignon, 27 octobre 1988–9 janvier 1989* (La Bibliothèque, 1988).

Hall, James Baker, 'The Last Happy Band of Brothers', *Esquire*, April 1974.
Hammond, John, with Irving Townsend, *On Record* (Ridge Press/Summit, 1977).
Hancock, Ian, *The Pariah Syndrome* (Karoma, 1987).
Hastings, Max, *Overlord* (Michael Joseph, 1984).
Haver, Ronald, *David O'Selznick's Hollywood* (Knopf, 1980).

Hegedus, Adam de, *Hungarian Background* (Hamish Hamilton, 1937).
Hemingway, Ernest, *For Whom the Bell Tolls* (Charles Scribner's Sons, 1940).
– *Selected Letters, 1917–1961* (ed. Carlos Baker: Charles Scribner's Sons, 1981).
Hemingway, Leicester, *My Brother, Ernest Hemingway* (The World Publishing Company, 1961).
Hemingway, Mary Welsh, *How It Was* (Alfred A. Knopf, 1976).
Hersey, John, *Life Sketches* (Knopf, 1989).
– 'The Man Who Invented Himself', *47: The Magazine of the Year*, September 1947.
Hertzstein, Robert E., *Henry Luce* (Charles Scribner's Sons, 1994).
Herval, René, *Bataille de Normandie* (Éditions de Notre Temps, 1947).
Herzog, Chaim, *The Arab–Israeli Wars* (Arms & Armour Press, 1982).
Higgins, Marguerite, *News Is a Singular Thing* (Doubleday, 1955).
Hofstadter, Dan, 'Profiles – Henri Cartier-Bresson', Part 2, *New Yorker*, 30 October 1989.
Hohenberg, John, *Foreign Correspondence: The Great Reporters and Their Times* (Columbia University Press, 1964).
Hotchner, A. E., *Choice People: The Greats, Near-Greats and Ingrates I Have Known* (William Morrow, 1984).
Howard, Noël, *Hollywood sur Nil* (Fayard, 1978).
Hughes, Jim, *Shadow and Substance, W. Eugene Smith* (McGraw-Hill, 1989).
– and Alexander Haas, *Ernst Haas in Black and White* (Little, Brown, 1992).
Huston, John, *An Open Book* (Alfred A. Knopf, 1980).

Ignotus, Paul, *Hungary* (Benn, 1972).
Inge Bondi, Chim, *The Photographs of David Seymour* (André Deutsch, 1996).
Isherwood, Christopher, *Christopher and His Kind, 1929–1939* (Farrar, Straus & Giroux, 1976).
– *Goodbye to Berlin* (Panther, 1977).
– *Journey to a War, With poems and photographs by W. H. Auden* (Octagon, 1972).
Ivens, Joris, *The Camera and I* (International, 1969).

Jaenecke, Heinrich, *Es lebe der Tod, Die Tragödie des spanischen Burgerkrieges*, (Gruner und Jahr, 1980).

Kantorowicz, Alfred, *Politik und Literatur im Exil* (Christians, 1978).
– *Spanisches Tagebuch* (Aufbau-Verlag, 1949).
– *Tschapaiew, das Bataillon der 21 Nationen* (Torrent, 1938).
Karnow, Stanley, *Paris in the Fifties* (Random House, 1997).
Keegan, John, *A History of Warfare* (Vintage, 1993).
– *The Second World War* (Penguin, 1989).
Kershaw, Alex, 'Up Close and Personal', *Guardian Weekend*, 18 July 1998.
Kershaw, Ian, *The Hitler Myth* (Oxford University Press, 1987).
Kert, Bernice, *The Hemingway Women* (Norton, 1983).
Kessel, Joseph, *The Lion* (Rupert Hart-Davis, 1959).
Knightley, Phillip, *The First Casualty* (Harcourt Brace, 1975).
Knox, Bernard, 'Remembering Madrid', *New York Review of Books*, 6 November 1980.
Koyen, Kenneth A., *The 4th Armored Division* (4th Armored Division, 1946).

Lacoutre, Jean, '*Introduction*' to *Robert Capa* (Pantheon Photo Library, 1989).
Lamarr, Hedy, *Ecstasy and Me* (Fawcett Publications, 1966).
Lang, Will, 'Doughboys' Beachhead', *Time*, 7 February 1944.
– 'The Story of Fort Schuster', *Life*, 25 October 1943.
Laqueur, Walter, *Weimar: A Cultural History, 1918–1933* (G. P. Putnam's Sons, 1974).
Le Goff, Hervé, *Pierre Gassmann: la photographie à l'épreuve* (Delory, 2001).
Le Vien, Jack, 'The Faking of War Pictures', *Sunday Times*, 5 October 1975.
Leamer, Laurence, *As Time Goes By: The Life of Ingrid Bergman* (Harper & Row, 1986).
Lechenperg, Harald, 'Hochzeit beim Maharadscha', *Die Dame*, August 1932.
Lee, Laurie, *Moment of War* (The New Press, 1991).
Lee, Lawrence, and Barry Gifford, *Saroyan: A Biography* (Paragon House, 1988).

Lessing, Erich, *Fifty Years of Photography*, exhibition catalogue, 1955.
Lewinski, Jorge, *The Camera at War* (Simon and Schuster, 1978).
Liebling, A. J., 'Reporter at Large', *New Yorker*, 8 July and 15 July 1944.
– *The Road Back to Paris* (Doubleday, 1944).
LIFE: The First Decade, 1936–1945 (New York Graphic Society, 1979).
Loengard, John, *Life Photographers: What They Saw* (Little, Brown, 1998).
Loyd, Anthony, *My War Gone By, I Miss It So* (Doubleday, 2000).
Lucas, Jim, 'Bob Capa Planned to Leave Indo-China by Sea', *Washington Daily News*, 27 May 1954.
Lucas, Jim G., *Dateline Vietnam* (Award Books, 1966).
Lukacs, John A., *Budapest 1900: A Historical Portrait of a City and its Culture* (Weidenfeld & Nicolson, 1988).
Lynn, Kenneth S., *Hemingway* (Simon & Schuster, 1987).

MacKinnon, Stephen R., and Oris Friesen, *China Reporting* (University of California Press, 1987).
Man, Felix H., *Man with Camera: Photographs from Seven Decades* (Schocken, 1984).
Marinovich, Greg and Silva, Jaoa, *The Bang Bang Club* (Heinemann, 2000).
Markos, György, 'My Friend Capa', *New Hungarian Quarterly*, Winter 1976.
Matthews, Herbert L., *The Education of a Correspondent* (Harcourt Brace, 1946).
– *Two Wars and More to Come* (Carrick & Evans, 1938).
Mauldin, Bill, *The Brass Ring* (Norton, 1971).
Mayall, David, *Gypsy-travellers in Nineteenth-Century Society* (Cambridge University Press, 1988).
Mayo, Gael Elton, *The Mad Mosaic* (Quartet, 1983).
Mecklin, John, 'Forward Lies the Delta', *Time*, 7 June 1954.
– 'He Said: "This Is Going to Be a Beautiful Story"', *Life*, 7 June 1954.
Mellow, James R., *Hemingway: A Life Without Consequences* (Addison-Wesley, 1992).
Messenger, Charles, *The Chronological Atlas of World War Two* (Macmillan, 1989).
Meyers, Jeffrey, *Hemingway: A Biography* (Harper and Row, 1985).

Mieth, Hansel, *The Singing Hills of Jackass Flat* (unpublished manuscript, quoted courtesy of Georgia Brown and Center of Creative Photography).

Miller, Arthur, *Timebends: A Life* (Harper & Row, 1987).

Miller, Lee G., *An Ernie Pyle Album* (William Sloane Associates, 1946).

– *The Story of Ernie Pyle* (Viking, 1950).

Miller, Russell, *Magnum: Fifty Years at the Front Line of History* (Grove Press, 1998).

Miravitlles, Jaume, *Notes dels meus arxius: Episodis de la Guerra Civil Espanyola* (Collecio Portic, 1972).

Modern Photography, July 1969.

Montgomery, John Flournoy, *Hungary – The Unwilling Satellite* (Vista, 1993).

Moorehead, Alan, *Eclipse* (Coward–McCann, 1945).

Morath, Inge, 'Meeting Magnum', in *Paris/Magnum – Photographs 1935–1981* (ed. Irwin Shaw: Aperture, 1981).

Morris, Benny, *A History of the Zionist–Arab Conflict* (Knopf, 1999).

Morris, John, *Get The Picture* (Random House, 1998).

– 'Magnum Photos: An International Cooperative', *U.S. Camera Annual*, 1954).

– 'A Two Quart Bottle of Spirits', in *Robert Capa* (ed. Anna Farova: Grossman, 1969).

Mydans, Carl, *More Than Meets the Eye*, New York: Harper & Brothers, 1959).

Mydans, Shelley Smith, *The Open City*, Garden City: Doubleday, Doran, 1945).

Natchwey, James, *Inferno* (Phaidon, 2000).

Oestreicher, J. C., *The World Is Their Beat* (Duell, Sloan & Pearce, 1945).

Ogden, Christopher, *Life of the Party: the Biography of Pamela Digby Churchill Hayward Harriman* (Little, Brown, 1994)

Oldfield, Colonel Barney, *Never a Shot in Anger* (Capra Press, 1956).

Orwell, George, *Down and Out in Paris and London* (Harper & Bros., 1933).

– *Homage to Catalonia* (Secker & Warburg, 1938).

Parini, Jay, *John Steinbeck* (Heinemann, 1994).
Parks, Gordon, *A Choice of Weapons* (Harper & Row, 1966).
Payne, Robert, *The Life and Death of Trotsky* (McGraw-Hill, 1977).
Penrose, Antony, ed., *Lee Miller's War* (Little, Brown, 1992).
– *The Lives of Lee Miller* (Holt, Rinehart & Winston, 1985).
Penrose, Roland, *Portrait of Picasso* (New York Museum of Modern Art, 1971).
Pettifer, James, ed., *Cockburn in Spain* (Lawrence and Wishart, 1986).
Photo (Paris), June 1983, 'Robert Capa: 124 Photos Retrouvées'.
Photo Technique, November 1977.
Popular Photography, September 1954, 'Robert Capa: A Memorial Portfolio'.
Prochnau, William, *Once Upon a Distant War* (Times Books, 1995).
Pyle, Ernie, *Brave Men* (Henry Holt, 1944).
– *Here Is Your War* (Henry Holt, 1943).

Quirk, Lawrence J., *The Films of Ingrid Bergman* (Citadel, 1970).

Radnoti, Miklos, *Foamy Sky* (Corvina, 2000).
Radzinsky, Edvard *Stalin* (Doubleday, 1996).
Rand, Peter, *China Hand* (Simon & Schuster, 1995).
Regler, Gustav, *The Owl of Minerva* (R. Hart-Davis, 1959).
Renn, Ludwig, *Der Spanische Krieg* (Aufbau-Verlag, 1955).
Reportage, Spring 1995.
Reynolds, David, *Rich Relations: The American Occupation of Britain, 1942–1945* (Random House, 1995).
Reynolds, Quentin, *Quentin Reynolds* (McGraw-Hill, 1963).
Riss, Françoise, 'Robert Capa: Les Photos Retrouvées du Tour 1939', *Photo Revue* (Paris), September 1982.
Rodger, George, *George Rodger*, Introduction by Inge Bondi (Gordon Fraser, for the Arts Council of Great Britain, 1975).
– 'Random Thoughts of a Founder Member', *Photo Technique*, November 1977.
Rolfe, Edwin, *The Lincoln Battalion* (Random House, 1939).
Rollyson, Carl, *Nothing Ever Happens To The Brave* (St Martin's Press, 1990).
Rooney, Andy, *My War* (Public Affairs, 2000).

Rosenbaum, Ron, *Explaining Hitler* (HarperCollins, 1998).
Ryan, Cornelius, *The Longest Day* (Simon and Schuster, 1959).

Salter, James, *Burning the Days* (Random House, 1997).
Sanders, Marion K., *Dorothy Thompson: A Legend in Her Time* (Houghton Mifflin, 1973).
Sante, Luc, *Evidence* (Farrar Strauss Giroux, 1992).
Saroyan, William, Letter to the editor, *'47': The Magazine of the Year*, October 1947.
Schaber, Irme, *Gerta Taro: Fotoreporterin im spanischen Bürgerkrieg: eine Biografie* (Jonas Verlag, 1994).
Scherman, David, ed., *Best of Life* (Time-Life Books, 1972).
– *Life Goes to War* (Simon and Schuster, 1977).
– *LIFE Goes to War: A Picture History of World War II* (Little, Brown, 1977).
Shaw, Irwin, Letter to the editor, *'47': The Magazine of the Year*, October 1947.
– *Paris/Magnum; Photographs, 1935–1981* (Aperture, 1981).
– *Paris! Paris!* (Harcourt Brace Jovanovich, 1977).
– *Report on Israel* (Simon and Schuster, 1950).
– 'Retreat in Indo-China', *Picture Post*, 12 June 1954.
– *Views of Paris; Notes on a Parisian* (Aperture Books, 1981).
Sheean, Vincent, Letter to the editor, *'47': The Magazine of the Year*, October 1947.
– *Not Peace But a Sword* (Doubleday, Doran, 1939).
Shirer, William, *A Berlin Diary* (Knopf, 1941).
– *The Rise and Fall of the Third Reich* (Simon & Schuster, 1960).
– *Twentieth Century Journey: The Nightmare Years, 1930–1940* (Little, Brown, 1984).
Shlaim, Avi, *The Iron Wall* (Norton, 1999).
Shnayerson, Michael, *Irwin Shaw* (G. P. Putnam's Sons, 1989).
Smedley, Agnes, *Battle Hymn of China* (Alfred A. Knopf, 1938).
Sommerfield, John, *Volunteer in Spain* (Lawrence & Wishart, 1937).
Sontag, Susan, *On Photography* (Penguin, 1977).
Sorel, Nancy Caldwell, *The Women Who Wrote The War* (HarperCollins, 1999).

Soria, Georges, Robert Capa, David Seymour-Chim, *Les grandes photos de la guerre d'Espagne* (Editions Jannink, 1980).
Southworth, Herbert Rutledge, *Guernica! Guernica!* (University of California Press, 1977).
Spoto, Donald, *The Dark Side of Genius: The Life of Alfred Hitchcock* (Little, Brown, 1983).
– *Notorious: The Life of Ingrid Bergman* (HarperCollins, 1997).
Steele, Joseph H., *Ingrid Bergman: An Intimate Portrait* (McKay, 1959).
Steichen, Edward, ed., *The Family of Man* (Museum of Modern Art, 1955).
– *Memorable Life photographs* (Museum of Modern Art, 1951).
Stein, Louis, *Beyond Death and Exile: The Spanish Republicans in France, 1939–1955* (Harvard University Press, 1979).
Steinbeck, John, *Once There Was a War* (Viking, 1958).
– *A Russian Journal* (Viking, 1948); new edition, with an introduction by Susan Shillinglaw (Penguin, 1999).
Stone, I. F., *This Is Israel* (Boni and Gaer, 1948).
Sulzberger, C. L., *World War II* (Houghton Mifflin, 1969).

Tanenhaus, Sam, 'Innocents Abroad', *Vanity Fair*, September 2001.
Taylor, John, *Body Horror, Photojournalism, catastrophe and war* (New York University Press, 1998).
The Magnum Story, BBC2.
Thomas, Hugh, *The Spanish Civil War* (Harper & Row, 1977).
Thompson, Edward K., *A Love Affair with Life & Smithsonian* (University of Missouri Press, 1995).
Tobin, James, *Ernie Pyle's War* (The Free Press, 1997).
Tregaskis, Richard, *Invasion Journal* (Random House, 1944).
Tuchman, Barbara W., *Stilwell and the American Experience in China, 1911–45* (Macmillan, 1971).

US Army, *83rd Infantry Division, Thunderbolt Across Europe* (Munich, 1946).
Ullstein, Hermann, *The Rise and Fall of the House of Ullstein* (Simon and Schuster, 1943).
Utley, Freda, *The China Story* (Henry Regnery, 1951).
– *China at War* (Faber and Faber, 1939).

Viertel, Peter, *Dangerous Friends* (Viking, 1991).
Volkogonov, Dmitri, *Stalin, Triumph and Tragedy* (Grove Weidenfeld, 1991).
Voss, Frederick S., *Reporting the War, The Journalistic Coverage of World War* (Smithsonian Institution Press, 1994).

Wallace, Robert, and the editors of Time-Life Books, *The Italian Campaign* (Time-Life Books, 1978).
Weber, Eugen, *The Hollow Years, France in the 1930s* (Norton, 1994).
Wertenbaker, Charles C., *The Death of Kings* (Random House, 1954).
– *Invasion! Photographs by Robert Capa* (Appleton, Century).
– 'Paris Is Free!' *Time*, 4 September 1944.
Wertenbaker, Lael, *Death of A Man* (Random House, 1957).
Weyden, Peter, *The Passionate War: The Narrative History of the Spanish Civil War, 1936–1939* (Simon and Schuster, 1983).
Whelan, Richard, *Robert Capa: A Biography* (Alfred Knopf, 1985).
White, Theodore H., and Annalee Jacoby, *Thunder out of China* (William Sloane, 1946).
Winneaple, Brenda, *Genet: A Biography of Janet Flanner* (Ticknor & Fields, 1989).
Woff, Milton, *Another Hill* (University of Illinois, 1994).

Zeman, Z. A. B., *Nazi Propaganda* (Oxford University Press, 1973).

Index

Aarons, Slim 118, 157
Anzio landings 113–15
and Capa 93, 146, 168–70, 229
Abrams, Lieut.Colonel Creighton 152
Adams, Eddie 38n
Adler, Larry 160–3, 166n, 168
Allan, Dr Norman 60
Allan, Ted 43, 55–61
This Time a New Earth 57
Allen, Jay 53
Allen, General Terry 100
Alliance agency 27, 31, 51
Aly Khan 227
Ambrose, Stephen 133
Anzio landings 113–15
Aragon, Louis 61, 235
Arnold, Eve 215, 226
Auden, W. H. 67
Auschwitz 193n

Balenciaga 216
Banks, Dennis 129
Barcelona 34–5, 78–9
Battle of the Bulge 150–2
Belden, Jack 106
Belsen 154
Ben-Gurion, David 201, 207
Benny, Jack 160
Bergman, Ingrid 158–76, 229, 254
Arch of Triumph 172–3
Casablanca 159
Gaslight 159
Joan of Arc 173–6
Notorious 167
Spellbound 166
The Four Companions 162
Berkovits, Julianna Henrietta *see* Julia Capa
Berlin 15–21, 162, 208
Berliner Illustrierte Zeitung 26
Besnyö, Eva 11–16, 20, 27, 62, 68, 83, 219
Bethune, Dr Norman 51, 56
Beumelburg, Werner 59
Bilby, Kenneth W. 201, 204, 206–7
New Star in the East 28, 212n
Bischof, Rosellina 253
Bischof, Werner 215, 223n, 252–5
Blum, Léon 30
Bogart, Humphrey 168, 237–8
Bohen, Frau 16
Bondi, Inge 216, 252, 254
Borkenau, Franz: *The Spanish Cockpit* 36, 42, 46
Borrell, Everisto 45
Borrell, Federico 45
Bosshard, Walter 68
Bote, Hans 25
Bourke-White, Margaret 88, 234
Boyer, Charles 172–3
Bradlee, Ben 228, 231
Bradley, Major General Omar 100
Bradshaw, Braddy 128
Brandt, Bert 128

Brecht, Bertolt 18, 21
Brereton, General Lewis 153
Brothers, Caroline 46
Brotons Jorda, Mario 45–6
Brown, Georgia 85
Buchwald, Art 229
Budapest 6–10, 192, 209–10
Burke, Don 82
Burrows, Larry 250n
Butler, E. K. 128

Capa, Cornell (brother of RC) 13, 82, 233, 253
  emigrated to New York 82
  and *Falling Soldier* 38, 39
  photographer 28, 230, 255
Capa, Julia (mother of RC) 9–11, 13, 16, 28, 91, 230, 255
  Capa's funeral 253
  emigrated to New York 82
Capa, Robert
  LIFE
    birth 8
    change of name 28–9
    marriage 83–5
    Ingrid Bergman 158–76
    death 249–51
  WORK
    Berlin 15–21
    Budapest 11–14
    China 66–72
    England 90–7, 116–20
    exhibitions 29
    FBI file 234–7
    France 132–39
    Germany 149–65
    Hollywood 167–70
    Israel 201–7, 210–13
    Italy 107–12
    Japan 241–2
    Magnum 179–3, 214–16, 219–25
    Mexico 86
    North Africa 98–102
    Omaha Beach landings 2–4, 120–32
    Paris 22–32, 139–51, 158–9
    Sicily 106–8
    Spain 26, 33–66, 73–80
      Falling Soldier 37–47
      Gerda's death 59–62
    USSR 177–9, 182–90
    Vietnam 245–51
    World Video 196–7, 199
  Death in the Making 53–4
  Images of War 2, 3–4
  Report on Israel 212–13
  Russian Journal 178, 194–6
  Slightly Out of Focus 41, 52, 90–1, 96, 149, 168, 189
Capote, Truman 237–9
Cartier-Bresson, Henri 23–4, 28, 43, 215
  and Capa 23–4, 61, 146, 181n, 225n
  Magnum 152, 180, 181, 221–2, 255
Ce Soir 33, 55, 61, 65, 81, 235
Cerf, Ruth 25–8, 44, 52, 56n 61–2
Chaplin, Sydney 230
Chardack, Willi 27
Cherbourg 135–8
Chiang Kai-shek, General 67, 71
Chiang Kai-shek, Madame 68, 70, 237
Chicago Tribune 102
China 66–74
Churchill, Pamela 94, 198, 228
Churchill, Randolph 94
Churchill, Winston 95, 177
Clavadetscher, Flury 239
Cockburn, Claud 56, 58
Cogny, General René 245–6, 251
Cogny, Marie-Robert 245
Collier's 73, 90, 100–1, 103, 104–5, 201
Collins, Larry 236
communism 12, 86, 195, 234–5

Cooper, Gary 167
Cunningham, Jack 201

D-Day landings 120, 138
Daily Express 42
Daily Herald 40
Daily Mail 63
Daily Worker 57, 58, 196n, 234
Davis, Floyd 145
Davis, Myron 91
de Rochemont, Richard 53
  Rehearsal for War 54–6
Delahaye, Luc 254
Delmer, Sefton 63
Dephot agency 17, 73
Der Welt Spiegel 19
Descamps, Michel 244–5
Dien Bien Phu 243–4, 246
Dietrich, Marlene 158
Dior, Christian 197–9
Dollfuss, Engelbert 21
Dos Passos, John 56
Duhamel, Marcel 146
Duncan, David Douglas 223n

Ehrenburg, Ilja 56, 79
Einstein, Albert 21
Eisenhower, General 118, 121
Eisner, Maria 27, 31–2
  Magnum 179–80, 219, 221
Eldans, David 203
Elisofon, Eliot 100
England 90–7, 116–20
Ernst, Morris 234, 235, 238
Erwitt, Elliot 215, 221

The Falling Soldier 37–47
Fath, Jacques 197–9
Fernhout, John 66, 69–71, 83
Fischer, Béla 147
Fischer, Suzy 22–3, 147
Fischer, Szeren 22, 147
Flanner, Janet 145, 226n
Fox, Jimmy, *The Falling Soldier* 39–40
France 129–39
  political crises 24, 30
Franco, General 32, 48, 49, 65
Freiburg, Judy 193, 253
Freund, Gisèle 18, 42, 179, 219, 232
Friedmann, André *see* Robert Capa
Friedmann, Angela (sister-in-law of RC) 192
Friedmann, Cornell (brother of RC) *see* Cornell Capa
Friedmann, Dezsö (father of RC) 8, 14, 28
Friedmann, Julia (mother of RC) *see* Julia Capa
Friedmann, László (brother of RC) 192

Gallagher, O'Dowd 42–3, 79
Garbo, Greta 237
Gassmann, Pierre 24, 61, 146, 152, 154
  Magnum 152, 179–80, 181
Gavin, General James M. 104
Gellhorn, Martha 33, 79, 94, 154, 174, 224
  and Hemingway 73, 87–8, 140n 148–50, 167
  Till Death Do Us Part 74
Germany 149–65
  invades Poland 81
  martial law 19
  Nazi revolution 20
  surrender 157
Gilmore, Ed 182
Gilot, Françoise 217
Glinn, Burt 215, 228–9
Goalen, Barbara 198
Goetz, William 168
Goldman, Paul 202–3
Goodwin, Carl 163
Gorin, Raymond 27

Gould, Beatrice and Bruce 195
Graffis, Bill 147
Graham, Sheila 170
Graziani, Bettina 198–9, 231
Groce, Benedetto 110
Grosvenor, Rita 45
Guernica 53
Guler, Hans 226
Gunther, Thomas 31
Guttmann, Simon 17, 19, 24, 26

Haas, Ernst 216
Halstead, Dirck 238n, 254–5
Hamill, Peter 140
Hammond, Jemmy 214, 218–1, 230, 237, 252, 253n
Hammond, John 214, 218
Hammond, John Jnr 214, 218, 230, 252
Harrison, Colette 231
Hawks, Howard 167, 168, 227
Hawks, Slim 167
Hayward, Leland 167
Hecht, Ben 165
Heim, Peter 7, 13
Hemingway, Ernest 56, 94, 139–3, 145, 235
- *A Farewell to Arms* 52
- and Capa 52, 118–19, 139–40
- *For Whom the Bell Tolls* 54n, 87–8
- and Gellhorn 73, 87–8, 140n, 148–50, 167
- reporting for *Collier's* 119
- Spanish Civil War 63, 75–6
- *Spanish Earth* 64
- and Steinbeck 139, 145, 199–200
- *The Sun Also Rises* 52

Hemingway, Leicester 118–19, 146
Herald Tribune 195–6, 201, 235
Herrera, Lieutenant Colonel Emilio 26
Hersey, John 22, 28, 30–1, 153
Hiroshima 5
Hetényi, Imre 13
Heute 216
Hicks, Wilson 80
Hitch, Peter 231
Hitchcock, Alfred 165–6
Hitler, Adolf 20, 65, 73
Holiday magazine 6, 210, 225–6, 230, 231, 234
Hollywood 167–70
Holocaust 192–3
Holt, Henry 189
Hopper, Hedda 167
Horthy, Admiral 7, 10, 13
Howard, Noel 208, 231–5, 234
Hughes, Howard 168
Hungary 8, 12, 209
Huston, John 168–70, 227, 229, 237–8
- *An Open Book* 238n
- *The Battle of San Pietro* 109

Huston, Ricki 237
Hyde, Henry 236

Illustrated 96, 173, 197, 201, 206
- Hungary 209
- Israel 203, 205n , 210, 212
- Italian campaign 108, 113

Illustrated London News 40
International Brigades 73–4
International Center of Photography 255
International Writers' Conference 56
Isherwood, Christopher 67
Israel 201–7, 210–13
Italy 107–15
Ivens, Joris 66–71, 235
- *The Camera and I* 67

Izvestia 79

Jacobs, Fenno 219
Japan 241–2
Jaramillo, Miguel Angel 46
Jarreau, Charles 125, 127

Jerusalem 203–6
Jeudy, Patrick 38–9, 132
Jews 10, 165, 192n, 201, 203n 207
Justin, Elaine (Pinky) 97, 101, 116–17, 120, 149, 156
Justin, John 97

Kandinsky, Wassily 21
Kantorowicz, Alfred 54, 58
Kavitkes, Georg 25
Kawazoe, Hiroshi 241
Keating, Jeffrey 113
Keleti, Eva 29
Kelly, Gene 227
Kerr, Deborah 231
Kertész, André 30
Kilner, Dr Thomas Pomfret 93
Knightly, Philip, *The First Casualty* 42
Koester, Peter 73
Koltsov, Michail 58
Korchein, Polly 83
Koyen, Ken 151

Lacapelle, Lieutenant Colonel Jean 246–8, 250
Ladies Home Journal 182, 192, 195, 233
Lamarr, Hedy 228
Landry, Bob 120
Lang, Fritz 18
Lang, Will 107–9, 113
Lanham, Colonel Charles 'Buck' 140
Laurie, Annie 197
Leamer, Laurence 170
Lechenperg, Harald 19
Leica cameras 18
Leigh, Vivien 231
Lewinski, Jorge 43
L'Humanité 61, 79
Liebling, A. J. 106
  Life magazine 111, 146, 179, 215, 241–2
  and Capa 82–3, 88, 242, 252–3
  China 67–71
  D-Day landings 120, 122, 126–9, 139
  invasion of Europe 132–4, 139, 152, 161
  Israel 202
  Italy 107–12
  London office 102, 127–9
  Los Angeles office 172
  Mexico 86
  Moscow 190
  New York office 103
  Robert Capa Medal 254
  Sicily 104–6
  Spanish Civil War 42, 51, 54, 61, 80
  Vietnam 244–8, 254
Lindstrom, Petter 159, 169–70, 175
List, Herbert 219
Lister, General Enrique 76
Litvak, Anatole 168
Llewellyn, Lieutenant Richard 92
  How Green Was My Valley 92
Lorant, Stefan 68, 78
Lubitsch, Ernst 18
Lucas, Jim 246–9
Luce, Henry 54, 55n, 69, 192, 242n
Lukacz, General 49
Luttwitz, Lieutenant General Heinrich von 151

McAuliffe, General Anthony C. 151
McCombs, Holland 86
McCullin, Donald 254
Madrid 49–51
Magee, Commodore 91
Magnum 179–82, 208, 214–16, 219–24, 238, 252, 255
  Capa president 219, 232–3
  clients 225
  foundation 111, 152, 226n
  Paris office 221
Mainichi Press 28, 239, 241
Malraux, André 34

Man, Felix 17–18
Mann, Thomas 21
Marcus, David Michael 203–6
Markos, György 8, 62, 73
Marquis, Suzy 16, 73, 213, 222, 223, 229, 240
Martinez, Romeo 181
Matisse, Henri 217
Matthews, Herbert 63–5, 76, 79, 105, 110
Mauldin, Bill 115, 150n
Mayne, Richard 208
Mayo, Gael Elton 220–1
Mecklin, John 246–51
Melgar, Manuel 46
Mexico 86
Mieth, Hansel 40, 62, 84–5
Mieth, Otto 40, 84–5
Miles, Blossom 96
Miles, Frederick 97
Milestone, Lewis 172
Mili, Gijon 217, 229
Miller, Henry 23
Miller, Russell 222
Miravitlles, Jaume 34
Morath, Inge 215–16, 227, 232, 239–40
Morris, John 118, 141–4, 145–6, 252–3
  Ladies Home Journal 182, 192, 195, 233
  Life 83, 110, 126–30
  Magnum 220, 233, 237, 242
Moscow 183–4, 189–90
Müncher Illustrierte Presse 17
Murrow, Edward R. 94, 154

Namuth, Hans 48
Nance, Lieutenant Ray 4, 124
Naples 107–9, 113
Natchwey, Jim 254
Naudet, Jean-Jacques 202
Navarre, Lieutenant Colonel Jacques 250–1
Nazis 18–20
Neruda, Pablo 56
New York Herald Tribune 76, 102, 229
New York Times 63, 76, 88, 105, 122, 189, 194
New York World-Telegram 39, 41
New Yorker 106, 210
Newsweek 228, 236
Nin, Anaïs 23
North, Sterling 194
North Africa 98–102

Observer 45
O'Hara, John 200
Omaha Beach landings 1–3, 120–32
Operation Overlord 120
Orchard, Tom 54
Orkin, Ruth 198
Orwell, George 34, 35, 63
Overseas Press Club 254

Page, Homer 219
Palestine 201
Paris 22–32, 158–9
  Café du Dôme 23, 26, 28
  liberation 139, 144–6
Paris-Match 244
Paris-Soir 42
Parks, Gordon 88
Patrick, Ted 225, 230
Patton, General George 99–101, 151
Pearson, Bill 227
Philadelphia Inquirer 189
Photo News 190
Picasso, Pablo 146, 217
Picture Post 68, 77–81, 225, 237
Piscator, Edwin 18
Pohorylles, Gerda *see* Gerda Taro
Poltoratsky, Comrade 187, 188, 191, 194
Prescott, Orville 194

Puttnies, Professor Hans 41, 42
Pyle, Ernie 99, 106, 113–15, 118, 133, 135–8, 156

Regan, Edward K. 130–1
Regards 23, 33, 42, 53, 234
Regler, Gustav 34, 49
Reinhardt, Max 18
Reis, Irving 117, 167
Reuter, Walter 58
Reynolds, Quentin 92–5, 201
Riboud, Marc 215, 238
Rich, Captain Oscar 122
Ridgway, Major General Matthew 104, 106
Robert Capa Medal 238, 250n, 254–5
Rock, Bobby 83
Rodger, George 110–11, 118, 146, 154
  Magnum 111, 179–80, 182, 255
Rodger, Jinx 110, 222, 238, 241
Rommel, General 121
Ronis, Willy 62
Rooney, Andy 151
Roosevelt, Franklin D. 87
Roosevelt, General Teddy 100, 105
Rossellini, Roberto 171–2

Salter, James 218
Saroyan, William 117–20, 146, 167
Schaber, Imre 43
Scherman, David 128
Scherschel, Frank 120, 202
Schlieben, General von 138
Schmeling, Max 26
Schneider, Agnes 236
Scripps-Howard 106, 137, 246
Serrano, Carlos 43
Seymour, David 'Chim' 28, 146, 229
  Holocaust 193
  Magnum 152, 179–80, 182, 221–2, 255
  Regards 23–4
  Spanish Civil War 43, 74
Shaw, Irwin 173, 230, 231
  and Bergman 158–60, 164
  and Capa 82–3, 117, 139, 207, 217–18, 227, 229, 232, 239
  Evening in Byzantium 218
  Malibu beach house 168, 172
  Report on Israel 210–12
Shaw, Marion 217–18
Sheean, Dinah 89, 96
  The Battle of Waterloo Road 89
Sheean, Vincent 53, 76, 80, 89, 96
Sherekh, Yuriy, 'What Did You Not Want To See, Mr Steinbeck?' 187
Shipley, Mrs 236
Shirer, William 145
Shnayerson, Michael 218
Shockley, Orion 136
Sicily 104–6
Sino-Japanese War 66
Smedley, Agnes 71
Snow, Edgar 71
Sochurek, Howard 241–2, 254
Sorel, Toni 83–5
Soria, Georges 44–5, 61, 79
Spain 26, 32
Spanish Civil War 33–65, 73–81
Spiegel, Irene 60
Spooner, Len 96
Spoto, Donald 160
Stanton, Arthur 227–8
Steele, Joe 160, 169–71
Steichen, Edward 253
Steinbeck, John 106, 139, 145
  A Russian Journal 178, 187, 191, 193–4
  and Capa 102, 252, 255
  and Hemingway 139, 145, 199–201
  in Russia 177–9, 182–90, 234
  World Video 196–7, 199
Stevens, George 117, 167

Stevens, Sergeant Roy 1, 134
Stilwell, 'Vinegar Joe' 71–3
Stokowski 237
Stuart, Jozefa 202, 214, 218–19, 230

Taro, Gerda 25, 27–9, 253
  death 59–62
  la Paquena Rubena 55
  in Spain 33–5, 43, 48–9, 52–60
The 400 Million 66–7
The Spanish Earth 66
Thompson, Edward 82–3, 85, 235, 241–4, 247
Thorne, Judy 226, 237
Tilton, Martha 160
Time 229
Time and Life 106, 133
Time-Life 54, 86, 168
Tobin, James 156
Toller, Ernst 18
Trabant, Warren 116, 216, 220–1, 236
Trotsky, Leon 19, 87

Umbehrs, Otto 16
US Camera magazine 93
USSR 177–9, 182–90
Uzcudun, Paolino 26

Vachon, John 192
Vandivert, Bill, Magnum 180
Vandivert, Rita, Magnum 180
Viertel, Peter 141n, 167, 198, 217, 220, 230–7
Vietnam War 243–51
Vogel, Lucien 30, 31, 33, 42, 50
Vu magazine 26, 30, 33, 42, 44

Walters, General 58
Washington Post 228
Weber, Eugen, *The Hollow Years* 24
Weizmann, Chaim 210
Welsh, Mary 94, 102–3, 146, 148
Wertenbaker, Charles 122, 124–5, 130, 133–6, 139, 142–5
Whelan, Richard 38, 192
White, Harry S. 198
White, Theodore 208–9
Whitehead, Don 122
Wild, Hans 128
Wilder, Billy 229
Wilkie, Wendell 87
Wilson, Don 244–5
Winocour, Jack 201, 204–6
Wolff, Milton 75
World Illustrated 50
World Video 196–7, 199

Yank 93, 113

Zachary, Frank 225
Zalka, Mate 49
Zuckmayer, Karl 18